CW00501860

For CLUB and COUNTRY

Welsh Football Greats

FOR CLUB and COUNTRY

WELSH FOOTBALL GREATS

Edited by Peter Stead and Huw Richards

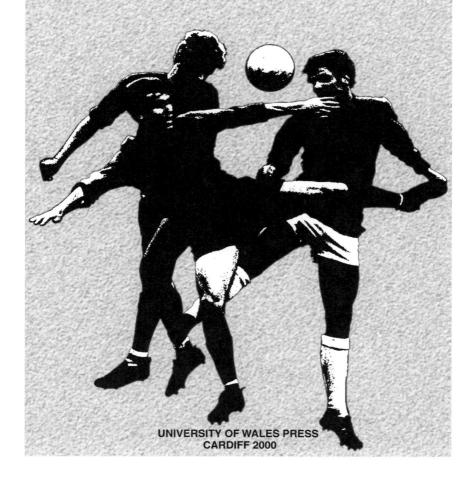

UNIVERSITY OF WALES PRESS
CARDIFF 2000

© The contributors, 2000.

All rights reserved. No part of this book may be reproduced, stored in a retrieval system or transmitted, in any form or by any means, electronic, mechanical, photocopying, recording or otherwise, without clearance from the University of Wales Press, 6 Gwennyth Street, Cardiff, CF24 4YD.
www.wales.ac.uk/press

British Library Cataloguing-in-Publication Data
A catalogue record for this book is available from the British Library.

ISBN 0-7083-1624-7

Typeset at University of Wales Press, Cardiff
Printed in England by MPG Books Limited, Bodmin

CONTENTS

ACKNOWLEDGEMENTS

Many of these chapters could not have been written without the considerable help and co-operation of the players, their families and their friends. We thank them for their time and inspiration. Research assistance was willingly tendered by Ceri Stennett and Dick Williams. The staff of the University of Wales Press were unfailingly helpful and, as always, Susan Jenkins was a firm and genuinely creative editor.

The photographs in this book have been reproduced by kind permission of the following:

Associated Sports Photography: Mark Hughes (p.210).
Colorsport: John Charles (p.100), John Toshack (p.140), Ian Rush (p.168), the Millennium Stadium, Wales v. Brazil, 2000 (p.224).
Popperfoto: Terry Yorath (p.154).
Press Association: Jack Kelsey (p.74).
Public Record Office: (COPY 1/479) Billy Meredith (p.10).
Richard Shepherd: Wales v. England, 1951 (p.2), Fred Keenor (p.34), Terry Medwin (p.112), Mike England (p.126).
Sportsphoto Ltd.: Neville Southall (p.184).
Western Mail and Echo Ltd.: Ivor Allchurch (p.86), Trevor Ford (p.59), Mel Charles (p.74), Ryan Giggs (p.196), and the silhouette (Cardiff City v. Birmingham, 1968, showing John Toshack on right) used throughout the book.

PREFACE

Once Nick Hornby had made explicit what many of us had always known, that psychologically we are moulded by our football allegiances, there was an explosion of writing about football. In Wales we needed to catch up, to fill in the details in the story initially outlined by Peter Corrigan, Geraint H. Jenkins, Gareth M. Davies, Ian Garland and Ceri Stennett. In these pages a group of writers who care about Welsh football evoke and celebrate particular heroes who were important in their own lives.

The selection reflects the long history of Welsh football excellence as well as its geographical diversity; thankfully soccer has always been an all-Wales game, far more inclusive than rival codes. More space would have allowed us to pay homage, too, to Bob John, Tommy Jones, Dai Astley, Ron Burgess, Roy Paul, Alf Sherwood, Mel Charles, Robbie James, Arfon Griffiths, Brian Flynn, Kevin Ratcliffe and other Welsh greats. Certainly we want this volume to prompt further reflections even as it inspires renewed glory.

Our title was suggested by Ron Burgess who in 1952 dedicated his autobiography to 'my club, my country, and my pals'.

July 2000   Peter Stead

CONTRIBUTORS

HUW V. BOWEN Senior lecturer in economic and social history at the University of Leicester.

DAVID EASTWOOD Chief executive of the Arts and Humanities Research Board and formerly pro-vice chancellor of the University of Wales Swansea.

ALED EIRUG Head of news and current affairs, BBC Wales.

JOHN HARDING Writer, sports biographer and teacher in North London.

ROB HUGHES Sports writer for the *International Herald Tribune* and *The Sunday Times*.

GERAINT H. JENKINS Director of the Centre for Advanced Welsh and Celtic Studies, Aberystwyth.

MARTIN JOHNES Lecturer in sports studies at St Martin's College Lancaster.

BARRIE S. MORGAN Director of external relations, King's College, University of London.

KENNETH O. MORGAN Labour peer, historian and former vice-chancellor of the University of Wales.

HUW RICHARDS Freelance writer, historian and sports correspondent for the *International Herald Tribune* and *Financial Times*.

ROB STEEN Author and sports reporter for *The Guardian*, *Sunday Telegraph* and *Financial Times*.

PETER STEAD Writer, broadcaster and historian of popular culture.

JOHN WILLIAMS Director of the Sir Norman Chester Centre for Football Research at the University of Leicester.

The Welsh Football World

In June 2000, as the leading football nations of Europe prepared for Euro 2000, the supporters of Wales were yet again left to reflect on their team's failure to qualify for the finals of a major international tournament. There was, however, a moment of consolation, for the press carried photographs of John Charles in cap and gown on the day he had received an honorary doctorate from Leeds Metropolitan University. The fact that Wales's greatest ever player was being honoured in this way, and indeed the knowledge that he was fit enough to attend the ceremony, warmed the hearts of a football nation that had increasingly lost out in vital matches and accordingly slipped in the world rankings.

This story was a reminder that at least we had produced one of football's all-time greats, a player who in his day would have been picked for any World XI either as a centre-half or centre-forward. The news of this latest honour occasioned special joy in the player's home town of Swansea, but citizens there were well used to sharing their hero with the wider world. It was wholly fitting that Charles should be honoured in Leeds where he was for so long the star attraction. But it was the degree of his reputation in Turin, the most knowledgeable soccer city in the world, that most fully confirmed Charles's global status. In Turin they have never understood the British reluctance to honour *il buon gigante*: if it had been up to the Italians he would have been 'Sir John' long before now.

John Charles has been our greatest player and his career serves as a general reminder of how football has operated in Welsh life. We may have slipped in the FIFA rankings but, traditionally, the very fact of a distinct national team, one which had played its first game in 1876 and which for many years had played in the most distinguished of all international kits, had been one of the most explicit confirmations of identity in international terms. Success had never come easily but the prospect of success was ever present, not least because the small nation could at any one time rely on the presence of a handful of players whose value was suggested by their star roles in the leading English club sides.

From the days of Billy Meredith on it was the presence of genuine star quality in the national team that made supporting Wales such a pleasure. In national terms the game peaked in Wales in those Home International matches played against England and Scotland in the 1950s when crowds of over 50,000 would fill Ninian Park, not least because Jack Kelsey, John Charles, Ivor Allchurch, Trevor Ford and Cliff Jones, Swansea boys all, were regarded as being world class. There was to be a reprise of that kind of satisfaction in a later decade when Neville Southall, Ian Rush, Mark Hughes and Ryan Giggs injected class into the Welsh line-up, but the context of international football had changed and support for Wales was less focused. The decline in the rankings together with the extensive television coverage of football and a huge emphasis on club loyalty, especially for the superclubs, had fragmented Welsh football loyalty.

Certainly, in the old days, the identification of stars was one's first response to any Welsh side running onto the park, for it was only international fixtures which brought the top Welsh players to Ninian Park, the Vetch or the Racecourse. We would also look for the newcomers, always checking the programme to see where they were from. It was this particular exercise which taught us the geography of Wales; we would take pride in players who came from what we thought of as scattered parts of the land. In those days programme editors relished birthplaces, and in doing so they filled out our sense of Wales. The first Welsh team I saw in the flesh was based on the usual Swansea core but there were also representatives from Pont-henri, Gelli, Aberaman, Brecon, Merthyr and Cwm. Later games had me checking the whereabouts of Wrexham, Caersws and Ffynnongroyw.

My favourite entry in an imaginary atlas of Welsh 'song-lines' would be one on Jack Evans, a player affectionately recalled during Cardiff City's centenary celebrations in 1999. The Welsh-speaking Evans was born in Bala in 1889 and had already played for Bala Wanderers, Welshpool and Wrexham before a serious shoulder injury forced him to abandon the game. He came south to work in the Rhondda and was soon fit enough to play for Cwmparc and Treorchy. He was spotted by the newly named Cardiff City and he became that club's first professional signing. In 1910 he scored the first City goal in the refurbished Ninian Park, he was the first Cardiff player to be capped by Wales and he played regularly for the club until 1926; he was in the first City team that went to Wembley in 1925. As a youngster Evans had trained as a printer's compositor, a career he continued first in the Rhondda and then for thirty-five years in Cardiff. He was a regular at Ninian Park until his death in 1971. He had played only eight times for Wales, but there is a way in which his career encapsulated much of the dynamic of Welsh society in the early decades of the century. One can imagine the pride experienced in Bala, Welshpool, Wrexham, Cwmparc and Cardiff itself as Jack Evans ran out for his first cap against Ireland in 1912.

As a native of Barry I shared in the town's joy in 1954 when local lad Derek Tapscott was picked to play for Wales against Austria in Vienna. Quite remarkably, Tappy had been playing for his home town until 1953 when he had signed for Arsenal; his first-team debut for the Gunners, playing alongside Tommy Lawton, came only three days before his call up for Wales. At a time when Wales was well-blessed for goal-scoring forwards, Tappy was to be in and out of the Welsh team, and this was a matter I was to discuss in detail with his father who delivered our Sunday papers. I was slightly in awe of the diminutive Mr Tapscott Senior who had fathered seventeen children, and I was fully prepared to share his indignation whenever his son was dropped. On one such occasion in 1956 he opened the *Sunday Express* and proceeded to take pleasure in pointing out in the matchless Barry idiom that a significantly bigger crowd had watched 'our Derek' playing for Arsenal at Highbury than had turned up to support Wales at Ninian Park. This was the first time that I realized that there was a club and country tension: there were dimensions to the game over and above the call of country.

For those of us who played our soccer in streets and parks it was tempting to assume that there was a direct progression from the informal to the organized, from the public place to the enclosed stadium and from the amateur to the professional. We soon realized, however, that football needed to be organized and that, in Wales, such matters were in the hands of middle-aged men in blazers. At the first level of organization, and this surely had been the case since the start of the twentieth century, it was teachers who were vital. It was they who taught skills, picked teams, shouted increasingly frantic touch-line instructions and took us to Ninian Park to watch schoolboy internationals. It was they who taught the Welsh to love football, and in any analysis of national decline the question of why that teaching tradition disappeared in the 1980s would have to be broached.

After the teachers came the local businessmen who became the backbone of club soccer in Wales, the men whom we saw taking tea, biscuits and perhaps something a little stronger at half-time and whom we knew would be paying the wages, buying the kits and trying to install floodlights. Inevitably there was a politics of Welsh football and we all became experts on that, courtesy of international programmes in which the photographs of committee men were given greater prominence than those of the players. We all sensed that Ron Burgess and Ivor Allchurch came lower in the hierarchy than Mr Milwyn Jenkins, Mr T. E. Russell, Mr T. H. Squire and Mr D. C. Rees. Years later we all laughed at the famous Berlin scandal when an overbooked flight led to a player being left behind whilst all the FAW officials travelled on. In truth, however, we knew then as we know now that the logic of football demands entrepreneurs. At the start of the twenty-first century it is 'tycoons' that the Welsh game most urgently requires. If they invest millions let them have full-page photos in the programme.

Our football was nurtured in a complex society where harsh economic realities were accompanied by a range of agencies specializing in identifying and encouraging talent. It was preponderantly a village and small-town culture, but one which naturally fed into a British urban framework. In recent years the world's media tycoons have bought sport and, in particular, fully exploited the universal popularity of football, which remains the most simple and accessible of all sports. A post-urban and deindustrialized Wales has been left behind and consequently many Welsh football fans find it easier to support Manchester United or Liverpool rather than Wales or any team in Wales. At the start of a new century attention has focused on the need for the National Assembly for Wales to promote economic regeneration. In truth, however, the battle to redefine Wales is essentially a cultural one. As we save our football and our culture we save our nation.

In supporting our national team and glorying in the club successes of our favourite players, followers of Welsh football became citizens of the world, fully qualified to air views and express prejudices in the company of experts from Manchester, Liverpool, Turin, Barcelona, Rio and Buenos Aires, indeed anywhere the beauty of the sport is appreciated. In our hearts we know that we are better than the crude rankings suggest: no wonder we try to suppress our knowledge of them. I have never recovered from a shock experienced on Christmas Day 1997. Just as my plane was about to land in Hanoi I noticed that the *Viet Nam News* had printed the most recent FIFA rankings. Knowing that the Vietnamese were passionately interested in the game I checked their standing: they were 104th in the world, between Singapore and India. To my horror I then saw that Wales was in 102nd place. During my subsequent stay in Viet Nam I never quite shook off the shame of that statistic, although there was some consolation. Every child seemed to support Manchester United and one particular urchin in Hoi An, who every day reeled off for me the Premiership League table, worshipped Ryan Giggs. Following my hurried course of instruction the young lad came to understand that Giggs was Welsh, while I was left to reflect on wider issues. How many teachers and tycoons will it take to earn a Welsh club side a following in the Far East and to guarantee global fame for a new generation of stars from Bala, Ffynnongroyw, Manselton, Barry and Tiger Bay?

Billy Meredith

John Harding

In late 1999 Patrick Barclay, writing in the *Daily Telegraph* about England's paucity of left-sided players, expressed his bemusement at Ryan Giggs being 'so oddly pledged to Wales, after captaining England Youth'. Yet, the idea that playing for Wales might be a waste of time and talent (particularly if the talent be a great one) and that, given the option, anyone with sense would choose England, is not new. In 1910, while walking the deserted streets of Cardiff with journalist Jimmy Catton after Wales had been beaten yet again by the old enemy, Billy Meredith muttered, 'I wish I had been born in England.' Catton wrote: 'This surprised me. Meredith added, "You know the house where I was born was only three hundred yards or so over the border. What a time I should have had if I had been born an Englishman. I'm sick of being on the losing side." Then, after a silence, he burst out again, "Here, take my jersey," and he gave me the red jersey of wild Wales in which he had played against England. I thanked him for the sporting treasure and stored it away at the bottom of my kit-bag as soon as possible in case he repented.'

In Meredith's era, wearing an England shirt brought none of the tangible rewards to be gained today. Back before the First World War, the Home International Championship provided the only opportunity to earn a cap and, with just three on offer per season no matter what your nationality, money hardly entered into the equation. Yet Meredith was a perfectionist who hated losing at anything. He was also a consummate, if reluctant, professional whose job it was to win. Playing for Wales made no sense on either of those counts, hence his frustration and bitter anger at the way fate had dealt him such a poor hand. Those few tantalizing yards . . .

And yet, of course, it is not as clear cut as that. The meandering border separating Denbighshire from Shropshire threw up many an anomaly in the early years of Welsh international football. The first ever Welsh eleven to play England in 1879 included six players from the town of Oswestry which, being some three miles inside England, led to considerable doubts as to whether all six were, in fact, Welsh. And as late as 1910, R. E. Evans played ten games on the left wing for Wales before it was discovered that he had been born marginally outside the Welsh border near Chester. England then claimed him, much to Evans's chagrin. Yards, or miles: nationality has always been as much about mind and mood as geography. Jimmy Catton's anecdote continued: 'More silence until he said with dramatic eloquence, "I would like to be on the winning side for once against England. Mind you, we did win at Fulham in 1907 if the referee had given us our dues. But there, never mind, little Wales will win some day. May I be there at the death."'

If anything, the outburst tells us more about Meredith's occasionally shocking candour than it does about his allegiance to Wales. And it certainly does his home village of Chirk, where he was born on 24 July 1874, a great disservice. Indeed, from a purely footballing point of view, there was more than a touch of good fortune to his having been born there. By the time that Meredith joined their first-team ranks, in the early 1890s Chirk was the pre-eminent Welsh side in a period when north Wales, with its close proximity to the football hot-beds of Stoke, Liverpool and Manchester, was the cradle of Welsh soccer. Between 1887 and 1894, Chirk won the Welsh Cup six times; what is more they were fashioned and controlled by T. E. Thomas, a pioneer administrator of Welsh football who also happened to be Meredith's schoolmaster. The school itself, which looked out on to Chirk's ground, might be deemed an early football academy for it would produce some twenty internationals in the first twenty-five years of Welsh soccer.

Thus the Welsh team that Meredith was to grace for a record forty-eight times (fifty if you include, as he always did, two Victory Internationals in 1919) was, particularly in these early days, almost a local side. Its members were often related by blood or marriage, the majority (including Jimmy Trainer, Dai Jones, Billy Lot Jones as well as Meredith's brother, Sam) hailing from a ten-mile stretch of country south of Wrexham where soccer, according to Welsh football historian Peter Corrigan, 'found its first fertile ground in Wales'. The resulting camaraderie may well have accounted for some of the remarkable results achieved by the team – though rarely against England. It certainly imbued in Meredith an almost manic desire to be a part of it. In 1948, then in his seventies, he recalled on Radio Wales that he had often had to take 'dog's leave' to play for his country, defying his (English) club management. In fact, his grand total of appearances would have topped the seventy mark had he been permitted to play each time he was picked. It was an issue that would always rankle with Meredith: English officialdom denying him his rights. He would battle against it in one form or another throughout his long and tempestuous career.

Once again, his relative good fortune at having been born those few hundred yards across the border provided him with a perspective denied many of his English counterparts. Welsh football, whether local or national, drew strength from its lack of unnecessary formality and debilitating class divisions. The clear distaste felt by certain members of the English FA for professionals, for instance, had no counterpart in Wales. Meredith would have found such attitudes unacceptable whatever his national allegiance. That they should impinge upon his relationship with his 'gallant little Wales' he considered intolerable.

There was more to Chirk, of course, than just football. It was a mining village and Meredith's was a mining family, although by the time he joined his father at the local Black Park Colliery, his elder brothers Sam, Elias and Jim had taken alternative routes out of the pit. Meredith began full-time work aged twelve as a pony driver and 'hutcher' (hooking on empty tubs at the pit-bottom). He later becoming a boiler-firer and even had ambitions to become an engineer. And even though professional football offered a great deal, and though he had a perfect role model in his brother Sam, who would have a long career with Stoke City and Leyton Orient, Meredith was at first reluctant to embrace the game full time. Perhaps his parents' lack of interest in football was a factor (Meredith claimed his father only ever saw him play once) and his own natural caution certainly played a part. That he would have to uproot himself, leave his family home and go to live in a distant industrial English city certainly held little attraction for him. Chirk is situated amid breathtaking countryside and Billy Meredith was a great walker, loved fishing, and revelled in the slow pace of village life. That he did not drink and eschewed gambling also made the strange world of the professional footballer less than compelling.

Nevertheless trouble in the mining industry, strikes, lock-outs and the resulting hardships that followed saw him move tentatively but steadily towards signing professional forms. After winning a Welsh Cup medal for Chirk in 1894, he played briefly as a semi-professional for Wrexham and then professionally for Northwich Victoria in the English Second

Division. Finally, in late 1894, Manchester City officials plucked him from under the noses of Bolton and Everton. For a year or so he commuted happily back and forth between Chirk and Manchester, down the pit during the week, football on Saturdays, and he always maintained that having a job outside the game was beneficial to players. In 1896, however, the club insisted he give up his colliery job. He would remain a full-time professional playing for both Manchester City and United until his retirement in 1924.

His record in purely statistical terms is awesome: in more than thirty years of almost continual playing, Meredith notched up some 650 League appearances plus fifty-three FA Cup ties (including two finals). During this time he scored almost 200 goals. He appeared for Wales on fifty occasions, scoring another ten goals and helping Wales to win two Home International Championships. Meredith's own statistics, which include four years of war-time appearances plus testimonials, exhibitions and local cup competitions put his career appearances at well over a thousand. He climaxed this marathon by turning out, aged almost fifty, in an FA Cup semi-final for Manchester City in 1924 which, had City won, would have seen Meredith at the newly opened Wembley Stadium.

Longevity and statistics do not guarantee immortality, however, and Meredith's reputation has endured partly because, with his speed, his breathtaking goals, and his ball-playing skills, he succeeded in catching the public's imagination, thrilling, puzzling and perplexing crowds, commentators and fellow players alike. Sadly, it is also true to say that his fame might not have lasted quite so long and his impact on the game might not have been quite as profound if, on 15 March 1904 while playing for Manchester City, he had not attempted to bribe an opposing captain into 'throwing' a vital League match. The scandal that followed shocked the football world and, though he protested his innocence vehemently, there can be little doubt that he was central to a conspiracy to pervert both the course of a game and the destiny of a championship. It may have been a half-hearted and poorly executed scheme to offer Aston Villa captain Alec Leake a mere ten pound note to secure a favourable result for Manchester City, but Meredith had acted as go-between and it was his immense good fortune that he was not banned from the game for life. As it was, he spent a year and a half kicking his heels before returning, this time in the colours of Manchester United.

His re-emergence on New Year's Day 1907 has probably only been matched by the return of that other brooding, temporarily fallen Gallic hero, Eric Cantona. And, like Cantona, Meredith returned not as a penitent, but as the aggrieved party determined to make up for lost time and to repay his various enemies in full.

Meredith was convinced that he had suffered suspension and financial loss not because he had done wrong but because he was Welsh and because he had been playing for a team from the then unfashionable city of Manchester. His troubles were thus the result of jealousy and hypocrisy. Consequently, he derived great pleasure in helping to propel Manchester United from obscurity to League and FA Cup glory, as well as leading Wales, in March 1907, to her first-ever Home International Championship. These were victories for underdogs, and Meredith enjoyed the idea that he, the 'outsider', was their champion. His popularity, needless to say, suffered hardly at all – indeed, his ignominious fall and phoenix-like resurrection simply added to his fascination. That he was a thrilling player to watch, one who rarely failed to give the men and women on the terraces value for money, must also have played a considerable part in his rapid rehabilitation.

David Jack wrote in the 1930s: 'Centring as an art seems to be dying out. There is not a William Meredith in present-day football for example. Meredith was a first-class winger in every way, but his crossing of the ball was par excellence, true in delivery and directed towards his colleagues with almost uncanny accuracy and strength. He rarely dropped a ball behind.' Later still, Meredith, writing in *Titbits* in 1947, reflected a little tongue-in-cheek perhaps:

In my day I could play on the wing with only one eye. I only had to look ahead, not all around me. Once I had the ball, I knew what was expected of me – to beat the wing-half and full-back, take the ball down to the corner-flag and centre. The other forwards knew my intentions and kept up with me.

Such direct, fast and spectacular football was what the fans came to see, he felt, whereas:

Nowadays wingers cut in and you get a lot of bunched-up play and frenzied kicking around the goal mouth. The corners of the field are there to be used. We did use them when I was playing. Now you can almost pick mushrooms there . . .

This may suggest a simpler, less complicated time, but it is also probably misleading. Meredith was frequently man-marked, sometimes with two men deputed to deal with him during a period when robust physical contact was accepted as essential to the game. His solution to such obstacles, the key to his success, was control of the ball. In 1924 a *Manchester Guardian* reporter described 'the strange feat' Meredith could perform 'of magnetising the ball round his toes in a half-circle and then running down the field to the goal-line with a ferocious half-back somehow kept always on the off-side of him'. Almost twenty years earlier in 1906 Meredith himself had commented in the prestigious *Association Football and the Men Who Made It* on the qualities that made a successful forward: 'That he has the ball completely under control is the motive power of his energies, the current showing him the shortest and best cut to goal.'

As the statistics show, going for goal was very much a part of Billy Meredith's game. He enjoyed nothing better than to volley the opposing winger's cross into the roof of the net, his power of shot being such that he was once credited with snapping a crossbar. Yet, how he managed to score quite so many while apparently hugging the touch-line remains one of football's unsolved conundrums.

Such puzzles mattered little to those who flocked to watch him, drawn to see a real sporting celebrity: for Meredith was a star during a time when publicity was rudimentary. He was also familiar to many who had never seen him in the flesh before because, during an era when sports photography was unknown, Meredith was a perfect subject for newspaper cartoonists. His bandy legs and tricky back-heel were ideal 'hooks' for professional and amateur caricaturists alike, while his toothpick, which he chewed incessantly while playing, was a readily identifiable trademark. He claimed that he chewed toothpicks and matches instead of the traditional miner's tobacco 'twist', the latter being considered inappropriate for a footballer as there were no convenient spittoons at pitch-side. Fans would send him packs of toothpicks.

It is fair to claim that Meredith was more than a sportsman: he was a national celebrity. In 1904, he was voted footballer of the year ahead of

Englishmen Steve Bloomer and Bob Crompton by readers of the *Umpire* Sunday newspaper; he was also a favourite of music-hall star George Robey who paid for both the Manchester City and United Cup Final jerseys and had the winning teams appear on stage with him in the West End. Other music-hall stars such as Fred Karno and Harry Wheldon were good friends and a catch-phrase from one of Karno's stage plays, *The Football Match*, 'Meredith, We're In!' became a popular cry on the terraces. He had various nicknames from the Welsh Wizard to Old Skin; songs of praise were composed in his honour. He sold own-brand footballs and boots from his sports shop in Manchester's St Peter's Square, and he even appeared on railway posters advertising football excursions. His return from 'exile' was a great success, therefore, and his fame and relative fortune were guaranteed. Yet, he wanted more. As we have already seen, he felt an abiding sense of grievance over the bribery scandal and his target for revenge would be those football administrators whom he held responsible for his temporary disgrace.

On 7 January 1907, at the Imperial Hotel, Manchester, Meredith took the chair at a meeting to re-establish a football players' union. That the idea stemmed directly from his suspension and disgrace cannot be doubted. He had been back in the game for no more than a few weeks before the idea was floated. He was, one senses, a man in a great hurry, anxious to change things, to assert himself, maybe even to cleanse himself.

Insurance against injury and the establishment of a pension fund were important items on the new union's agenda. The ending of restrictions on the freedom of movement of players between clubs and the recognition by the FA that professional footballers were bona fide workers with the same rights of access to employment law as other workers were other key demands. Yet the organization was by no means egalitarian-minded. The abolition of the maximum wage (then but a few years old but the source, Meredith was convinced, of most of the evils blighting the game) was clearly the driving motive behind the new organization. It was certainly top of Meredith's agenda. As he wrote in a newspaper article some days after the union's reformation: 'What is more reasonable than our plea that the footballer, with his uncertain career, should have the best money he can earn? If I can earn £7 a week, should I be debarred from receiving it?'

A year later, when there appeared to be a chance that League clubs might abolish the maximum wage, he wrote in the *Bradford Argus*:

At last! At last the large cities and the biggest crowds are to have football of the best, and at last the players are to have a genuine inducement to show for the benefit of the public all the skill that is in them. The day of the man who is content to exert himself one week in four is over. Men will now be paid according to their ability and conduct.

Meredith's fitness was legendary: in his thirty-year career at the top he could have missed no more than a dozen matches through injury. But he did not attribute this to good fortune. He was a strict teetotaller, a non-smoker (a legacy of his Primitive Methodist background) and a keen dietician. He liked to prepare various ointments to treat his own injuries, usually herbal-based, comfrey and country style, although his favourite application, according to his daughter Winifred, was a vile-smelling jelly used on the gears of coal-mine machinery. He would remain happily married all his life to his childhood sweetheart, Ellen Negus. He was, in every respect, the model professional – organized, dedicated, abstemious.

It was hardly surprising that such a man should feel insulted at being told that he could not negotiate his own salary, that he could not receive what his employers were happy enough to pay him, that he should be considered morally suspect for receiving money to play a game in the first place. It was, Meredith considered, this unnatural, deeply hypocritical situation that had led to his ultimate disgrace. His union, he was sure, would force through sensible, rational reforms and thus create a healthier, more honest game. For two years, the union busied itself with recruiting members and devising schemes to end the transfer system and liberalize wages. Meredith held no formal office in the new organization, but railed away at FA councillors and League management committee members from his column in *Thomson's Weekly News*. Changes were few and minimal and, for a time, the game's rulers considered Meredith and his organization mere irritants to be tolerated. In 1909, however, annoyed at the union's insistence on taking clubs to court without asking its permission, outraged at the union's approach to England players before an England–Scotland match to secure compliance with possible strike action and unnerved at the union's insistence on affiliating to the General Federation of Trades Unions, the FA decided enough was enough. It ordered all players to resign from the union forthwith, or face permanent exile from the game.

Meredith, though no socialist, had some experience of industrial disputes. The year 1894 had seen strikes and lock-outs in his home region, and bitter divisions between the two local coal-mines, Black Park and Brynkinallt. He knew about solidarity, about struggle, about standing firm. And so Meredith and his Manchester United colleagues refused to resign from the union as demanded and were, with some reluctance on Manchester United's part, 'locked out'. In September 1909, faced with a possible national strike by players in support of 'The Outcasts', as the United men had become known, the FA relented and allowed the union to continue, albeit in emasculated form. Meredith, however, was scornful of the compromise reached by players less radically inclined than himself and he wrote of his disgust shortly after the crisis had ended: 'I confess that the bulk of the players have not shown much pluck in the matter . . . A man said to me the other day, "Ah, the players have not the pluck of the miners," and he was right, of course.' Nevertheless, the establishment of the union would remain Meredith's proudest achievement: in the 1940s and early 1950s, when well into his seventies, he could be found on the door at the union's annual general meeting in Manchester, checking identities and collecting subs, a sort of spectral presence reminding players of their heritage and responsibilities.

During the First World War, aged forty and too old to be enlisted, he played more than a hundred games for Manchester City as a 'guest'. His career reached its apogee, however, in 1920 when he was part of a Welsh side including Ted Vizard, Fred Keenor, Moses Russell and Stan Davies that at long last defeated England at Highbury Stadium to take the Home International Championship for only the second time. Tears were shed in the dressing-room. He had been there 'at the death' after all. Meanwhile, power in Welsh soccer had now moved irrevocably south, ushering in an epoch when Welsh players and teams would move to the very forefront of the British game.

Meredith had little luck as a businessman. His sports goods shop in Manchester closed in 1909, having been badly damaged by fire; a revolutionary rubberized football design that might have saved him from bankruptcy had previously been bought by the secretary of the Players' Union, who developed it independently. In 1914, he took a public house, the Church Hotel in Longsight, Manchester, and during the 1920s and 1930s he and his wife managed a second public house, the Stretford Hotel on the Stretford Road, close to Old Trafford. It was a popular 'sportsman's' pub, and a venue for celebrities of all kinds, from jockeys to boxers to music-hall stars. In 1926 he starred in a feature film, *The Ball of Fortune*, a tale of football skulduggery and bribery. He also featured in training films and appeared on stage to take questions from the floor. In his last years, he did a little scouting and often accompanied journalists to Wembley to lend a little colour to match reports. He died on 19 April 1958, two months after the Munich air-crash had taken the lives of the Busby Babes, many of whom Meredith had come to know first as schoolboys.

Meredith's contribution to Welsh soccer, in terms of the prestige and credibility he lent it during its formative years, is incalculable. But like all great players, he transcended national boundaries. He is one of the game's truly legendary figures, ranking alongside Matthews, Best and Baxter. In that sense, Billy Meredith was Wales's first, perhaps finest, contribution to the world game.

Leigh Richmond Roose

Geraint H. Jenkins

It is one of the commonplaces of sport that a goalkeeper is rather different from the rest of mankind and certainly from his fellow footballers. From the days of William ('Fatty') Foulke, the gargantuan Shropshire-born international custodian who used to get his retaliation in first by waddling naked into visiting dressing-rooms to intimidate opponents and referees, to René Higuita (El Loco), the eccentric Colombian keeper whose surges upfield and scorpion kicks passed into folklore, goalkeepers have taken pride in being deemed a breed apart. Arguably the most gifted superman of them all was Leigh Richmond Roose, the 'Prince of Goalkeepers' in Edwardian Wales, whose *curriculum vitae* was a thing of wonder. No other member of the Welsh Hall of Footballing Fame can claim to have sat at the feet of the father of modern science fiction H. G. Wells, won nineteen of twenty-four international caps playing alongside the incomparable 'Welsh Wizard' Billy Meredith, represented clubs as diverse as Stoke, Everton, Sunderland, Huddersfield, Aston Villa, Woolwich Arsenal and Celtic, entertained the music-hall star Marie Lloyd, and prompted the dry-as-dust Welsh historian Thomas Richards to refer to him in awe as 'this wondrous Hercules' ('Yr Ercwlff synfawr hwn').

Born on 27 November 1877, Roose was a native of Holt, near Wrexham. His Anglesey-born father, Richmond Leigh Roose, was a Presbyterian minister and the author of *The Five Senses of the Body* (1875). He sent his son to Holt Academy, whose prospectus offered 'a sound English Education, together with Greek and Latin, or German and French'. Under its principal, James Oliver Jones, discipline at the academy left much to be desired, and when the young H. G. Wells was appointed master in 1887 the menacing attitude of some of the older pupils unnerved him. While refereeing a football match on a wet Saturday afternoon, Wells fell on the muddy field and was severely kicked in the back by Edward Roose, Leigh's brother, and spent several weeks incapacitated with a ruptured kidney. Wells left shortly afterwards, but it may well be that his provocative independence and obsession with the bizarre fruits of science left their mark on Leigh Richmond Roose and that this prompted him to read science when he arrived at the University College of Wales, Aberystwyth, in 1895.

Although the 'College by the Sea' was not, as the embittered Goronwy Rees liked to claim, 'a theocratic society, ruled by priests and elders', the Nonconformist way of life was a powerful influence on staff and students alike. When R. Williams Parry, later to become one of Wales's most celebrated poets, confessed to Principal T. Francis Roberts that he smoked cigarettes and played billiards, he was asked: 'What other sins have you Mr Parry?' Most students worshipped regularly and the historian R. T. Jenkins recalled seeing Roose many times in his sober dark blue suit in the English Presbyterian chapel. However, since his father had failed to pass on the native language, Roose never darkened the meetings of the Celtic society (Y Geltaidd), and wild horses would not have dragged him to the coy soirées and at-homes which figured so prominently in the social round of staff and students. He had the reputation of being a self-possessed, rather aloof loner. From time to time, however, he figured in tempestuous student debates, interjecting on one occasion 'at a speed of some 300 words per minute' in order to demolish the argument of a priggish Liberal, and, on another occasion, winning thunderous applause by vigorously opposing a motion that athletics was 'detrimental to the best interests of the nation'. In February 1899 he was persuaded to take part in a mock trial, 'The Ass and the Ass's Shadow: The Great Case of John Jones v. John Jones in re the Shadow of the Ass'. Cast as a policeman, his sole contribution was to roar 'Silence in Court!', which he did with such panache and authority that many believed it was the highlight of the evening. Roose was also one of the few students who dared to twit the head porter, Sergeant Wakeling, a tragicomic Falstaffian figure who ruled the quad with a rod of iron and whose malapropisms provoked much private hilarity.

As a result, although 'Mond' Roose kept his distance from fellow students, he became an iconic figure. Women students adored him and flocked to sporting events in order to cheer on and flirt with their hero. Puerile rules and regulations designed to restrict the mingling of the sexes were ignored or circumvented at the Vicarage Fields where, summer and winter alike, Roose was the principal focus of attention. At cricket his superlative fielding more than compensated for his Tufnell-like batting (his average was 3.83 in 1898) and his bowling was brisk and lively. During the annual Sports' Day he basked in the adulation of his admirers, proving invincible at throwing a cricket ball and winning the shot putt, high jump and piggy-back events in May 1899. Only when other mortals fell below his high standards did he lose his composure. At a gymnastic display held in the examination hall, a dishevelled Roose failed to rally the Science team in a tug-of-war competition and was reported to have been 'uncertain whether to stand on his head or his feet'.

But it was as a brave, unorthodox, idiosyncratic and marvellously athletic goalkeeper that Roose gained his reputation as a genius. While playing for the College, he particularly savoured the bruising contests against the students of Bangor, and such was his prowess that Aberystwyth Town FC also captured his signature. Roose represented the 'Old Black and Green' on eighty-five occasions, and on 16 April 1900 he was carried shoulder-high from the field when Aberystwyth trounced the Druids 3–0 in the Welsh Cup Final. By the time of his departure from the College, the *Cambrian News* had exhausted its fund of superlatives in recounting the exploits of this extraordinary figure. Roose moved to London to train as a doctor at King's College Hospital, but although James A. H. Catton, who wrote under the pseudonym 'Tityrus', referred to Roose in the *Athletic News* as 'this eminent bacteriologist' he never qualified as a doctor and thus earned a living as an extremely expensive 'amateur' player for a host of illustrious clubs in the First Division of the Football League. He made 144 League appearances for Stoke in 1901–4 and 1905–8, helped Everton to reach the runners-up position in the League and the semi-final of the FA Cup in 1904/5, and during four seasons at Roker Park helped Sunderland to finish in third place in the League on two occasions. When the *Daily Mail* invited nominations for a World XI to challenge another planet, Roose was the undisputed choice as goalkeeper. His League career ended with Woolwich Arsenal in 1911.

By his twentieth birthday, Roose had established himself as an international reserve to Jimmy Trainer of Wrexham and (later) Preston North End. He won the first of twenty-four caps in February 1900, when Ireland were defeated 2–0 at Llandudno, and the last – also against Ireland, when Wales won by a three-goal margin – at Wrexham in 1910. But for injury and other 'social' commitments, Roose would have won many more caps. His record – won nine, drawn six and lost nine – was extremely respectable and was marred only by some severe and painful drubbings at the hands of England (0–6 in 1901, 1–5 in 1905, 1–7 in 1908). Yet he proved a tower of strength in the memorable 1907 season when Wales won the Home Championship, following which each player was rewarded with a gold medal by the Welsh Football Association. In the Edwardian period Roose and Billy Meredith were not only the most gifted but also the most valuable members of the Welsh team. Roose, the son of a Presbyterian, and Meredith, the son of a Primitive Methodist, were also no strangers to controversy and Welsh international fixtures would have been much staider events without them.

Nabokov once maintained that, by sheer force of personality as well as footballing skills, outstanding goalkeepers in Russia and the Latin countries impose themselves on every game: 'He vies with the matador and the flying ace as an object of thrilled adulation.' He might just as easily have been referring to Roose, for he was the first (and perhaps the last) of the Welsh goalkeeping entertainers. To him, every game was a piece of human drama in which he was the principal player. This meant that he felt obliged to entertain, as well as protect his goal. Unlike his immediate predecessor Jimmy Trainer, who had been safety and reliability personified, Roose turned demonstrative goalkeeping and un-predictable behaviour into an art. As James A. H. Catton shrewdly observed, he was 'dexterous though daring, valiant though volatile'.

Like wicketkeepers, goalkeepers are born rather than made, and Roose certainly possessed all the necessary physical attributes. Standing 6ft 1in. tall and weighing 13st 6lbs, he cut an impressive figure and could both physically and literally look down on most of his fellow players. Roose's jutting browline, small intense eyes, well-groomed moustache (at least in his student days) and wide, powerful shoulders oozed authority and defiance. His phenomenal reach and huge hands – Thomas Richards referred to his 'prehensile grip' – enabled him to make saves which lived long in the memory. Moreover, his sharp eyesight, startling reflexes, competitive instinct and reckless bravery made him an extraordinarily daunting opponent. Goalkeeping is a demanding position and Roose's flamboyance should not blind us to his athletic and technical prowess.

Yet throughout his career (and even unto death) there remained an air of surprise and mystery about Roose. A repertoire of well-rehearsed, though sometimes impromptu, eccentricities were an integral part of the Roose legend. The fact that he was a middle-class amateur in a largely professional game did not mean that he played purely for pleasure, for his 'amateurism' was a token of his social exclusivity as well as a passport to financial gain as a roving 'guest' player. He expected, indeed demanded, extravagant expenses and lavish hospitality for his services. Often he would awaken public interest by arriving at the ground in a horse and carriage, which was followed through the streets by entranced young supporters. On one occasion he hired a special locomotive to transport him from London to Stoke, and charged the costs of the journey to the club. A born self-publicist, Roose knew how to add thousands to the gate. When Wales were due to play Ireland in March 1909, he arrived at Liverpool for the journey to Belfast with his hand heavily bandaged. He claimed that although two fingers were broken he would be fit to play the following day. His two closest friends, Billy Meredith and Charlie Morris (both from Chirk), were too street-wise to be taken in and, peeping through the keyhole of Roose's room in their Belfast hotel, they saw the great man remove the bandage and wiggle his fingers without any sign of discomfort. News of Roose's 'disability' spread like wildfire and on the following day, before a huge crowd, the Welsh goalkeeper played a blinder and Wales won 3–2.

Like many (perhaps all) goalkeepers, Roose was highly superstitious. His attire was strikingly different: he wore white sweaters, twin-peak caps and padded knee-bandages. Although he carried white gloves onto the field, he seldom wore them, preferring to catch and fist the ball with his bare hands. Like Neville Southall, his dishevelled appearance at the beginning of a game gave the impression that he had just completed another. He preferred to play in unwashed shorts and during his season at Everton it was noticed more than once that his pants 'carried about them the marks of many a thrilling contest'. He insisted on wearing another shirt (some claim it was the old black and green shirt of Aberystwyth Town FC) under his international jersey and he never allowed charwomen to wash it.

Whereas most goalkeepers in the Edwardian era walked on to the field of play, Roose used to run briskly, acknowledging the applause before pacing the goalmouth like a restless tiger. Though jealous of his craft, he was also conscious of his vulnerability in an arena where ruffianly conduct was the norm. He once observed ruefully: 'There is a proverb which says, "Before you go to war say a prayer; before going to sea say two prayers; before marrying say three prayers." One might add: "Before deciding to become a goalkeeper say four prayers." He's the Aunt Sally.' Association football in the early twentieth century was generally a game of long passes and crosses, cunning dribbling (Meredith was the master of the 'dribbling code') and brutal tackling, and the emphasis on 'kick and rush' encouraged repetitive and unimaginative patterns of play which were often enlivened when goalkeepers deserted their goalmouth by venturing upfield. Until 1912, by which time Roose had retired, goalkeepers were permitted to use their hands outside the penalty area. All eyes would be on Roose as he sallied forth. He revelled in leaving his penalty area to become a third back or sweeper behind defenders, and his cavalier style often exasperated his experienced colleagues and infuriated his own supporters. Notoriously tetchy and unforgiving, supporters of Aberystwyth used to complain bitterly about his erratic sorties upfield, for during dull periods of play Roose liked to venture forth and indulge in 'a little fancy play' which sometimes led to costly blunders. He also used the tactic to nip attacks in the bud or to floor dangerous opponents. During his first international, against Ireland at Llandudno, Roose inexplicably sprinted from the goalmouth and unceremoniously bundled the Irish right-winger over the touch-line, knocking him unconscious. Roose had honed this tactic to perfection during inter-college matches between Aberystwyth and Bangor, en-counters which were characterized by over-zealous tackling, tripping, hacking, frayed tempers and bloody noses. The 1896 fixture proved to be one of the roughest ever seen in Aberystwyth. Relishing the hurly-burly, Roose was his own dashing, reckless self, and in the muddy conditions fierce clashes occurred. According to the match report:

> . . . an unpleasant incident happened, reflecting no credit on the feeling between the teams. Roose had run the ball out almost as far as the centre line. R.E., steering in a bee line across the field, intercepted his progress. Both went down. The Aber man, highly incensed, was up first, and at once deliberately kicked the Bangor man as the latter was in the act of rising.

A pitched battle ensued and Roose eventually returned to his goal 'in a rather knocked about condition'.

Even though the heavy brown footballs used in Edwardian days virtually became medicine balls in wet conditions, Roose could kick and throw them prodigious distances. On dry days he sent thumping kicks the length of the field and punched the ball well beyond the half-way line. According to James Ashcroft, an intelligent goalkeeper with Woolwich Arsenal, nothing gave a goalkeeper greater satisfaction than fisting the ball long distances: 'It is more than a sensation. It is an ecstasy.' But one suspects that Roose derived even greater pleasure from plunging headlong among flying feet and bruising bodies. 'Rushing the goalkeeper', particularly from corners, and heavy shoulder-charges were part and parcel of the game. But aggressive forwards held no terror for Roose and when, for instance, a scrimmage developed when Stoke met Arsenal it was 'all Lombard Street to a halfpenny orange that the Reds would score', only for Roose to emerge from the ruck with the ball clasped to his chest. Roose deliberately intimidated opponents with his fists and during his spell at Aberystwyth liberal quantities of Robert Ellis's celebrated embrocation 'for sprains, stiffness and bruises' were required by chastened forwards.

Roose's physical presence was a powerful psychological advantage for his teams. Like Peter Schmeichel, he oozed confidence, filling the goal with his mighty frame and 'psyching' opposing forwards. He exercised a strangely hypnotic influence over hesitant strikers, forcing them to scuff their shots or blast them wide of the goal. He enjoyed taunting experienced international forwards, some of whom felt the full force of his fist in goalmouth mêlées. On his day, he was an extraordinary shot-saver. In his first international he saved a point-blank drive from six yards by trapping the ball between his knees. Crowds marvelled at his spectacular leaps across goal and his mysterious ability to change his body posture in mid-air. If contemporary accounts are reliable, the save which Roose made while representing Aberystwyth against Builth in the Leominster Cup in April 1897 was at least the equal of that made by Gordon Banks against Pelé at Guadalajara in the 1970 World Cup. Some of his most breathtaking mid-air saves were from penalties. When Thomas Richards, the son of a Cardiganshire cottager who became Wales's foremost authority on seventeenth-century Puritanism and Dissent, was persuaded by a fellow student to attend a memorable en-counter between Aberystwyth Town and Glossop North End, a professional team from the Midland League, he was so intoxicated by Roose's performance that, many decades later, he was able to describe the match as if it had occurred the previous day. In a Cardus-like portrait, written in Welsh and entitled 'Gŵr o Athrylith' ('Man of Genius'), Richards depicted with subtle scriptural nuances an astonishing penalty save by Roose:

> . . . one of the full backs committed an unforgivable foul in the penalty box; the harsh blast of the referee's whistle, his finger pointing to one of the most calamitous places in the purgatory of this life – the penalty spot. The heavy odour of death hung over this fateful spot: did you not hear a crowd of thousands suddenly become dumb mutes, did you not see the players standing in a half circle as if they were at the graveside . . . Everyone holding his breath. I have always believed that Roose grew to his full height as a man in the purgatorial crisis of a penalty, drying off the clay around his feet, washing away the dross which entered his character with the gold . . . Arthur's sword against the bare fist. Then came the signal; the ball travelled like a bolt from the foot of the penalty-taking forward, and in the blink of an eyelid, revolution, a thump, and the ball landed in the heather and gorse of the Buarth.

At no time were Roose's instinctive reflexes, feats of agility and thunderous fists more evident than when he was called upon to save penalties. Large crowds would gather behind his goal and, playing to the gallery, Roose would acknowledge their warm applause with an arrogant wave both before and after completing the save. Throughout the land Roose's saves from the penalty spot lived long in the memory of supporters.

Since Roose thrived on physical contact and courageous showmanship, he despised dull games against inferior opposition. On such occasions he would lean on a goalpost and engage spectators in conversation. Warned of approaching marauders, he would embellish an easy save and goad opposing fans by lamenting the deficiencies of their team. Whilst playing for Sunderland at Everton, he incensed the home supporters by regularly kicking the ball into the deepest recesses of the stand. In April 1910 he tempted fate not only by 'guesting' for Port Vale against their deadly enemies, Stoke Reserves, but by insisting on wearing a Stoke shirt. He saved every shot with such arrogant ease that the furious crowd spilled onto the field and only the brave intervention of the local constabulary saved him from a ducking in the River Trent. It was not unusual for him deliberately to mistime jumps, fumble the ball or miskick clearances in order to add to the entertainment value of a tedious encounter. His insouciant attitude was redolent of that of the equally flamboyant Hon. Alfred Lyttleton, who declared during an England v. Scotland international in 1877: 'I am playing purely for my own pleasure, Sir!' The only goal in an international against Scotland in 1910 was scored when Roose was so preoccupied with baiting home supporters that he failed to notice a forty-yard piledriver from Devine rocketing into the roof of the net. Even then, his own players (save for the prickly Meredith) were reluctant to take him to task, and those fans who idolized him were also only too ready to forgive his indiscretions.

Off the field, too, Roose was very much his own man. He set little store by loyalty to club and his reputation for mischief was matched by his contempt for authority. In the company of football directors he burned on a short fuse: he pummelled a Sunderland director so roughly in March 1906 that the Football Association banned him for fourteen days. When, during his ninety-ninth appearance for Sunderland in November 1910, Roose broke his wrist, the club's attempts to arrange a testimonial match in his honour were scuppered by the FA who were not only mindful of his much-vaunted amateur status but also his rooted aversion to the governors of English football. Like his great friend Billy Meredith, Roose was a free-thinking rebel who expressed his views in a forthright manner. When the Football League summoned him to provide a weekly account of his expenses at Sunderland, he noted as the first item: 'Using the toilet (twice) . . . 2d.' Many tales, apocryphal and otherwise, of his combative style and rebellious spirit litter the pages of the *Athletic News* and the national newspapers.

By the time of the Great War, Roose had hung up his cap, gloves and boots. Recruited by the 9th Battalion Royal Fusiliers, he was dispatched to the Western Front. Characteristically, his telegrams to friends bore his *nom de guerre* 'The Archdeacon' and it is easy to imagine Roose playing a full part in the impromptu kickabouts in No Man's Land during Christmas festivals and exasperating German soldiers with his unorthodox tactics and volatile behaviour. At Pozières on the Somme in August 1916, his battalion came under heavy fire and Roose was badly burned. Ordered to fall back to the dressing station, he insisted on remaining in the front trench from which he tossed bombs and flame-throwers with the same unerring accuracy as he had thrown soccer balls in peacetime. On Saturday, 7 October, however, the seemingly indestructible Lance-Corporal Leigh Richmond Roose was cut down on the Somme. He was thirty-eight. He was awarded a posthumous Military Medal and his name (spelt Leigh Rouse) figures on the Thiepval Memorial to those who lost their lives on the Western Front. There is something both poignant and reassuring in the knowledge that this legendary Welsh goalkeeper, who had shown such complete mastery of psychological warfare on the football field, should have lost his life in the theatre of war. Better to have died in battle than to have suffered not only the indignities of old age but all the glorious memories fading into oblivion.

Fred Keenor

Martin Johnes

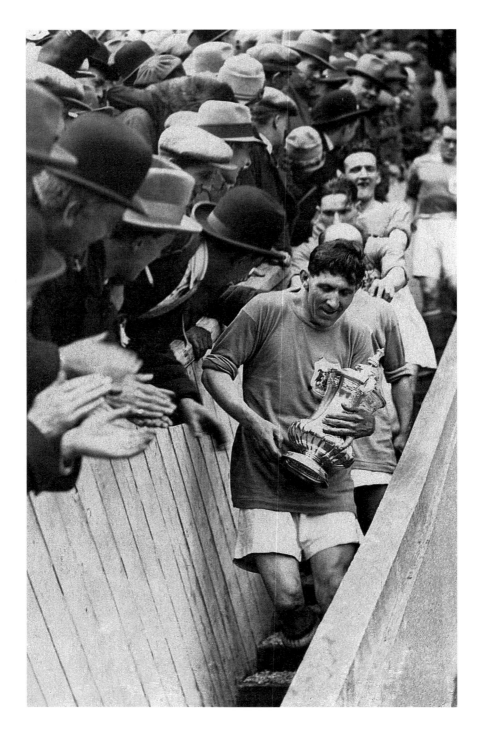

I would have liked to see him against today's fancy dans with their elbowing, shirt-pulling and poking out tongues. Fred would have tackled them once – they wouldn't have come back for more.

Ernie Curtis, team-mate

On 23 April 1927, Fred Keenor climbed the famous Wembley steps to receive the FA Cup from the king. His team, Cardiff City, had become the first, and probably the last, Welsh team to win the coveted trophy. That morning the *Western Mail* printed a cartoon, entitled 'the most important man in Wales', depicting Keenor pushing David Lloyd George aside. The game made Keenor a Welsh national hero as north and south celebrated Cardiff City's triumph. During the inter-war years, Keenor's name was synonymous with Cardiff City. He played for the club from 1912 until 1931, making 504 appearances as the team rose from the Southern League to the First Division of the Football League before falling back down into the Third Division South. His international career saw him win thirty-two caps and lead Wales to the 1924 Home Championship. By the time he retired from playing in 1936, he had become something of a legend in Welsh soccer.

Frederick Charles Keenor, the son of a bricklayer and mason, was born in Cardiff in July 1894. His rise to the status of professional footballer followed the conventional path of so many of his contemporaries. He graduated from the schoolboy game to the local Cardiff league where he eventually came to the attention of the young Cardiff City club. In 1912, aged seventeen, Keenor was 'pounced upon' by one of his former schoolmasters who was now a Cardiff City director. He signed amateur terms and, by the end of the year, had turned professional for a weekly wage of ten shillings. Like so many Edwardian footballers, he continued to work outside the game as well as playing. With his two wages he said that he felt like a millionaire. Just as Keenor was beginning to establish himself in Cardiff's first team, war was declared. Six months later Keenor enlisted alongside other professional players in the 17th Middlesex (Footballers') Battalion.

Like so many others, the Great War scarred Keenor, both physically and mentally, for the rest of his life. A leg wound threatened to end his footballing career before it had really started. In later years, he largely refused to speak of his experiences on the Western Front. As his son put it, 'Dad blotted it out. He had lost too many friends. He often said that he was one of the lucky ones who came back.' On being demobbed, the 'land fit for heroes' was no more apparent to Keenor than it was to most other returning soldiers. He found work in a gasworks and on a milk-round before rejoining Cardiff City when professional football restarted in 1919.

The 1920s saw Cardiff City establish itself as one of Britain's leading clubs. With the help of a vast support across the Valleys, the club attracted large attendances and purchased quality players. The team rose rapidly from the Southern League to the First Division of the Football League, missing out on the Championship in 1923/4, under the system then used, on a goal average of 0.024. But it was in the FA Cup that the club achieved its greatest glories. After being beaten semi-finalists twice and runners-up in 1925, Cardiff City finally won the trophy in 1927. It was to be the pinnacle of their success, as the depression that had engulfed south Wales took its toll on the belligerent soccer club. Gate receipts had already begun to tumble and the income from the successful years was invested in the ground not the ageing team. After 1927, the club's decline was rapid. Four years after lifting the FA Cup, Keenor found himself captain of a team relegated to the Third Division South.

Keenor played an integral role in Cardiff's successes during these years. He became the inspiration and captain of both club and country and a favourite amongst supporters. Yet Keenor was not the type of player who normally attracted adoration. He was neither a skilful dribbler nor a prolific goal-scorer. Instead, he was one of soccer's hard men, a rugged and uncompromising performer, playing usually at centre-half or half-back. Skill on the ball was not his forte and, at 5ft 7in, neither was size, but he more than made up for it with his resolve, strength, fitness and energy. A team-mate said of him,

> . . . he was one of the hardest tacklers in the game, some said he was dirty but he was just hard. Nobody took liberties with old Fred . . . [He] could run all night, he couldn't run with the ball mind you, but he could run all day.

In 1928, it was said that 'He might not be a stylish player but his doggedness and determination makes him one of the most effective centre halves in the country.' Such levels of fitness required hard training, particularly when, liking a drink and being a heavy smoker, the rest of your life was not always dedicated to staying in peak condition. While the other Cardiff players were doing ball practice, he was lapping the pitch in old army boots. He would often turn up late for training and, ignoring the trainer and other players, just begin running around the ground to build up his stamina and work off the previous night's beer. His robust style may have won him friends in Cardiff but he was not always so kindly treated by supporters of the teams which had to oppose him. While at Crewe, Keenor was assaulted at the end of a match, then followed to the train station and had to be given a police escort. Alongside his strength and stamina, Keenor was renowned for his courage. In 1929, he injured his neck on the morning of a match between Wales and Scotland. With Wales unable to call a reserve in time, Keenor played with his neck strapped and under orders not to head the ball, enduring the pain in order not to let the side down.

Keenor's ability to inspire others made him a natural choice as captain of both club and country. Although he did not become captain of Cardiff City until 1925/6, his influence and length of time at the club made it later seem as if he had always led the team. He was said to have 'marshalled his men magnificently' in the 1927 FA Cup Final, and in 1928 was described as 'a leader in every sense of the word, he commands respect of colleagues and sets an inspiring example by his whole hearted enthusiasm'. No doubt such leadership skills were also instrumental in pushing him towards management as his playing days drew to a close. Yet he could also be a domineering leader, angrily shouting and swearing at his team-mates. He was nearly sent off playing for Wales against Scotland in 1930 for swearing at the rest of the Welsh team, but the referee accepted that Keenor was so involved in motivating the others that he did not realize what he was saying. When Cardiff City's goalkeeper was chipped from the half-way line in a match against Blackpool, Keenor ran back and began shaking him roughly while the crowd shouted at them to get on with the game. Such a belligerent temperament did not always endear him to the Cardiff City management, and the end of his career at the club was marked by arguments with staff and other players. He even had a transfer request granted during the FA Cup winning season after being unhappy about being dropped for several matches. Keenor had his opinions and standards, and he expected fellow players and club officials to conform to them. Thus he was very much the quintessential 'British' player: physical, committed and determined, making up in strength for what he lacked in skill. And he expected the same from those around him.

It was in this style of play that Keenor's popularity originated. He embodied the working-class masculine ideal: strong and brave, an individual yet part of a team. He displayed all the virtues that the supporters on Ninian Park's Bob Bank valued. The agile deftness of a rugby fly-half may have been admired and even revered in south Wales, but it was the more down-to-earth but directed brute strength of a prop-forward, a boxer or a soccer centre-half that was in touch with what working men experienced in their daily lives. They valued and celebrated the artists of the game, but it was to the skilled artisans whom they related most closely. There are obvious parallels between the characteristics that Keenor embodied and those of the coal industry that dominated the lives of so many Cardiff supporters. Keenor may not have been a master of ball-control, but he still had a degree of skill that enabled him to become a professional player in the first place. There was a talented player beneath the rough veneer. Much as miners were proud of the physical side of their work, they were also quick to point out the technique involved. Strength and courage were admirable, but one still had to know how to apply them.

There was nothing particularly Welsh about the attributes and values that contributed to Keenor's popularity. They were characteristics shared by working-class communities across Britain. Yet Keenor's popularity also owed much to his roots. Although the professional nature of soccer created teams made up of players from across Britain, this did not prevent players from becoming representatives of the towns they played for. It was the team that was important not the individual. But when a local player did stand out it was something to celebrate. Keenor was a true 'Cardiff boy', and the local press repeatedly proclaimed how the city could be proud that one of its sons was an integral part of its multinational, star-studded soccer team. Reporters used Keenor to deflect the accusations of the rugby fraternity that soccer's success was imported into Cardiff and, in so doing, they helped mould him into a local hero.

Keenor's pride in playing for Wales ensured that his popularity extended beyond Cardiff. Like all good Welshmen, he saw England as the primary enemy. As he once said, 'We Welshmen do not mind much if we have to bow the knee to Scotland or Ireland but we do take a special delight in whacking England'. He also acknowledged the importance of Cardiff City to Wales at large and when the club was elevated to the Football League he said, 'We had made up our minds that, come what may, we'd do our best to shine and show England that Wales could run a big club successfully'. Before the 1927 Cup Final, he talked of bringing the trophy to Wales not Cardiff. Keenor was not alone in such rhetoric but, none the less, he was telling people what they wanted to hear and this helped ensure that it was not just Cardiff who appreciated him.

The maximum wage helped to ensure that players remained part of the community from which they came. They earned limited wages and thus tended to live in the locality, with the result that there was not the inseparable gulf between the stars and their supporters that exists today. Yet even between the wars, leading professional footballers enjoyed comforts and a lifestyle that set them apart from their working-class roots. Keenor built a house he had designed himself in a select part of Cardiff and developed a passion for the more middle-class recreations of motoring and shooting. The maximum wage may not have made Keenor rich but it, together with money earned from putting his name to articles and products, and the free time a professional player enjoyed, enabled him to develop tastes that were hardly typical of his background. Nevertheless, his fame and success did not remove him from his roots or take away the prejudices that they had instilled. In 1927 he visited his old school to show children the FA Cup. He described foreign tours as a pleasant break but complained that the food was strange. Such gestures and rhetoric were genuine and ensured that, while Keenor may no longer have led the life of a typical working man, both he and his supporters regarded him as someone still firmly located in his working-class roots.

The south Wales press ensured that Keenor also enjoyed a good reputation amongst the middle classes. In a world of industrial disputes and increasing commercialism in sport, Keenor was held up as an old-fashioned working man and footballer, committed to community rather than class or money. After Cardiff's defeat in the 1925 FA Cup Final, Keenor said that the best team had won. Such notions of fair play were emphasized by the press and helped to endear him to those who believed in 'traditional' values in sport. In 1937, a series of articles ghost-written for Keenor stressed his commitment to such values. One article revealed his refusal to become involved in match-fixing while another told of his detachment from threats to strike by Cardiff players in 1915. He was asked by the club to raise a team in the event of a strike and claimed that he did not even really know what the dispute was about. Keenor did argue against the maximum wage and admit that he had been tempted by some of the underhand inducements offered to him to join other clubs. However, he had been resilient and not accepted them while the maximum wage remained part of the game's legislation. Thus, for those who valued the 'respectable' ideals of sport, Keenor could be looked upon as not just a good player but also an honest man, untainted by the more unsavoury aspects of the professional game.

Keenor stayed at Cardiff City for nineteen years. To a generation of supporters he came to embody the club, fighting on loyally for them until no longer needed. While his team-mates came and went, he remained, building a special and lasting relationship between himself and the supporters. Keenor was certainly aware of the way he was viewed and talked of 'hero worship' after the Cup win. Yet he remained modest and shared the supporters' pride in the honour that winning the FA Cup had brought to Cardiff. When the press used Keenor as the face of the club in cartoons, they were not so much creating a new symbol but reflecting how people already saw him. Keenor's ability had made him a transfer target for other clubs and, by 1928, financial pressures meant that Cardiff City had to sell several of its leading players. Keenor, however, stayed on until long past the peak of his career. Had he left it is unlikely that people would have blamed him personally; after all the Depression meant that insecurity, poverty and unemployment were familiar fears for the inhabitants of south Wales. Just as there was sympathy with Welsh rugby players who left for professional rugby league, any desire on the part of Keenor to seek greater financial rewards and stability elsewhere would have been understood. Yet by staying in Cardiff and resisting the English riches on offer, Keenor ensured he remained the local hero and the popular face of Cardiff City.

By 1930, Keenor, past his best and in his mid-thirties but still earning the maximum wage, was an obvious target in Cardiff City's efforts to trim its wage bill. However, as the club's main star it would have been difficult for them to sell him without causing some discontent amongst supporters, so Keenor was told that he would have to take a wage-cut of two pounds a week. The club expected him to refuse and ask for a transfer in the hope of receiving the maximum wage elsewhere, but Keenor accepted the pay cut, perhaps aware that his age meant that any move would only be short lived. It was probably better to be the fading star somewhere where you had a reputation, than at a new club where supporters did not fully appreciate your former glories. A player not wanted by a club was likely to have an unhappy time and the end of Keenor's career at Cardiff City saw not only internal arguments but some supporters losing patience with him. He still commanded respect but, with the team sliding down the league ladder, his old legs were becoming a liability. As early as 1929 letters had begun to appear in the press blaming Keenor for Cardiff City's declining form. Reputations did not win matches and there was a limit to the sympathy that even a hero could expect. After relegation at the end of the 1930/1 season, Keenor was released by Cardiff City. There was no outcry from the fans; the time had come to move on for both club and player.

As Keenor went off to join Crewe Alexandra, no one emerged to take over his mantle as club hero. Throughout the 1930s Cardiff City had a rapid turnover of personnel as it looked for a winning combination. The few talented players that were discovered by the club did not stay long as their own ambition and the club's financial plight meant that they were quickly sold to leading English teams. Despite changes in management, frequent new signings and promising starts to the season, Cardiff City remained firmly rooted in the Third Division South. With no new stars or successes to celebrate, Keenor began to take on an almost mythical status at Cardiff City as the press transformed him into the figurehead of a golden era that had passed away. As Cardiff City embarked on new Cup and League campaigns, newspapers printed cartoons of the shadow of Keenor, a representation of past glories, looming large over Ninian Park and the current team. While society was haunted by the ghosts of a booming coal trade and a vibrant national culture, Cardiff City was haunted by the achievements of Keenor's era. It mattered not that Keenor had been obstinate, not always even in the team and towards the end of his career blamed for poor results – the press had a selective memory and supporters needed no encouragement to swallow the message. They were not inventing a new persona for Keenor, for he had been a great player, but they were only remembering the good times. Alongside a team that kept fading towards the end of the season and was incomprehensibly inconsistent, Keenor's virtues of courage, persistence and effort seemed the ideal salvation.

After leaving Cardiff City Keenor briefly enjoyed some popularity at Crewe. In 1934, the club decided not to announce that an injury would prevent him from playing for fear of harming the gate. At the age of thirty-eight, he even added one final Welsh cap to his collection. He then moved on to become player-manager, first at Oswestry Town, and then at Tunbridge Wells, where he combined football with working as a farmer. He was not a success at Tunbridge and resigned in 1936 after disputes with his players. By then he was suffering because of his physical commitments to the game; he had given his all to football and was left battered and ill. In 1937, Keenor was admitted to hospital with diabetes. He had been suffering from the disease for some time but, courageous as ever, had kept it secret. The news was published in south Wales, together with the information that he had been out of work for some time, with not even the dole to support his wife and seven children. This was greeted with genuine shock and an appeal was launched immediately. Such was Keenor's esteem that the FAW itself ran the fund and made a donation. The fund-raising served to revive affection for Keenor, and he seemed to illustrate the whole plight of south Wales. Like so many who had revered him, he was now un-employed and helpless through no fault of his own. In the gloom of the 1930s, even a hero had fallen to the depths of despair. Keenor now represented not just Cardiff City's golden era, but the fate of a whole society. The press continued to use him as an emblem of the club's former glories, and the knowledge of what had happened to him since made that symbolism all the more poignant.

After the Second World War, Keenor's fame subsided as a new Cardiff City team established itself in the First Division. Supporters and the press, now with new heroes, no longer had to look back to past triumphs. Keenor returned to his native city in 1958 and worked as a builder's labourer. His fame and the Cup win still brought him some attention but he was now just part of the community that had once revered him. News of his death in 1972 made the front pages of the local press and revived interest in his career. Subsequently his reputation continued to live on because of the Cup win. A *Who's Who* of Cardiff City players, written in 1987, described him as 'quite simply the greatest Bluebird of all'. Yet he is not remembered by as many, or with the same nostalgia, as Dixie Dean or any of the other inter-war greats. The goal-scorers and providers are remembered long after their careers end, but the hard tacklers tend to die with the memories of those who saw them play. Keenor's name stands out from football's record books because he captained the only Welsh FA Cup winners. Had Arsenal's goalkeeper, Dan Lewis from Maerdy, saved the weak shot that gave Cardiff City the only goal of that game, then Fred Keenor would have been remembered today even less.

Thus Fred Keenor was a different kind of hero to the best-remembered players of the inter-war years. He was not the only popular aggressive defender of the era. Every club had its hard man, appreciated by his own supporters but vilified by the opposition. There were other players who, in their day, were just as much heroes at their own clubs as the spectacular stars whom history remembers. Yet Keenor stands out from his contemporaries, not just because of how good a player and leader he was, but because of what he came to represent to supporters in and around Cardiff. He was an example to all of the virtues of never giving up. In the trying circumstances of the Depression, it was a lesson that was much appreciated. There was a message in him for both soccer and society. By the 1930s the press had turned him into a symbol of a glorious past which owed more to myth than reality. Cardiff City were already past their best by 1927 and during their heyday Keenor had been just one of many stars in the team. He was even rivalled by Billy Hardy for the position of most popular defender at the club. But, as an Englishman, Hardy could not be turned into a local figurehead to the same extent as Keenor. It was not so much who players were that counted but what they meant, and Keenor meant far more than the sum of his career really deserved. His career therefore illuminates a different facet in the popularity of football's heroes; where the sporting and economic needs of a society and the supporters who were part of it, meant that the power of symbolism could overtake the reality of fact. Keenor's own personal fall then served to reinforce this symbolism, illustrating just how deep the plight of south Wales was during the Depression. He remained not just a symbol of past glories but also a reminder of what had happened to those triumphs. Yet beneath all this symbolism there still had to be a great player and Keenor was undoubtedly that.

Jack Fowler

Huw Bowen

During the 1920s, the spectators who stood on the rough stone-and-ash banks that formed three sides of Swansea Town's 'rubble heap' of a Vetch Field ground often indulged in enthusiastic bouts of community singing. The songs they sang echoed the Welsh hymns and arias usually associated with the crowds that gathered in rather smaller numbers at the nation's rugby football venues. Indeed, followers of the 'dribbling code' gave as good as their rugby counterparts, and observers were often moved by the strength and passion of their impromptu renditions of 'Cwm Rhondda', 'Mae Hen Wlad Fy Nhadau', 'Sospan Fach' and other favourites. It was reported that the volume of noise generated by the Vetch Field crowd could be heard 'ordinarily' as far away as Fforestfach, and the effects of massed Welsh voices on opposition players and supporters could at times be quite overwhelming. One Stoke City supporter was taken aback when he heard a section of the Swansea crowd launching wholeheartedly into 'Yn y Dyfroedd Mawr a'r Tonnau' and, on finding that he was listening to a funeral hymn, he was moved to suggest that the visiting contingent from the Potteries should perhaps starts humming 'Show me the way to go home'. These choral outpourings allowed many spectators to give vocal expression to their identity and celebrate their Welshness, if only for ninety minutes on a Saturday afternoon, and visiting English teams often felt that they were playing in an unfamiliar foreign land.

The Vetch Field, however, was not an exclusively Welsh sporting theatre. The changing and expanding nature of Swansea, the 'dirty witch' of a town evoked by Edward Thomas, was such that many immigrant working men of English, Irish and Italian descent also took their place in a cosmopolitan crucible. Alongside the deep-rooted influences of chapel and choir was also to be found a liking for choruses of a quite different type, and this enabled Swansea supporters to find a place for themselves within mainstream popular British culture. 'I'm for ever blowing Bubbles' was taken up with gusto during the early 1920s, and the crowd swayed vigorously, and often dangerously, from side to side in time with the chorus. Only later did 'Bubbles' become more exclusively associated with the followers of West Ham United. Swansea supporters, who before 1914 had sung their own 'war song', also adapted a favourite contemporary ditty by supplying appropriate words of their own which served to elevate one player, Jack Fowler, to the status of popular hero. To the tune of 'Chick, chick, chick, chick, chicken, lay a little egg for me', the Vetch Field crowd often sang 'Fow, Fow, Fow, Fow, Fowler, score a little goal for me. We haven't had a goal since the last match, and now it's half past three.' On the North Bank terraces of modern times it often has been loudly proclaimed that there is only one Alan Waddle, or one Alan Curtis, but during the mid-1920s there was, in both song and deed, most definitely only one Jack Fowler. He was Swansea Town's first footballing hero of the professional era, a talismanic figure who became the idol of thousands.

Jack Fowler earned canonization for the remarkable goal-scoring feats he achieved with Swansea Town between 1923 and 1930, and especially those he recorded in his most productive years between 1924 and 1927. He played in a largely successful side that contained a number of players, most notably Joe Sykes, Wilf Milne, and Billy Hole, who would find a place in any all-time Swansea XI, but it was Fowler who became the main focus for the adulation of supporters. In the League alone he scored 101 goals in 167 games, and this gave him a strike rate bettered only by Cyril Pearce, Wilf Lewis, and Frank Rawcliffe, who all played far fewer games. Only Ivor Allchurch and Herbie Williams have scored more League goals for Swansea than Fowler, but their careers were considerably longer.

John Fowler was born in 1899 in Cardiff, where he grew up in a large family with seven brothers and six sisters. Like many of his contemporaries he lied about his age and saw late service in the First World War as a member of the Royal Naval Air Service. The return of peace saw him begin to make his mark as a footballer with Maerdy, and in 1921 he followed in the footsteps of the great Welsh stalwart Moses Russell and transferred to Plymouth Argyle of Division Three (South). Many Plymouth supporters felt that Fowler was never given a fair opportunity to shine, but he managed to score twenty-five goals for the Pilgrims in thirty-seven League games, including two in April 1923 against promotion rivals Swansea. The Swans' manager Joe Bradshaw was impressed and, in February 1924, he secured Fowler's services for a fee of £1,280, a figure which stood as a record until 1938 when Newcastle United were paid £1,500 for Bill Imrie.

The first clause in Fowler's Swansea contract stated that the player agreed to 'play in an efficient manner and to the best of his ability'. There can be no doubt that he more than fulfilled his obligations on both counts. During his first full season, in 1924/5, he was the leading marksman in the Division, scoring twenty-eight goals in forty-two games as Swansea were promoted as champions. In the next campaign, in Division Two, he took advantage of the change in the offside law to record a further twenty-eight goals in only thirty-two appearances. The following year he returned figures of eighteen goals in thirty-eight games, and even though his powers then declined somewhat, he still managed to score, on average, once every two games during his remaining time with the Swans. Impressive by any standard, these outline statistics only conceal the concentrated bouts of scoring that became Fowler's trademark. He scored nine League hat-tricks between April 1924 and September 1927, setting a still unbroken club League record when he netted five goals in a 6–1 thrashing of Charlton Athletic in September 1924. He also set an individual club scoring record in the FA Cup when he scored four times in the 6–3 defeat of Stoke City in 1926; a feat that has only been equalled by David Gwyther, against Oxford City in 1969.

At 5ft 10in. and 12 st. Fowler was powerfully built, and his portrait carries more than a hint of aggression, determination and menace. He certainly relished the physical aspects of the game and he was regarded as a player who 'put himself about'. Yet it would be quite wrong to suggest that he was merely a bludgeoning or barnstorming type of forward. On the contrary, observers commented on his speed, constructive play, quickness of thought, and 'weaving' skills. He was regarded as a 'clever' player who made use of all his attributes, most notably when, with his characteristic bursts of speed and physical strength, he carried the ball between defenders into goal-threatening positions. He developed the ability to unleash ferocious shots when in full flight, and the adoption of a shoot-on-sight policy meant that he peppered the goal from all angles and distances. Those who saw him play recall a player who would explode into action, and 'always have a crack', and it is little wonder that an adoring crowd took him to their hearts. The Welsh selectors adopted a somewhat different view, however, and Fowler won only six caps, failing, along with other aspirants, permanently to dislodge Len Davies of Cardiff City who occupied the centre-forward position for much of the 1920s. Nevertheless, Fowler managed to score three international goals, including two in a rare Welsh away victory over England at Selhurst Park in March 1926 when he was at the very height of his powers.

The bulk of Jack Fowler's Swansea career was spent in Division Two of the English League, and this might suggest that he never performed at the very highest level. This cannot be denied, but several Swansea Cup runs during the mid-1920s enabled Fowler to demonstrate that he was able to continue his high goal-scoring record against some of the best sides in the country. More generally, Swansea's success, sandwiched between Cardiff City's Wembley appearances in 1925 and 1927, represented a sustained Welsh challenge on the English FA Cup. This captured the imagination of the nation and offered association football the prospect of a permanent place in the sun alongside a rugby game that was experiencing dismal times at both national and club level in Wales. Indeed, Fowler played a leading part in effecting a near-total eclipse of the 'national' game, not least in 1926 when the eight goals he scored in five successive ties carried Swansea through to the semi-finals of the FA Cup.

In Swansea, the FA Cup served fully to illustrate the powerful hold that soccer was establishing on the sporting public of south-west Wales. Indeed, as Martin Johnes's research demonstrates, it was the Cup rather than international fixtures that attracted most attention and carried the Welsh nation's hopes against English opposition. In 1915 Southern League Swansea had beaten League Champions Blackburn, and between 1920 and 1925 epic encounters were played out once more against sides from higher divisions in front of packed Vetch Field crowds of more than 20,000. In 1925, however, not only did Aston Villa administer a dose of disappointment by beating Swansea for the second year in succession, but also the west Walians could only watch with envy as Cardiff City progressed as far as Wembley. It was against this background that, in 1925/6, Swansea embarked upon a campaign that promised to bring them a promotion and Cup 'double', enabling Jack Fowler to step forward as the figure who represented the sporting hopes and ambitions of town, region and nation alike.

There were many remarkable aspects to Swansea's FA Cup adventure of 1925/6, but perhaps most extraordinary was the fact that the team personnel remained unaltered through seven ties. Even today, it is a line-up recalled with ease by those who saw them play: Denoon, Langford, Milne, Collins, Sykes, McPherson, Hole, Deacon, Fowler, Thompson and Nicholas. This mainly English side, constructed by manager Joe Bradshaw over the previous two or three seasons, was noted as possessing two particular attributes. Opposing managers considered that Swansea were, in the words of Major Frank Buckley of Blackpool, a 'tough lot' and this equipped them for the demands of away ties which often required a robust approach. Sykes, a small man for a centre-half, was regarded as a supreme organizer and marshal of the defence, while Wilfie Milne was widely respected for the quality of his tackling. The team was not, however, in any way negative in its outlook and it developed the ability to score plenty of goals. As centre-forward, Fowler benefited from this approach, but Thompson and Deacon also contributed their fair share to an impressive goals tally in both League and Cup. London-based critics agreed that no side could visit Swansea with any degree of confidence, and it was reported that the better the quality of opposition, the better the side would play.

The 1925/6 Cup campaign began with two relatively low-key victories, 3–1 away at Exeter and 3–2 at home against Watford, with Fowler scoring one goal in the latter game. Momentum began to develop when, away from home, Blackpool were defeated 2–0 (Fowler scoring once) and then Stoke City were brushed aside 6–3 at the Vetch Field, with a rampant Fowler scoring four times. At this point Cardiff City fell by the wayside and Swansea were left alone to carry Welsh hopes. In the fifth round Millwall were defeated 1–0 in London with Fowler scoring a dramatic winner in the last few minutes, and this set up a home quarter-final tie against First Division Arsenal. Charlie Buchan's team was unable to cope with the Swans on the day, the headline in *The Times* declaring 'The Arsenal beaten for pace'. Fowler, it was reported, 'outwitted the Arsenal backs to score' and amid scenes of great excitement and tension Swansea clung on desperately to record a famous 2–1 victory. This earned the team a semi-final place against Bolton Wanderers at Tottenham's White Hart Lane ground in north London.

Newspaper accounts of this enthralling Cup run reveal much about the nature of football at this time. The players' preparation for the ties was, for example, based upon a training regime supplemented by 'tramps around the bays', walks at nearby Mumbles, water polo and so many 'brine baths', that local wags suggested that the team was spending more time in the tub than on the training ground. The team might not reach the final, it was declared, but they would certainly be the cleanest in the competition. The players themselves became the focus for considerable press and public interest, and this manifested itself in a variety of different ways, not least in the form of 'behind the scenes' photo-opportunities. One such 'humorous interlude' at the Vetch Field revealed that, much to the amusement of Fowler and his great friend Lachlan McPherson, Jock Denoon had joined the ranks of 'spectacle-wearing goalkeepers'. Local entrepreneurs were swift to take advantage of this interest, and it is recalled that one enterprising confectioner in Morriston produced a range of boiled sweets, each of which, in seaside-rock fashion, had the name of a Swans' hero running through it.

The excitement of supporters knew no bounds. They gathered at newspaper offices to hear first news of Cup draws; they cheered visiting teams at High Street station; they flocked to Swansea on match days to queue for hours to gain entry to the ground; they sang their hearts out; and at the Vetch Field they let their emotions run wild. Against the Arsenal, the crowd was 'packed' onto the banks by a megaphone-wielding police force that would shortly be dealing with crowds of a different type during the General Strike. This 'packing' strategy, based on the notion that 'The closer the crowd, the less danger there is', was undoubtedly distressing and dangerous for those crushed at the front of the bank, but it had the effect of greatly enhancing the atmosphere as the crowd swayed, surged and sang together. The success of the team, the drama of the occasion, and the vigour of the action all combined to create a rich brew of heady excitement that at times was translated into extraordinary scenes of rejoicing. At the Stoke match, it was reported that 'as the clever Fowler piled up a continuous succession of goals, the enthusiasm passed all limits. The frantic fervour of the crowd was a wonderful thing. It must have left thousands of people hoarse and voiceless long before the end.' But this was surpassed by the scenes following the victory against the Arsenal, a game that ended with Swansea pressed back and resorting, rather shamefacedly, to booting the ball as far as possible up the field. The match report in the *South Wales Daily Post* declared that 'The final whistle at the Vetch Field on Saturday was the signal for the most amazing outburst of enthusiasm that Welsh soccer has ever known. It was roar of relief as well as joy. A dense mass of almost hysterical supporters – shouting, cheering, brandishing flags, rattles, sticks, and even leeks – yelled in unison for the heroes of the afternoon. Several women were in tears of joy.' Not surprisingly, Fowler was mobbed as he left the field.

The Swans were representing the town and its industrial hinterland, and the enthusiastic celebrations of victory can be seen as expressions of local pride, but the team was also taken up and supported by large numbers of people drawn from across south, west and mid Wales. As such, it can be said that Swansea carried the hopes of a significant part of the nation, including those in Cardiff. This much can be inferred from the elaborate transport arrangements that were put in place on match days. With a precision and timing of the type associated with military manoeuvres, the GWR and LMS provided trains to carry supporters into Swansea and out of Wales. For home ties, football excursions arrived in the town from all points near and far, with services running from Craven Arms, Gowerton, Llandovery, Llandrindod, Llanelli, Loughor, Pontarddulais and Pembroke. Trains from Cardiff and Newport brought in large numbers from the east and the Valleys. As groups of supporters from Caernarfon and Colwyn Bay mingled with those from Ireland and the north of England, the cosmopolitan nature of the crowds was a matter for comment.

The number of supporters travelling away was also increasingly substantial and they were carried on excursions which offered discounted prices, guaranteed match tickets, and all the 'steam-heated comforts' of fast modern 'corridor expresses'. On the day of the Millwall match five day-excursion trains were booked from Swansea and a half-day trip ran from Cardiff to London. With the game being for the Swans 'an event calculated to be the biggest moment in their history', supporters went to great lengths to get to the match. These were reported in the local press as 'astonishing stories', especially the tale of the '200 South Wales men who left their pits on Friday night without bothering to change, went straight to their reserve carriages, and arrived in London in their "Yorks"'. It was thought by some that this story was 'scarcely credible', but it was reported on good authority that the miners had in fact been seen driving in a specially hired charabanc to the game in New Cross. Popular folklore in Swansea still suggests that the Millwall game was marred by punch-ups with South London dockers, but reports of violence did not make their way into the local press.

In the event, Swansea's Fowler-inspired Cup run ended at the semi-final stage of the competition, although by that point many confident supporters were already planning their trips to Wembley and worrying about the size of ticket allocations for the finalists. Indeed, it was reported in the press that some people remained at home in Swansea over the semi-final weekend because they were saving their money for the excursion to the final. Others were no doubt offended by the fact that the price of tickets was more than double the amount they were used to paying. Those who did travel to London formed part of an 'early morning invasion' and a 'human avalanche at Paddington'. More than 2,300 football supporters travelled by train from Swansea, and more than 700 from Cardiff, to take their place in a 25,000 crowd. As the Swans' followers poured onto the platforms at Paddington, they held aloft a replica of the FA Cup with Fowler's picture on it. They carried daffodils, flags, leeks, miniature swans, and rosettes decked out in blue, a choice dictated by the fact that Swansea had been obliged to change their playing colours because of a clash with the white of Bolton. Rugby supporters and players from Llanelli – soccer converts for the day – carried 'sospans' with them. As they spilled out onto the streets of London, groups of supporters struck up the Fowler song. Local residents were taken aback by the sudden arrival of this seething mass of humanity and were baffled by the unfamiliar Welsh accents they could hear. 'Who are the Swans?' asked one old woman, to which a supporter in an 'Ystalyfera muffler' replied, 'Wales!' Two Londoners listened intently to the words of the Fowler song. Not surprisingly, they could not understand them, one declaring to the other 'It is Welsh they are singing, Bill'. Logic dictated to one bystander, a 'precocious youth', that the many blue favours in evidence belonged to those who had come to watch the university boat race, also taking place that day. He was put firmly in his place by three 'women of Wales' wearing large blue hats who 'promptly reminded him that they were members of the proletariat'.

As the crowds mingled in central London any class tension was overridden by a general sense of excitement, and it was reported that 'The 'varsity drawl blended with musical accent of the Welsh'. The meeting of two quite different class and athletic cultures passed off peacefully enough, although some fifty undergraduates were charged with drunk and disorderly behaviour as they celebrated Cambridge's boat race victory. In contrast, the Swansea supporters were described as being 'boisterous' and 'feverish' and only two men from south Wales found themselves detained at Marlborough Street police station. One of the men, a miner, was discharged with a caution after being arrested for pushing people off the pavement, while the other was fined £3 for being in possession of a revolver. The magistrate does not seem to have been impressed with the latter's defence that he had brought the weapon to London 'for safety as he was going to the cup semi-final'. Quite what this man expected to encounter in London is not clear, although perhaps tales of violence in circulation after the Millwall game had heightened his fears about the dangers awaiting him in the metropolis.

While two Swansea supporters spent an uncomfortable night or two in the cells, the rest of the human avalanche melted away and trickled back to Wales feeling dejected and dispirited. The Swans fell badly at the penultimate hurdle, as they put in an uncharacteristically limp performance during a one-sided defeat. The Welsh cause was not helped by an early Denoon error that gifted a goal to Bolton, and a further two goals were conceded before twenty minutes had elapsed. Observers, including the reporter from *The Times*, agreed that all of Bolton's goals were 'lucky' but it seemed that the Swansea team was also badly affected by an attack of nerves. The players were 'in a flustered condition' and they watched their opponents in a 'kind of trance'. Although the Swans rallied in the second half, Fowler, like his team-mates, was unable to rise to the occasion and he failed to find the back of the net for the first time in six cup ties. After the Millwall tie, Fowler had been carried on the shoulders of supporters when the team arrived back at High Street station; on this occasion his sense of failure and humiliation was such that he chose to leave the returning train at Landore.

The side's confidence was badly dented by the Cup defeat and the promotion campaign suffered. The Swans eventually finished in a very disappointing fifth position in Division Two and a season that had promised so much in February and March ended on a decidedly flat note. Indeed, in retrospect, it can be seen that the quarter-final victory against Arsenal marked something of a watershed in the fortunes of both Swansea Town and Jack Fowler himself. Although football in Wales continued briefly to offer a serious challenge to rugby, none more so than in 1927 when Cardiff won the FA Cup, Swansea and Fowler performed only fitfully during the second half of the 1920s. Fowler continued to score regularly, but he recorded only one of his League hat-tricks after the end of 1926. Of great importance in Swansea's slump was the departure of Joe Bradshaw to manage Fulham and the subsequent decision of the board of directors to take over responsibility for team affairs. This was a mistake to rank with the worst of many made by Vetch Field boards over the years, and an opportunity was lost to build on the solid foundations laid down by Bradshaw. Instead, in a steadily worsening economic climate, Swansea Town marked time, selling good players and failing to entertain in the way that they had during the early 1920s. Slowly but surely, there was a resurgence in both national and local rugby fortunes, and the pendulum swung back towards the union game in the town. This movement appeared to be complete when the All Whites recorded their famous victory over the All Blacks in 1935. By that time, the Swans were engaged in a grim annual struggle to avoid relegation and there were no cup runs to offer much by way of solace.

Fowler left Swansea Town in June 1930, his hundredth League goal for the club scored in a 4–0 victory over Tottenham Hotspur in November 1928. As with several other Swans of the period, he signed for Clapton Orient, having secured an additional 7s. 6d. on top of the £7 a week he earned with Swansea. He started his career in East London with a characteristic bang, scoring five goals, including a hat-trick, during his first three appearances. In total, Fowler made eighty appearances for Clapton, first as centre-forward and then as centre-half. He was appointed captain and scored fourteen goals, including the first one to be recorded at the Lea Bridge Ground. These were unhappy times, though, and the hard-pressed club did not always pay the players' wages. Fowler, always a generous man, found it necessary as club captain to distribute his own wages among his junior team-mates.

Fowler remained popular in Swansea, where he had often organized boxing matches and performed on stage during benefit concerts. Thus, after retiring through injury in 1932, he returned to run The Rhyddings Hotel in Brynmill. Always with an eye for the main chance, but never as accurate as he had been with a football, he was an enthusiastic small-scale entrepreneur dogged by bad luck. He moved easily in theatrical and popular entertainment circles, however, and he continued to perform on stage, where, as a local favourite, he told jokes and read his own monologues. His theatrical connections ensured that popular performers of the 1940s and 1950s such as Billy Cotton and Robb Wilton found their way to The Rhyddings, and the hotel became the watering hole of Kingsley Amis and his university circle. As a landlord of thirty-five years standing, Fowler is remembered as having 'stood no nonsense', but his establishment also became renowned as a venue for Saturday-night singing. For a Swansea sporting hero whose own exploits had been so loudly celebrated in song, this seems peculiarly appropriate.

In his later years, Jack Fowler lost interest in football in general and the Swans in particular. While always happy enough to reminisce about his glory years or to act as a referee in charity matches, he turned his attention to other sports, notably rugby, cricket and horse racing. Nevertheless, he must have been dismayed by Swansea's desperate plight during the mid-1970s. The feeble performances produced by a team of anonymous players in front of tiny crowds stood in marked contrast to the thrilling exploits performed by Fowler and his team-mates. The success of the Swans during the 1920s had helped to galvanize the support of town, region and nation for the association game, and Swansea had been etched firmly onto the football map. By the time Jack Fowler approached the end of his days, however, the outlook for professional football in Swansea could not have been bleaker. When the former hero died in February 1975, the club whose playing ranks he had graced with such distinction was stuck firmly in the lower reaches of Division Four, destined shortly to suffer the indignity of having to apply for re-election to the Football League. This humiliating experience for the Swans could not have been further from the heady days of 1926 when a rampaging Jack Fowler was so often able to satisfy the vocal demands of Swansea supporters to 'score a little goal for me'.

I am indebted to Jack Fowler's daughter, Maureen, David Farmer, Martin Johnes, John Conibear and Bertie Miller for their help with this chapter.

Trevor Ford

Peter Stead

In every childhood there are those moments of truth and embarass-ment that stay with one for life. In 1954 a group of us were walking through the town, picking that day's Great Britain XI. When we came to centre-forward I made my regular selection: 'Trevor Ford.' Evidently my friends felt that enough was enough, for this time I was challenged: 'Why do you always pick him? He's not the best.' Almost half a century later I can still hear my defiant reply: 'He is the best; my father says so.' Understandably, inevitably but nevertheless hurtfully, the spokesman of the gang shuffled off his eleven years and with schoolmasterly authority told me to start thinking for myself.

This was a scene that I was to replay many times. Of course, to a degree I had been echoing automatically my father's enthusiasm for Trevor Ford, but I was also invoking his name and undoubted authority to back up my own judgement. And, what is more, that judgement was based on personal experience, for since the age of nine I could claim to be a legitimate member of Trevor Ford's fan club. The story starts in October 1952 when my father, a well-built 6 ft tall police sergeant, came home from seeing Wales lose to Scotland at Ninian Park and, as furniture was moved, my mother and I were ordered to one side of our small kitchen. What followed was a quite remarkable re-enactment of the goal that Ford had scored an hour or so earlier. Perhaps in order to punctuate the amazed silence that prevailed in the kitchen my father, as he turned to take off his mac, casually uttered the words that were to result in my lifetime devotion to football: 'I must take you to see him play.'

And so it was that a couple of weeks later I was taken to Ninian Park to see my first game in the English Football League. I would be starting at the top for, after twenty-three years, Cardiff City were back in Division One and we were due to play the mighty Sunderland for whom Ford was expected to play at centre-forward. Before the big day there were several briefing sessions in which the nature of First Division football was explained. Aged nine, I was already a veteran of several seasons in the Southern League and at Barry Town's Jenner Park I had already graduated from the directors' box (with tea and biscuits at half-time) to a terrace behind the goal from which Barrie Morgan and I would direct abuse at referees. Apparently First Division football would be very different: the crowd would be 30,000 rather than 2,000, the pace of the game would be furious, and I was never to take my eye off the ball as my position in the children's enclosure would be right behind a goal and therefore very much in the firing line, not least of Ford himself.

Two things happened to me on that December afternoon. Cardiff City, playing in a blue with which I have ever since associated myself, comfortably won the game 4–1 and in so doing became my team. Barry Town, who played in green and were then known as 'the Linnets', had been relegated to a secondary position. I had been inducted into a routine of Bluebird nostalgia and analysis that I quickly came to think of as the core of my identity. Certainly the newly acquired knowledge that we had won the Cup in 1927 made me feel a little more important. Nevertheless, my becoming a City fan was not the most important thing that happened to me that afternoon. What was of far greater significance was my interaction with the Sunderland team.

First and foremost there was the one man on whom all 31,500 pairs of eyes were riveted throughout the afternoon, the only player whose photograph appeared in the threepenny programme (although a note paradoxically commented that he 'needs no introduction to Ninian Park where he has played many brilliant games for Wales'). Trevor Ford was the whole point of the afternoon. My father had deposited me in the front row of the Grangetown Stand before he retreated to a better vantage point, but I was soon in deep conversation with a stranger whose presence in the enclosure owed more to his size than his age. He explained that he had only come to the game to see Trevor Ford, whom he hero-worshipped, and he proceeded to outline the great centre-forward's career. The teams came out and, for a moment, there was a panic as we failed to identify the great man. We both spotted the other two Sunderland stars, the English cricketer Willie Watson and the already legendary Len Shackleton, but of Trevor there was no sign. Finally a player turned and we saw the number 9 on his shirt. 'Blow me,' said my new mate, 'he's smaller than I thought.' And he was right: Trevor was smaller and slighter than one would have wanted. But immediately I was struck by the dark intensity: here was a pent-up energy, a dynamo waiting to be activated. Something was going to happen.

We had to wait a long time but happen it did. With the game well and truly won play was perceptibly winding down when suddenly, some 120 yards away, there was a roar as the whole Canton Stand crowd stood up. Whatever had happened was well beyond my ken but my new mate and others were piecing together a scenario. Ford had scored with a rocket but it had probably taken a deflection. One contributor suggested that the shot might have broken the leg of the hapless City defender, Billy Baker. The whole crowd first roared with excitement and then purred with pleasure. The afternoon had been justified; we had all seen (some in far more detail than others) what in truth was the one thing we had come to see. The great man, one of the most expensive players in the history of the game, the player who had scored four goals in his last four matches for Wales, including one against the Rest of the UK and two only a month before against England at Wembley, had now scored for us.

We had gone to see him in his own right , but it was not irrelevant that on the day he was wearing the red and white striped shirt and black shorts of Sunderland. Quite apart from anything else the colours beautifully suited his raven-black hair and greatly intensified his dark good looks. Even at that tender age I sensed that his physical attractiveness and distinctiveness had marked him out as someone beckoned by destiny. Moreover those splendid colours, which had brought a distinct hint of promise to a dull December afternoon, were entirely appropriate for what we thought of as a great club. And this was very much the point. Our team was now playing the big boys, and at the time they did not come much bigger than Sunderland. The record books indicated that the club had not won the League since 1936 or the Cup since 1937, but it was not for want of trying. We all knew that this was 'the Bank of England' team who, ever since the war, had spent an enormous sum of money in an attempt to regain the glory of the past. We took the distant north-east, of which we knew little, to be the true home of English football, we envied the praise that was always heaped on their 'knowledgeable and passionate' fans and we appreciated that not the least of Sunderland's assets was the fearsome 'Roker roar'. There was a glamour about the visitors that day that we all sensed. For me, that glamour has lingered on and I have always been a fan of Sunderland, for I associate them with the day that I myself had 'entered' the Football League and felt the thrill of having access to big-time football. But over and above everything else there had been the fact that in 1952, on the first day I had ever seen top-level football, the star attraction had been a Welsh player. We had all wanted him to score that day, because transcending our club loyalty was the fact that he gave all of us who were Welsh a legitimate place at and interest in the top echelons of British football.

As the City programme had indicated there was a special thrill in anticipating Trevor Ford's running out at Ninian Park. He had certainly put a few thousand on the gate that day, but he was doing that at every First Division ground. In his book *The Golden Age of Football*, Peter Jeffs rightly describes Ford as 'one of the top attractions of the period'. That is why Aston Villa broke the record by paying Swansea £25,000 for him in 1947 and why Sunderland forked out £30,000 four years later. Above all, his home fans loved him for his goals: he obliged with fifty-nine in 121 matches for Villa and sixty-seven for Sunderland in 108 appearances including a providential last half-hour hat-trick on his home debut. When Ford was playing away from home, whether it be at Arsenal, Wolves, Everton or Spurs, huge crowds turned up expecting to see him at the centre of a drama. They were less concerned with his powerful two-footed shooting and graceful laying-off of balls and rather more anticipating his physical encounters with goalkeepers and centre-halves. At several points in the match he would hunch his shoulders like a boxer and crash into the goalkeeper, and throughout the game he would be involved in fearsome bone-threatening tackles with the opposing number 5. It was the physical aspect of his game that opposition fans loved to hate. He was 'fiery Ford', 'the two-footed firebrand', a 'hell-for-leather' non-stop and fearless opponent who injected a unique element of danger and tension into every game. By his own admission, that home debut against Sheffield Wednesday in 1951 had seen Ford 'bore into the defence like an armadillo'. Even after he had broken the jaw of centre-half Packard in a heading duel he went on 'playing like a madman'.

It was that potent blend of intensity, skill and danger that made Ford a real star in an era of stars and which gave him a rightful place in the pantheon. In that 'Golden Era' before television he was a key player at the very heart of the British game. As early as 1950 the *News of the World* identified him as 'the most dangerous centre-forward in Britain' and regretted that he was born the wrong side of the Severn. The paper thought his 'three-goal shooting' in a match against Belgium was 'an act that the Wild West could not have bettered'; throughout the land the dressing-room warning was 'Watch Ford or else'. The Home International Championship, in which he featured regularly between 1948 and 1956, pitted him against the best centre-halves in the land and gave him a high British profile. A 1951 report spoke of 'the buffeting' he had given the English centre-half Barrass and speculated that 'the English selectors must have yearned for a forward with his lion-heart, indefatigable spirit and football brain'.

In all, Ford played in seven games against England and only in the last of these was he on the winning side but his energy in those matches, not to mention his four goals, made him a particular threat to English supremacy. The way he was perceived in England was best encapsulated in his performance at Wembley in November 1952. Faced with the brilliance of Finney and Lofthouse the Welsh defence collapsed and conceded five goals, including two in the first eleven minutes. Wales had little to offer on the day other than 'the brilliance of Ford' whose 'robust' and 'electrifying' play enabled him to score two goals. For the first, 'the best of the match', he had rounded Jack Froggatt, the English centre-half, and 'crashed in a great shot' past a familiar opponent, Gil Merrick. A few minutes later Froggatt had to leave the field after clashing with Ford and could only return as a passenger on the wing. Ford, now regularly booed by a large section of the crowd, revelled in a new freedom and his repertoire of 'passing, heading, back-heeling and flicking passes to Allchurch or his wings culminated with a cheeky back-heeled goal'. In the photograph of that goal, one of the most treasured in Welsh football history, the agony of the defenders and especially Billy Wright is all too apparent. Wright, who was to become the best-known English defender of the era, played many times against Ford, first as wing-half and then as centre-half. Their clashes were never other than fearsome, but in his autobiography the Wolves player went out of his way to emphasize that his 'friend Trevor Ford' was 'amongst the cleanest and most sporting men I have ever played against'. That was a remarkable assessment from a Wolves player whose goalkeeping colleague Bert Williams had often been bruised by the Welsh tearaway. In that 1952 match at Wembley, the first that Wales had played at the stadium, the man of the match was England's Tom Finney who was confirming his position as the best British player of the 1950s. What he recalled about the day was that he had 'never seen a man try as hard as Trevor Ford'. In general he thought of Ford as 'the centre-half's nightmare, a fellow who never stops trying' but had noticed that 'when he pulls on the red jersey of Wales he seems to go twice as hard again'.

The glorious and indisputable fact that I now had First Division experience fully entitled me to pick Great Britain teams and to pass judgement on Ford and all the other stars of the era. But it was not all plain sailing, for increasingly my selections were being challenged not only by my schoolfriends but also by the Beaverbrook newspapers to which I had become addicted. There was, in particular, one large cloud on the horizon and ironically it was a Welsh cloud. The nature of the problem was manifested on the afternoon of 10 October 1953. Sitting in Ninian Park's Canton Stand I had my first glimpse of Wales, and magnificent they were in their imperial red shirts. All was set for a great battle between the respective 'greats', Paul, Burgess and Sherwood on one side and Finney, Wright and Lofthouse on the other. However, my afternoon had been ruined for there was a change from the Welsh side printed in the programme. Trevor Ford was indisposed, so John Charles was moved from inside-forward and Reg Davies of Newcastle came in at number 8. Not only was my hero not wearing that vital number-9 shirt but after the match, which Wales (lacking my full support) lost 1–4, there was uneasy talk of this youngster Charles, whom I was quite prepared to select at number 5, now developing into a great centre-forward. That afternoon I had seen John Charles wear the number-9 shirt of Wales for the first time but it was a historic moment that I would willingly have forgone. In the next five years that most revered of shirts was worn eight times by Ford and twelve times by John Charles. I was not a happy lad, for it seemed to me as if my handsome hero, of whom I thought in almost purely cinematic terms, had been replaced by someone who was just big. When I saw Charles play for Leeds at Cardiff my judgement was confirmed. The visitors looked gaudy in their blue and gold and the giant Charles anomalous in the forward line. Cardiff won 4–1 that day with Trevor Ford, then in his third season with City, scoring twice. Nevertheless, my confidence was eroding and in moments of honesty I had to concede that my preference for Trevor increasingly owed more to loyalty than to reason.

Much of my difficulty was related to that fact that Ford had signed for Cardiff in late 1953. In his three seasons at Ninian Park Trevor's record was extremely honourable. He scored thirty-nine goals in ninety-six League appearances, generally boosted the image of the club and helped to swell attendance figures. For me, however, he seemed a slightly less heroic figure: familiarity had stolen enchantment from the eye. His signing had smacked of desperation, as it was known that Tommy Taylor and John Charles had been the initial targets. Ford was now thirty and looked even smaller in blue than he had in stripes. In his third season a struggling City played him on the wing and I was in despair. I remember aching with frustration in one game when it seemed as if he had spent all his time nearer to me on the Bob Bank than to the goalposts. Fortunately we had a replacement number 9 who had fully captured my attention. In 1956 I thought the young Gerry Hitchens the most exciting thing in football. What had happened is that, aged thirteen, I had become first and foremost a Cardiff City supporter.

In one respect, however, Trevor Ford's place was beyond challenge. He had been the agent, the catalyst, who had sealed the bond between my father and myself. I had already sensed that the close relationship of childhood was something that could possibly only be sustained during conversations about and attendances at football. Only later would I read the considerable confessional literature in which writers, American writers in particular, spoke of sport as the only meaningful link they had developed with their respective fathers. It was another Ford, the writer Richard Ford, who in his novel *Independence Day* was to investigate most memorably the experience from the father's point of view. My father was from Merthyr, a town he regarded as being the centre of civilization. The great Bryn Jones was a neighbour and he was partly responsible for my father's view that all the best players came from Merthyr. However, it was at Ninian Park that he developed his fascination with centre-forward play and from my earliest days I had known about Lawton, Lofthouse and, above all, Ford.

Two further moments completed the Fordian connection. In September 1957 my father and I entered W. H. Smith's in High Street Merthyr and happened to see a copy of Trevor Ford's recently published autobiography *I Lead the Attack*. We found the title and the striking red-and-black cover irresistible and the 9s. 6d. was readily proffered. But as far as reading the volume was concerned I never progressed beyond the first chapter, although I can describe in detail every illustration. It had been acquired as a talisman and it proudly took its place in our one glass bookcase alongside *The Bible*, *Pear's Cyclopaedia*, six volumes of Dickens and Stone's *Justice Manual*. Having Trevor inscribe the book forty years later greatly enhanced its personal value.

By 1957 Trevor Ford had temporarily gone out of my life but there was to be one more sighting. Sometime in the 1960s there was a testimonial match at Jenner Park, Barry, the ground at which I had grown up. My familiarity with the complicated Jenner Park layout encouraged me to climb the few steps of the changing-room hut in search of post-match autographs. I went to the visitors' door and knocked. It was opened by an immaculately dressed Trevor Ford who had not played in the match but had obviously dropped by to chat to his chums in the All Star XI. I had never been so close to him and, quite frankly, I was stunned by the intensity of his aura. His black hair glowed and his dark eyes challenged me to justify my presence. I was admitted to a crowded dressing-room just as a totally naked and very pink John Charles emerged from the communal bath in the inner room. Clearly it was shaping up as an evening I would never forget, but it was the watchman at the door whose Raphael-like luminescence had given me the image of a lifetime. The man who had so often been compared to Hollywood's Tyrone Power had veritably become an icon.

The point about heroes is that they should retreat into a mythology. I was not very interested in the controversial post-1957 Ford. There had been every justification for my not persisting with the text of *I Lead the Attack*. It was written to confirm and exploit its author's new status as one of football's leading rebels. In what was to become one of the saddest chapters in the history of the game the last years of the maximum wage were marked by a whole series of rows regarding irregular payments made either when players joined new clubs or as a regular weekly bonus. The era was best summed up by Simon Inglis who wrote of how 'a continuous stream of articles in the popular press in which players "revealed all" in "no punches pulled" interviews, and chairmen abused each other' meant that 'the League and professional football's reputation seemed to sink in direct proportion to the rise in newspaper circulation'. The popular Sunday papers, concludes Inglis, gave the distinct impression that 'all footballers were rowdy, dishonest, greedy and corrupt'. Ford's own justification for publicizing his case was that the paradoxical twin processes of wage restraint and individual bargaining, of which he (like all professionals) became a part, constituted a massive hypocrisy which dominated the domestic game. He felt compelled to be totally honest, but the truth he was determined to tell was something that most of us Bob Bank fans did not want to hear. His initial signing for Sunderland had become a *cause célèbre* which ended with his being fined £100 for allegedly demanding more than the specified £10 signing-on fee. Now the fuller revelations in his book of under-the-counter payments led to an unprecedented fine being imposed on the Sunderland club and to the suspension of several directors and players, including Ford himself who was now at Cardiff. After reinstatement Ford was again suspended for not substantiating his claims. His reaction was to head for Holland where he signed for PSV Eindhoven. At a time when few British fans knew anything about continental football, and cared even less, this was regarded as an exile in the wilderness. The fact that he was to miss the 1958 World Cup and his nation's greatest moment of soccer glory seemed a sad ending to a great career in international football.

The whole Sunderland romance had crumbled. 'The Bank of England club' had become a nest of vipers. It seemed as if the national battle of professional footballers to shrug off that wage slavery, which had made them subject to the whim and ignorance of local butchers and bakers masquerading as football moguls, was being fought out at Roker Park. Ford's *I Lead the Attack* had only been one part of it, for a bigger stir had been caused by Len Shackleton's *Crown Prince of Soccer*. This most infamous of football's countless autobiographies revealed all the jealousy that the inside-forward had felt when Ford arrived to claim the glory at Sunderland, as well as something of the disappointment attending a career which, for all his unorthodox brilliance, had resulted in only five caps and no medals. For Shackleton, Ford was merely 'a goal-minded dasher' who finished off wonderful moves orchestrated by the true masters of the game like himself. In a cruel but pathetic overstatement he concluded that the club fine of £100 was 'the only real highlight of Ford's career at Roker Park'. Clearly there had been many tensions at the club, and perhaps it is not surprising that Sunderland's historian has argued that a full recovery came only half a century after these events in which its staff had 'dragged the name of football through the mud'. Quite understandably Roger Hutchinson's judgement on Ford is double-edged. He was a 'terrific footballer', but one who will be associated as much with the commercial story of the club as with its on-the-field activities. The centre-forward, we are pointedly reminded, had only signed for Sunderland on the understanding that he be given a house, a job and other benefits; his departure had become merely notorious.

Scott Fitzgerald once spoke of how few great American lives have meaningful second acts. Happily there was to be a second act in my relationship with Trevor Ford. Forty years after his departure to Eindhoven and thirty years after his manifestation at Jenner Park I saw him listed as a sidesman on a notice-board in the porch of my local Anglican church. Later I spotted him helping his wife at a stall in the annual church fête. Trevor was living at West Cross, Swansea, and was often to be seen jogging between Mumbles and Swansea Docks, 'from pier to pier' as he was to refer to it. In the years since his playing days I had read of his involvement in the car trade, seen his name on garages and was vaguely aware that his sons were prominent in Swansea affairs. Now I could hardly believe in his reincarnation, not least because he still looked impressive. His hair was grey but he had not lost a single strand of it; as far as weight was concerned he could have gained only a pound or two. He was in every respect a film star still.

For several years now I have relished my chats with Trevor, on the sea front, at his apartment and at various functions. It is a joy to see the life come into his soft brown eyes and his lovely smile as he recalls and invokes his cinema-manager father who worked hard to make him a two-footed player, his mother, a Londoner whom he nearly rewarded by initially signing for a London team, his teacher, Dai Beynon, who allowed football only after school lessons were completed, National Service days when he first became a centre-forward, and his friendship first with Bobby Daniel, who was killed in the RAF, and then with younger brother Ray, that elegant centre-half whom Trevor persuaded to join him at Sunderland, and finally with Ivor Allchurch who always laid on a constant flow of perfect passes. As we move from football to wider questions two themes predominate. The first is his enormous debt to his wife Louise, the convent girl and publican's daughter who first saw the 'devastatingly handsome' young Ford going into the Mannesman steel works at Landore where he was a gantry driver. Her father was against the match and advised her to marry an accountant. His other great joy is his sons, both of whom he educated at public schools. The fact that his grandson is now at Eton he sees as a perfect rounding-off of the story of the Ford family from Swansea's humble Townhill Estate.

The 76-year-old Ford is particularly interesting on the whole question of the status of footballers. For most of his career he was in the car trade, a notoriously risky business. During much of that time there was only the flimsiest of public interest in his soccer stardom. 'We old players were often regarded as fools', he once commented. It was in the 1990s that soccer nostalgia became big business and suddenly the media, charities and clubs, not to mention historians, 'couldn't have enough of us'. Particularly gratifying has been the generosity and warm welcome extended by Aston Villa, Sunderland and Cardiff City. Now there is a fully developed football culture, but in the old days, he explains, 'football was just a job'. The clear implication is that in that earlier era, the austere Cold War years, the working-class boy from Swansea had been forced to make a living as best he could. It might have been Landore and the steelworks, but instead it was the comforts of suburbia in Sutton Coldfield, an albeit arctic Sunderland, leafy north Cardiff and eventually Eindhoven, where incidentally he and Louise were well placed to visit her brother who worked in Brussels. Ford's commercial arrangement with the Philips Company at Eindhoven was perfect, and those four years when he was still scoring goals regularly were quite possibly the happiest of his career. Today, much of his memorabilia is packed away, but he prominently displays a portrait showing him in his Welsh jersey and a 1999 medal presented to him by the PFA which identified him as one of the '100 legends of League Football'.

Today, as always, he is essentially a family man and indeed one suspects that as far as the world of football is concerned Trevor tended to be something of a loner. All that passion and vigour on the field was a reflection of the Townhill boy's determination not to let down his father or his family. He is a man with strong *amour propre*, and his face will cloud at any hint of misunderstanding. We once talked at length about Len Shackleton, 'a brilliant player' but one who 'hated the Welsh'. In matches against Manchester City he would craftily set out to get his marker Roy Paul sent off. Playing with Ford at Sunderland he would deliberately place his pass an agonizing couple of feet beyond the centre-forward's reach. As we moved on to consider England–Wales rivalry generally Trevor bent his arm and waved his clenched fist saying: 'You've got to put it in on them'. Here indeed was the Red Dragon who had thrilled his nation and terrorized the English in that distant decade. Essentially, Trevor Ford was the leading Welsh romantic hero of that austere post-war world when the masses had yearned for sporting entertainment as never before or since. He symbolizes that era; and he happens to be my favourite footballer ever.

The Arsenal Welsh

Kenneth O. Morgan

'Post-war', the years after 1945, have been called the age of austerity. Historians and journalists tell us that they were a time of unrelieved gloom – rationing and shortages, whale meat and dried eggs, shivering with Shinwell and starving with Strachey. We read about a bleak age, presided over by Sir Stafford Cripps, vegetarian, teetotaller, high Anglican moralist who urged women to wear shorter skirts to conserve textile supplies. But to me the years from 1945 were an age of fun. My only memory was of the war when, alongside real scarcities, were danger and tragedy. We moved from Aberdyfi to London in 1944 in time for the V1s and V2s. A flying bomb landed nearby, killing twenty people and damaging our little house, 'Dolybont'. I woke up to see our front door blown off its hinges, dumped at the far end of the hallway. Compared with all this, the post-war years were sheer paradise. We had voted in the Attlee government, which my schoolteacher parents supported, my father passionately so. I was properly clothed and fed and, thanks to the NHS, healthy. I can understand a recent report that children in 1950 had a better nutritional intake than they do today. Bananas and pineapples returned to the shops, television sets were sold. There were treats like wonderful British films (we were given 'trailers' at school by David McCallum, later renowned as 'The Man from Uncle'), Tom Arnold's circus at Harringay, old-fashioned music hall at the Finsbury Park Empire – and always sport. Huge crowds, people in full employment, with a welfare state and decent take-home pay, flocked to sport of all kinds, and so did I. Marvellous cricket, always my favourite game, with Compton and Edrich on the rampage and miracles like seeing Don Bradman score 146 at the Oval in May 1948; athletics at the White City (I sat on on the tube next to a Dutch runner, Slykhuis, who had just beaten Sidney Wooderson and was still in his track suit!), and above all, football. Especially, and towering above all others, Arsenal. That famous club was important to the happiness I enjoyed in these supposedly grim years. The age of austerity was for me the age of Alexandra Park, Attlee and, especially, Arsenal.

In part, I enjoyed Arsenal because I enjoyed football. It may be politically incorrect in Wales today, but I have always preferred football to rugby. In my early years, Aberdyfi and Tywyn (Aberdovey and Towyn in those days), like the rest of mid and north Wales, were soccer territory. Probably the only rugby team within a fifty-mile radius was the university students team at Aberystwyth. Local people talked of the celebrated Aberdyfi team that won the Welsh Cup in 1936; its centre-half, Bob Dai, was our baker. I saw comparatively little rugby until I lectured in Swansea, at the age of twenty-four. Football also seemed much more fun to play. My school in Hampstead played rugby, a game in which, as a small Welsh boy, I seemed to have no chance against larger Englishmen. Some of us persuaded the school authorities to let us play something else. At Oxford, I played some soccer for my college: here, it seemed, was a game that offered an equal chance for large and small alike. I still recall a goal for the Oriel first eleven. A corner came in from the left, I missed the ball altogether with my weaker left foot, it struck me on the right knee-cap and, astonishingly, shot into the net at high speed, a feat which probably neither Pelé nor Maradona ever achieved. Football also seems to me more fun to watch. Rugby, a thrilling spectacle when Gareth Edwards or Barry John won games by brilliant tries, has become, from the evidence of the last world cup, a game of incomprehensible stoppages, long-drawn out penalty rituals, and a routine of 'big hits' by bionic men, amidst much licensed brutality. Football, judging from television, is more fluid, cleaner (despite the red cards) and more enjoyable.

No sport could match the atmosphere at Arsenal in 1945–52. As a young boy you could get in at the Laundry End at Highbury for six old pence (2½p now). You were amongst crowds of sometimes over 60,000, and, of course, you had to stand. But I felt entirely safe. I would go either with my father or with the boy next door, the same age and size as myself. In fact, the stewards looked after smaller children, adults let us move to the front, while there was none of the violence that marred soccer years later. A communal code kept rivalries within bounds (sometimes tested when Newcastle United came to Highbury). There were just two policemen present, one per 30,000. I felt in physical danger only occasionally when caught up in the throng departing through the narrow streets of Islington after the game.

The players were almost all British and white. I recall the total astonishment (not hostility, I think) when Cardiff played Spurs at White

76

Hart Lane with a black centre-forward, named, if I recall, Tommy Best. To my joy, Cardiff won 2–1 and Best scored the winning goal. Arsenal's players were all British other than an Icelander, Albert Gudmundsson, who played briefly in 1946–7 and lodged near us in Alexandra Park Road. He ended up as Iceland's foreign minister during the cod war of the 1970s. Peace on the terraces was matched on the field where the referee's view prevailed, sometimes meeting with verbal protest, but nothing more. The players wore long shorts and shirts with buttons. The Arsenal inside-right, a wizard called Jimmie Logie, a Scot, wore his white sleeves buttoned at the cuffs, as had his famous predecessor, Alex James. At half-time, there was Sousa from a marching police band, complete with a mace tossed high (and never dropped) or later airs from *The Desert Song* and Franz Lehar sung by Constable Alex Morgan (never promoted, no relation). Football then was a very British game. Matthews, Finney or Lawton were said be the world's best. The Rest of Europe was hammered 6–1 by a British combined team in Hampden Park. An afternoon at Highbury was an exercise in modulated patriot-ism. The hugely enjoyable Festival of Britain on the south bank in 1951 celebrated an inferred code of values and beliefs. It depicted a great country, technically inventive, neighbourly and tolerant ,with a powerful sense of its history from Boadicea to Dunkirk – and a love of sport. The Festival had a clear message to convey. It embodied a national auto-biography. To me, Arsenal was a significant part of it.

I am not altogether clear why I have supported Arsenal for the past fifty-six years. Aberdyfi people rather liked Everton because they had a famous Welsh centre-half, Tommy Jones. My father favoured Aston Villa, a great team in his Edwardian childhood. However, he had acted as a steward at Highbury while a teacher in the 1930s, and marvelled at James, Bastin and other heroes then. I still occasionally use his term 'The Arsenal', even though the definite article disappeared from the club's name in 1925. During a visit to London during the war he took me into the marble hall of Arsenal Stadium (an ARP civil defence centre at the time, somewhat damaged by fire-bombs) to see the bust of Herbert Chapman: Nelson's tomb in St Paul's was not more awe-inspiring for the 8-year-old boy. The main determinant, though, was surely the influence of the other boys in Alexandra Park. You either supported Arsenal or Spurs, and everybody I knew appeared to be an

Arsenal supporter. It was no doubt prudent to agree, although it chimed in with my own inclinations anyway.

In fact, I did not see them initially at the famous Art Deco stadium in Gillespie Road. Arsenal played at White Hart Lane, the ground of our rival Spurs, in the winters of 1944/5 and 1945/6. There I saw the swan-song of such pre-war champions as Ted Drake, George Male and Cliff Bastin (now deaf and playing at wing-half). But when play resumed at Highbury in September 1946 (Arsenal lost to Blackburn Rovers who had the former Arsenal goalkeeper, George Marks, in their team), the peculiar quality of watching Arsenal was unforgettable. The ground had atmosphere, even the cheap Laundry End. Arsenal also exuded a sense of metropolitan self-assurance which Spurs, Chelsea or West Ham simply lacked. For perhaps the same reason, I became a great fan of the New York Yankees, then in their great Mickey Mantle years, when at Columbia University in Manhattan in 1962–3; their World Series victories in the past few years gave me much pleasure. And, of course, Arsenal were successful. After 1945, they were not the obviously dominant team of the 1930s when they won five Championships and two Cup Finals. But they won the League Championship in 1948 with ease: I recall seeing their final home match – Grimsby Town were about to be relegated, and Arsenal swamped them by 8–0, their team including the wonderfully entertaining Denis Compton who played too in-frequently. The League was won again, narrowly, in 1953. In 1950 Arsenal won the Cup, defeating Liverpool 2–0, a great occasion since it was the first television programme I ever saw. They lost the final most unluckily to Newcastle in 1952 after Walley Barnes sustained a serious knee injury They played most of the match with ten, not very fit, men. I was playing in a school cricket match at the time, and we lost that, too. Not a good day.

My Arsenal period was really my school years. When I went to university I saw them much less frequently. From time to time I went to Highbury with Oxford friends, one of them being the later MP Brian Walden, a West Bromwich fan. One deeply sad match I saw in 1958 was the last Manchester United played before the Munich air crash – United won 5–4. But I have not been to Highbury since 1969: Manchester United were again playing and George Best scored a great goal. Deterred by the violence of the 1970s and high prices today, I have not seen any match since 1981 when I took my son to the Racecourse Ground to see Wrexham play Derby County. The latter included an old Arsenal favourite, Charlie George, whom indeed I had seen play in 1969. Even so, the team's successes still give me a frisson of excitement. An away win for Arsenal coupled with a home defeat for Spurs (not unusual these days) is the perfect day. Even though the team contains Frenchmen and Dutchmen, with a Nigerian and Croatian for reinforcement, it is still my team. My birthday in May 1998 saw Arsenal, already League champions, win the Cup as well by defeating Newcastle. My daughter had bought me a red and white scarf, and got me to wear it over my suit at the theatre that evening. It may have been a sartorial disaster. But I wore my scarf with pride.

One important reason for my attachment to Arsenal came from their having major Welsh players, then and earlier. It was not, to be truthful, the main factor in my allegiance. Thus Ron Burgess, a Welshman, was a fine left-half at the time. But he played for the enemy Spurs and I had, therefore, no regard for him. When Arsenal, very luckily, defeated Swansea Town 2–1 at Highbury in 1950, the year they won the Cup, Swansea's Welshness was of no importance. Standing right behind the net, I cheered Barnes's fierce penalty as it crashed past Swansea's diminutive goalkeeper with a few minutes to go. (Peter Stead's biography reveals that it was a very early game for Ivor Allchurch: I saw what was almost his last game, against Arsenal, with Peter in a Cup tie at the Vetch Field in 1968.) Even so, the Welshness of Arsenal was of some moment. For we were very much a Welsh-speaking family; indeed my mother who spoke Aberdyfi Welsh all the time to my Cardi father and also to several teachers at her school, seldom seemed to speak English much in our north London suburb. Nearly all holidays were spent at Aberdyfi, which indeed I hugely enjoyed. We celebrated VE Day in May 1945 with the only flag we had in the house, a giant red dragon, which flew bravely to the bemusement of our neighbours. With the Welsh at Arsenal, truly I had a special relationship.

Arsenal's Welsh connection lasted forty years. Their first major goalscorer in the 1920s, before they became famous, was Jimmy Brain, a Bristolian but signed up from Ton Pentre. In 1925/6, he scored no less than thirty-three goals, a club record surpassed by Lambert's thirty-eight in 1930/1. But the most celebrated Arsenal Welshman was Bob

John, born at Barry Docks, playing for Barry Town and Caerphilly before joining Arsenal in 1922. He played until 1937 and notched up a record 421 appearances, along with many Welsh caps. He played in the Cup finals of 1927, 1930 (when Arsenal won) and 1932 (when Arsenal lost to a non-goal and when he scored, playing as emergency outside-left). John was a very skilful left-half, one of the great team's real stars. He was also a strong tackler and gave his young team-mate, Cliff Bastin, a hard time when he played first for England, against Wales in 1931. John later became a club administrator and deserves his place in the Club's valhalla.

It could be claimed that in the great years 1932–4 the entire half-back line was Welsh. The right-half to balance Bob John's left-half was Charlie Jones from Troedyrhiw, who played for Cardiff City and Coventry. He had 176 games for Arsenal, won seven Welsh caps and was a most cultured performer. In between them was Arsenal's most famous defender, Herbie Roberts, the first stopper centre-half, an English international who hailed from Oswestry and played memorably from 1928 to 1937, winning four League and two Cup medals in the time. Since his name was Welsh and he came from just over the border in Shropshire, Welshmen could claim him also. Later in the decade, in 1937–9 when the team was beginning to show signs of decline, Arsenal had at inside-forward Leslie Jones from Aberdare, formerly of Cardiff City and Coventry. He gained eleven caps for Wales and after the war moved on to Swansea Town and then Barry Town. There were also fringe figures like L. Rogers from Wrexham and Horace Cumner from Aberdare, wingers who had a brief run in the first team.

The most notorious of the Arsenal Welshmen was surely Dan Lewis, the temperamental goalkeeper from Maerdy, who played for Arsenal from 1924 to 1930, and won three Welsh caps. His moment of disaster came in the 1927 Cup Final against Cardiff City, no less. Arsenal easily dominated the play but somehow failed to score. Near the end, a simple shot by Cardiff's Ferguson was allowed by Lewis to slip under his body and over the line. It was said that a smooth unwashed jersey caused this disaster: ever since, Arsenal goalkeepers (Bob Wilson, for instance) have supposedly worn recently washed jerseys. At the time, dark rumours abounded that Lewis had missed the ball deliberately to allow his countrymen to take the Cup to Wales for the first (and only) time.

When presented with the runners-up medal, he hurled it to the Wembley turf in anger, but Bob John picked it up for him. Lewis might have found solace in 1930 when Arsenal won the Cup for the first time, beating Huddersfield Town 2–0, but he was injured and Arsenal's goal was defended, after a fashion, by their third-choice keeper, Charlie Preedy. He was reckless, straying far beyond his goal area: by trade he was a taxi driver – the joke was that Charlie was never around when you needed him. But it was all more bad luck for Dan Lewis who never played again.

In my years after the war, Arsenal featured several eminent Welshmen. The saddest was Bryn Jones, born in Merthyr, transferred from Wolves to Arsenal in 1938 for a record fee of £14,000 which was said to weigh on him. Jones, an inside-left, was undoubtedly one of the finest players Wales ever produced: he was uncle to the later Spurs winger, Cliff Jones. But the truth was that he lost his best years to the war. When I saw him in 1946–8 he was a marginal figure in the team, outshone by Logie, replaced by Lishman. His career simply petered out. There was, however another Welshman rising through the ranks – Walley Barnes, born in Brecon, and a full-back, either on the left or right, of great authority. He became a fixture in the team from the end of 1946, playing for long in tandem with the English right-back Laurie Scott. He won a League medal in 1948 and a Cup medal in 1950. He also played in the 1952 final when his serious injury caused him to miss a whole season. However he played on for three more seasons. He won many caps for Wales, for whom he was captain and later manager, before becoming a BBC commentator. He was an orthodox defender who played in the full-back's accepted style, that is he seldom ventured far from his own penalty area. But Barnes could pass stylishly as well as hoof the ball upfield. He was outstanding in the 1950 Cup Final. He also became Arsenal's penalty-taker. He took penalties in the way that I always feel they should be taken, simply kicking the ball as hard as he could. He took a twenty-yard run-up and aimed for the goalkeeper's left ear. This makes it harder for the goalkeeper to make a save, in my view, than having to dive to one side. At any rate, Barnes never missed when I saw him. A fine, whole-hearted player was Walley Barnes, whose worried brow and receding hair gave him a sympathetic professorial look, or so I thought.

Another great Welsh player who came into the team in 1949 was Jack Kelsey, the famous goalkeeper from Llansamlet, signed by Arsenal from humble Winch Wen. He succeeded George Swindin in goal and played for Arsenal until 1962, appearing in 327 League games. He also won forty-one Welsh caps and played stirringly for his country, notably in the 1958 World Cup finals in Sweden. Kelsey was a courageous performer whose confidence inspired the whole defence. It was certainly not his fault that his time at Arsenal coincided with a period of steady decline. Another very skilful Welshman who appeared for the Gunners between 1949 and 1953 was Ray Daniel of Swansea, later to play both for Cardiff City and Swansea Town. His opportunities were restricted for years since he was long-term understudy to Leslie Compton. When he did become a regular in 1951–3 he proved to be a somewhat untypical Arsenal centre-half, not a robust stopper but a graceful, almost languid defender whose casual approach in the penalty area could terrify his colleagues. He played for Wales against England in 1950, when still in the reserves, outshining his opposite number, no less than Leslie Compton. It is somewhat mysterious that Daniel left Arsenal for Sunderland in 1953 when at the peak of his powers, perhaps persuaded to move by Trevor Ford. He was never perhaps quite the same player again after he left Highbury.

Another stalwart was David Bowen from Maesteg, signed from Northampton Town, a team which he later managed with some success. He was a left-half and thus had to spend many seasons in the Combination side, since Arsenal with Joe Mercer and Alex Forbes in their team were well equipped in that area. When Mercer broke his leg, colliding with a colleague in a game I saw, Bowen, a cultured, calm player, took over, playing 146 League games. He also won eighteen caps, and captained Wales with distinction in the 1958 World Cup in Sweden; later he was an excellent manager of the national team. There were two other notable Welshmen whom I saw play for the Gunners – but in the mid and later 1950s when my attendances at Highbury were becoming infrequent. Derek Tapscott from Barry and Barry Town, was a nippy goal-scoring centre-forward. He played in 111 games between 1954 and 1958, scoring the remarkably high tally of sixty-two goals. He later played for many seasons for Cardiff City and Newport County. For a time he appeared to be the centre-forward Arsenal had been looking for since the heyday of Reg Lewis (not a Welshman). Finally, I caught brief sight of Mel Charles of Swansea and brother of the great John, of course. He was a utility defender of great strength. But his time at Arsenal in 1959–62 was much disrupted by injury, and his best years were with Swansea Town. On balance, a record of sheer bad luck. After that, Arsenal's Welsh brigade seemed to peter out: John Roberts of Swansea played some games in the 'double'-winning side of 1970/1, Peter Nicholas of Newport played in the early 1980s. Swansea's distinctly limited John Hartson is the only recent player I can recall.

These Welsh players were part of a distinctive, memorable team. The fact that Arsenal played a defensive style of game, massing around the stopper centre-half, gave matches at Highbury a kind of Rorke's Drift quality which made them more exciting. But they scored plenty of goals in counter-attacks all the same. Matches at Highbury give a structure to my childhood memories. A home game offered a complete day, if not weekend. In the morning's *News Chronicle*, I would peruse the views of Charles Buchan, a famous Arsenal player of the 1920s. As we wended our way from Finsbury Park station, you might get a glimpse of Alex James, who ran a tobacconist and newsagents nearby. After the match, you could read a report on the early play by Bernard Joy (uniquely, an amateur centre-half with Arsenal), in a late-night edition of the *Star*. Then, back home, to a ritual of listening to the wireless to hear Buchan's monotone report on the day's matches. He would invariably end with words like the Toffees beat lowly Rotherham 3–0 and this is Charlie Buchan saying cheerio and good luck. The following morning meant a walk to Wood Green to buy our Sunday papers, *The Observer* and the left-wing *Reynolds News*, to read accounts of events at Highbury. Then I forgot all about it until the next home game. Football was not discussed at school. It was thought a proletarian game and our masters tried, totally in vain, to interest us in the exploits of Blackheath and Rosslyn Park, wherever they were.

I do not associate my schoolboy visits to Highbury with any of the adolescent angst so memorably described in Nick Hornby's *Fever Pitch*. His account of divorce and difficulties with girls does not relate to my own, no doubt duller, experiences at all. Anyhow, the timing of my rites of passage rather parallels that of Philip Larkin (1963). For me, a rare defeat for Arsenal brought disappointment but not disaster. Highbury just meant an evanescent private world of heroism and delight.

Francis Thompson's cricket poem 'At Lords' ends as follows:

> For the field is full of shades as I near the shadowy coast
> And a ghostly batsman plays to the bowling of a ghost,
> And I look through my tears at a soundless-clapping host,
> As the run-stealers flicker to and fro, to and fro,
> O my Hornby and my Barlow long ago!

I do not know what my bundle of sensations will be when (or, indeed, if) I reach that stage of life. My miasma of recollection may well feature academic activities, books or lectures, perhaps blurring into each other. But part of me will always be clinging excitedly to a barrier at the Laundry End on a misty autumn day, cheering Barnes's tackle or Kelsey's save, a time when life was innocent and it all seemed right, and mind, heart and soul could unite in celebrating the greatest team on earth.

I am much indebted to Leslie Stone for valuable information for this chapter.

Ivor Allchurch

Huw Richards

There is no hero like your first. I first became aware of Ivor Allchurch in the autumn of 1966, when my father took me to my first Swansea Town away game at Walsall. The match itself has rather faded from the memory except that we drew 1–1 and my father, whose essentially charitable nature is occasionally clouded by sporting partisanship, characterized Fellows Park crisply as a 'dump'. Nowadays one hears the Vetch Field described, not without justice, in the same terms. Maybe so, but it is *our* dump and we shall miss it much as Walsall fans, who have moved to a serviceable but featureless metal box a few hundred yards away, miss Fellows Park.

The match programme is still around somewhere, a tiny red booklet which listed the teams in one of those diagrams intended to represent positions on the field – albeit strictly in traditional 5–3–2 formation, grouped around a ball at the centre-spot. Next to the number 10 and the name Allchurch is scribbled in childish letters 'owt'. This was not some break into Yorkshire dialect, but a misspelt response to his absence. I knew nothing about Ivor, but I did get a sense of how disappointed dad was that he wasn't playing. No surprise there. At six years old you do not know much about football, but you do know whom your dad likes. Just as I inherited the family genetic defect, traceable back to my grandfather's move from Pembroke to Swansea in the days of Denoon, Fowler, Sykes and McPherson, which passes down the male line and makes Swans fans of us all, so I inherited Ivor. I did not know that he was a great player, but Dad told me he was, and that is more than good enough for any six-year-old. I saw him play only four or five times before the Swans let him go in 1968 after one of the more ignoble acts in the club's history – offering him a reduced contract. Aside from ingratitude for his services over the years, it was stupid even in the short term; he had been comfortably the leading scorer in the Swans' first ever Division Four season with seventeen goals from forty appearances.

If I saw him very little, I heard a great deal about him. One of the ways we acquire a sense of who we are and where we come from is listening to our parents' and grandparents' stories. I grew up on Dad's stories of the Swansea blitz, Mum's of being evacuated from East

London to Somerset and their shared experience as teachers in London, Norfolk and Oxfordshire. A sporting education was acquired in the same way. This was not exclusively in the hands of my father – I owed the lore of Bradman and Hobbs, the Arsenal teams of the 1930s and a whole range of improbable anecdote about cricket in Somerset to my grandfather. But what I really grew up on was the post-war Swans teams and their heroes, triumphs and setbacks. Rory Keane saving acrobatically on the goal-line at Arsenal with his keeper hopelessly beaten; Ron Burgess creating the conditions for the excellence of Ipswich's playing surface by a massive donation of blood; Mel Charles maddening big brother John by scoring in the first minute against Leeds; and how Tom Kiley's injured knee cost promotion to the First Division.

Two names stood out from this litany of heroes. One was Trevor Ford – my father's first hero, a ferociously bustling centre-forward who had scored forty-one goals in the first season after the Second World War. My parents first car was nicknamed Trev – what else would you call a Ford? And then there was Ivor. Always just Ivor. No qualification or surname was ever necessary. I heard about the extraordinary goals he scored, how he could pass thirty yards so that a team-mate did not even need to break stride, how he could swerve round opponents as though they were not there and dribble with the ball well in front of him without ever losing possession, and how everything he did was both elegant and gentlemanly. It was a learned, inherited hero-worship. When we did see him play I was much more conscious of him than of the other players around him. You could tell he was different – he seemed to find the game much easier than anyone else and while he was quick when he needed to be, he did not seem to have to run a great deal. And now I knew he was extraordinary – after all he was older than Dad and had been playing since 1950.

Other early heroes like Majid Khan, Gerald Davies and Gareth Edwards lasted long enough for me to be able to see why they were great and I have been able to judge for myself the virtues of sportsmen like Robert Jones, Ante Rajkovic, Peter Beardsley and Steve Watkin (both of him). But Ivor remained a slightly mythic figure, rooted as much in my relationship with my father – one reason why early football has such an impact is that it is one of the first adult activities you can take part in along with your parents – as in real memories or judgements of my own. Life also progressively erodes the tendency to hero-worship. A combination of a history degree, a career in journalism and some involvement in party politics is probably as good an inoculation as you get. Meeting people who are in some way famous is inherent in journalism, the essentially transactional nature of the contact an insurance against being over-impressed.

In 1995, during the Year of Literature in Swansea, Peter Stead organized a conference on sport, literature and national identity in a city hotel. The guests of honour at the conference dinner were Ivor Allchurch and Trevor Ford. A room full of distinguished academics sat in awe of the two elderly gents in blazers in their midst. It would have been easier to offer to interview the prime minister live in front of that audience than simply to go up to the table and introduce myself to Ivor and Trevor. I had to be introduced and doubtless chuntered away inconsequentially as one does when awe-struck. Both were warm and friendly, happy to sign a proferred copy of David Farmer's history of the Swans (hero-worship makes nine-year-olds of us all). Ivor, the more reserved of the two, was in his quietly dignified style reminiscent of Stanley Matthews. That conference was in some ways the origin of this series of books (*Heart and Soul* and *More Heart and Soul* the earlier ones) on Welsh sport and its heroes of which this is the third. My own enthusiasm for the project dates directly to that brief meeting.

One can only wonder at the forces which generate extraordinary efflorescences of brilliance at a single activity in a relative small community in a short space of time. Why should nineteenth-century Budapest have been so prodigiously productive of mathematicians, while at the same time Ireland was turning out an extraordinary stream of writers? How did the village of Trebanos, with a population of less than 2,000, produce four international sportsmen – three rugby players and a cricketer – in little more than a decade?

Swansea's mid-century production of footballers can stand with any of these explosions of brilliance. What did they put in the city's water between the late-1920s and the mid-1930s? While Ford, born in 1925, was slightly older the years between 1929 and 1936 saw the births of Ivor Allchurch, Jack Kelsey, Cliff Jones, Terry Medwin and the Charles brothers, Mel and John. Swansea's second rank from those years – Len Allchurch, Harry Griffiths and Johnny King – would have been considered a fair return of footballing talent in most communities of comparable size. Four Swansea-born players of that era were among the hundred chosen to mark the first hundred seasons of League football. It would be pointless to ask why such productivity was not maintained, since it has scarcely ever been paralleled. One mystery worthy of exploration is why a city and club which once specialized in the production of outstanding forwards should more recently have become a nursery for defenders like Chris Coleman and Andrew Melville.

The city in which that outstanding crop of youthful talent grew up was still scarred both physically and mentally by the Second World War. The Swans were undoubtedly much more of a force in the town than the All Whites, and had been so since their Cup runs of the 1920s. The segregated schooling of the time made rugby the game of the grammar schools, while the majority played football. A powerful schools league, whose results were faithfully reported in the *South Wales Evening Post* fed a Swansea Schools team which under the guidance of Dai Beynon regularly contended for the English Schools Championship, winning it in 1950, 1953 and 1955. Twenty Swansea boys won Wales Schools caps between 1947 and 1951.

Yet because his secondary school years coincided with the war, Ivor missed out on much of this. He did, however, after national service and spells with Wellington Town and Shrewsbury Town – both more convenient for his posting – join a club which in one sense, that of public interest, was at its all-time peak. Only three times in the club's history has the Swans' average gate topped 20,000 – the Third Division South championship season of 1948/9, the following season which saw Ivor's debut, and 1955/6. There were plans, thwarted by building regulations, to extend the Vetch Field to a capacity of 45,000 – hardly an improbable capacity at a time of booming gates nationally. After all, at one point, Newport County were talking about extending Somerton Park so that it could hold 60,000!

Ivor's arrival, in the visit to West Ham on Boxing Day 1949, filled the gap for a towering local hero, vacant since Trevor Ford's departure to Aston Villa more than three years earlier. Ironically, his debut attracted only limited notice in the *Evening Post* as its veteran correspondent 'Rolande' was unable to make the trip to East London. The London-based writer who filled in noted that Ivor and the veteran Billy Lucas 'both played workmanlike football. They schemed cleverly, and they dropped back to help an overworked defence', but he evidently had no idea that Ivor was a 20-year-old debutant. There was almost certainly a good reason for this. Rolande's reports make it clear that Ivor arrived as a ready-made star. Nor was this the perception of an uncritical admirer. His bi-weekly columns in the paper show us an old-style reporter who saw himself as an auxiliary club official, always ready to explain the club line and, in cases such as a violent falling out with the supporters club which occurred weeks before Ivor's debut, to rebuke those who were out of line. This loyalism did not deter him from commenting frankly on the team's limitations. For instance, his reports make it evident that Terry Medwin was not an overnight success and took time to develop into the outstanding player who contributed so much to the Spurs double of 1961.

In contrast, Rolande's comments during 1950 refer to the full repertoire of skills which Ivor was to display over a career that would encompass 694 League appearances (third on the all-time list behind Jimmy Dickinson and Stanley Matthews at the time of his retirement) and 251 goals, 68 Welsh caps and 24 goals. After only his third game, away at Southampton, Rolande noted that 'Allchurch was faster than he appeared to be for his long, raking stride was deceptive. But more important, his passes were well timed and well placed and his goal, which enabled the Swans to win, was cleverly obtained.' By the end of January Ivor attracted national notice with an outstanding performance at Arsenal, in a cup-tie which provoked the 'biggest exodus of football fans travelling from Swansea' according to railway authorities who handled seven special trains leaving High Street station between 9.35 pm and 6.25am. The Swans fans, around 4,000, who endured these ghastly overnight marathons to Paddington were rewarded with a match that has passed into folk memory for Keane's acrobatics in beating a shot out from under the crossbar with keeper Parry well beaten. They went down 2–1 to the eventual Cup-winners, but only after dominating for long periods, and Rolande reported that 'none quite captured the imagination like the young Allchurch'. He added the one occasional criticism sometimes made of the young Ivor, namely that 'he had a tendency to hold on for too long at times', but concluded that 'generally he played like a veteran instead of a newcomer lacking experience of big match play'. It was this performance that prompted the first transfer rumours, with Arsenal manager Tom Whittaker, quoted in one paper as calling Ivor 'the player of the century', enquiring about him as well as the Swansea skipper Roy Paul and the Irish forward Jim O'Driscoll. Rolande, in his column, warned sternly that 'Enquiries must not be construed as "offers". It is just as well to make that clear, for rumours of that kind do much to spoil players.'

Rolande need not have worried. By the end of October Ivor had been picked for his first cap and hailed by the *Evening Post* scribe as 'the 20-year old version of Charlie Buchan' and, in early November, Cardiff City were reported to have 'no answer' to his skills in a 1–1 draw which featured Ivor's 'intriguing body swerve, telling pass and lightning shot . . . subtle play . . . intriguing passes and almost easy elusion of sturdy tackles'. By now he was reported to be valued at £35,000 – well above the British transfer record of the time. Rolande, by implication at least, compared him favourably with the Vetch's previous idol Trevor Ford. The bustling centre-forward, disenchanted with Aston Villa, had sought a transfer. The Swans had first refusal, although they were always going to struggle to find the £30,000 asked, given that the club's total income for the previous season – one of the most profitable in the club's history, had been less than double that. Without spelling it out, Rolande makes it clear that Villa asked for Ivor in exchange and, following a 3–2 win at Leicester, pointed to the 'defence-splitting efforts of a wizard with the ball – Allchurch. How foolish the club would have been to part with such a player as a part of any transfer deal! . . . let the "bank" critics at the Vetch really look at what this young forward accomplishes to the advantage of his colleagues and, and not call for wild dashes to the goalmouth and impossible shots.' That admiration would be echoed by critics from far further afield. Percy Young, a beguiling combination of musicologist and football historian, recalled his performance on the opening day of the 1953/4 season in *Football Year*, a miniature gem of a book: 'Within three minutes of the whistle there was a goal. It was Allchurch's goal . . . The papers were correct. Allchurch was the finest inside-forward in the game.' Young subsequently injects a note of scepticism, uncertain whether the scoring effort was 'the single, unmistakeable sign of genius, or was it that a speculative ball . . . had missed its intention?' But his description leaves a vivid sense of Ivor's individual brilliance and the alarm he induced in opponents – West Ham on this occasion.

It had been this way. Allchurch, receiving the ball just beyond the half-way line veered north-eastward, feinting the while. Ten yards from the corner-flag the position was without hope. A posse of defenders harassed, and to contrive a neat, carefully pointed pass appeared as impossible as to outwit, single-footed, so many claret-coloured men, whose vigour at least could earn no reproach. Suddenly the right foot swung. The ball lifted and, wind-swept, went directly and certainly into the distant goal.

Whether or not that goal was a fluke, brilliant goals were among Ivor's trademarks – perhaps the most famous the ferocious volley which helped Wales into the quarter-finals of the 1958 World Cup at the expense of Hungary. Ian Wooldridge described how he converted a cross from John Charles: 'Downfield in a blaze of eagerness streaked Ivor Allchurch. He swung his left leg, smashed the ball on the volley at the very bottom of its arc . . . and hit Wales level with one of the greatest goals I shall ever be fortunate enough to see.' After Wales were knocked out by Brazil in the quarter-final Santiago Bernabeu, the architect of the great Real Madrid club of the period, asked Wales manager Jimmy Murphy for the autograph of 'the greatest inside-forward in the world'. Other inside-forwards who played in 1958 included Sweden's Gunnar Gren and Nils Liedholm, Hungary's Ferenc Puskas, Johnny Haynes of England and the Brazilians Didi and Pelé.

He also induced enthusiasm and respect among team-mates. Cliff Jones still enthuses about him more than thirty years after they played their last game together for Wales. Ray Powell, a Swansea team-mate in the very early days, recalls one training session:

> I was paired with this young fellow; soon I began wondering if I should have signed professional forms as he was doing things with the ball which I had not seen previously and could not imagine myself ever doing. When I lobbed the ball to him, he casually took it on his chest and rolled it down on to his knee, then to his instep before returning it to me.

This, it must be remembered, was with the heavy leather boots and ball of the post-war era, not the rather more user-friendly equipment which makes such control commonplace among the best modern players.

Ivor was a player who appealed to every shade of opinion, both visceral and cerebral, an elegant, creative stylist who also scored ferociously struck goals. And the Swansea Town teams he played in were, in spite of the greater achievements of John Toshack's teams, the most exciting the club has ever fielded with a forward-line often quoted as the best in the game. While Cliff Jones and Mel Charles, both several years younger, would eventually leave the club for larger transfer fees, accounts of the time leave little doubt who was the star, the totem and unchallenged local hero.

The affection of fans was reinforced by the close relationship between players and supporters. Footballers were not yet distanced from their communities by income and lifestyle. The Swans often trained on the beach, running back to the Vetch through the streets. A professional footballer may have been better paid than most working men, but the difference was one of degree rather than thousands of per cent. They were privileged, admired members of the community, but not greatly differentiated from their followers – one of my father's stories about the post-war Swans was of how he would often sit next to Trevor Ford, idol of the town, and soon to be the most expensive footballer in Britain, on the bus which took them back to their respective homes on Townhill.

That relationship has some bearing on one of the central questions about Ivor. Why did a player universally recognized as one of the best in Britain spend his best years with a Second Division club, only leaving after the 1958 World Cup, by which time he was twenty-nine? It has led some observers, in spite of the evidence of the World Cup and outstanding performances for Wales and against First Division clubs for the Swans in cup-ties, to question how great he really was. Certainly, it would not happen nowadays. A young player of comparable talent emerging with a lower division club would rapidly learn that his talents could bring him an income vastly beyond the means of his club, and act accordingly.

Those imperatives did not exist in the 1950s. Ivor commanded the maximum wage at Swansea, just as he would have done at Wolves, Aston Villa, Arsenal, Manchester City or any of the other clubs with which he was linked over the years. Even in a period of denser Welsh talent than the present, moving clubs would have made no difference to his prospects of international selection. He was more or less a fixture in the team from his first cap in 1950. Nor was it an entirely forlorn hope that he might make it into the First Division with the Swans. In the mid-1950s, as that brilliant generation of players came to maturity, they were credible promotion candidates. In 1955/6 they led the table with twenty-four points from their opening sixteen games, before Tom Kiley's knee injury derailed their season. They still finished only six points behind second-placed Leeds. In the following season they were nine points off the promotion places. It is not too hard to see why they did not rise further – at least eighty goals were conceded in eight consecutive seasons starting in 1952/3, and not even the free-scoring 1950s allowed teams with that sort of defensive record to rise much above mid-table.

The Swansea Town board's policy of developing younger players rather than speculating in the transfer market was not wholly ignoble, but their mistake was to allow a guiding principle to become a fetish. John Toshack, from his experience at Real Sociedad, has pointed to the difficulties created by an exclusive insistence on local youth: 'You might have three good players coming through in a year – all of them left-sided midfielders. It makes building a team difficult.' There is no doubt that the Swans produced an unrivalled wave of attacking talent, whose quality was evident in the 259 goals scored in three seasons between 1954 and 1957. Too bad they conceded 254. It is hard to escape the conclusion that a couple of judicious defensive purchases – not least in the immediate wake of Kiley's injury when the board first dithered then attempted to fill the vital gap in their defence with bargain-basement products – might have made the Swans serious promotion candidates. When saleable attackers eventually tired of the club's limitations and sought transfers, untried youngsters were expected to fill the boots of international-quality players.

Ivor did nearly leave in April 1952. The club, which was struggling to avoid relegation, had exceeded its overdraft and agreed to let him go for a fee expected to break the current transfer record of £34,500. Wolves looked the likeliest buyers, and the *Evening Post* reported that Ivor had visited Wolverhampton to look at houses. His departure was averted by a reconstruction of the Swans' board which brought new directors including Philip Holden, who would end up as a major Football League panjandrum, into the club. Wolves manager Stan Cullis attended the final match of the season, a 3–1 win over Rotherham which ensured the Swans' safety – a result, which the *Evening Post* recorded was greeted improbably by one of the 'biggest cheers' of the afternoon at Cardiff City. By now there were 'strong hopes' that Ivor would remain a Swansea Town player'.

In 1952 Wolves were on the verge of one of the best runs ever enjoyed by any British club. Between 1952 and 1961 they won three Championships and finished in the top three on five more occasions. One has to wonder how Ivor would have fitted into Stan Cullis's long-ball tactics, but the transfer would certainly have given him the chance of picking up several medals. When he did move – saying in somewhat resigned fashion that it was 'now or never' in 1958 – he joined Newcastle United, a club in decline who would be relegated at the end of his third season. A few years earlier Jackie Milburn had advised his sister Cissie Charlton against allowing her prodigously gifted son Bobby to go to Newcastle, advice for which Manchester United remain eternally grateful. Ivor's three seasons with Cardiff were also spent in the Second Division, before he returned to the Vetch for three final years. The last of his 694 matches was at the Vetch, at home to Hartlepool on 5 May 1968. This is even more of a memorable day in Hartlepool history than it is in Swansea's – Hartlepool's win clinched their first ever promotion after forty-seven years in the Football League. The *Hartlepool Mail* recorded that Ivor made a point of going into the visitors' dressing-room to congratulate them – a gent to the end, he also knew what it was like to wait a long time for promotion. He went on playing after he left the Swans – playing a season in the Southern League for Worcester City – Roy Paul's refuge from League football a decade earlier – leading them to fourth place. He then enjoyed a long association with Haverfordwest, the club his elder brothers Syd and Arthur had played for when Ivor was breaking into League football, and well into his fifties he was still playing in the lower reaches of the Welsh League.

This might be seen as underachievement. Should one of the two or three greatest footballers produced by Wales have ended up working as a storeman and playing part-time football well into his fifties? There is no evidence that Ivor himself expressed any disattisfaction with his lot – and the immense length of his football career seems to have been based on the simple fact that he loved playing and was happy to go on for as long as he could. Perhaps he should have demanded more for himself, should have pushed for the transfer that would have brought him

League Championships and achievements commensurate with his talents. It is tempting to quote the manipulative theatre director Tom Chester, a character created by Michael Blakemore in his novel *Next Season*. Explaining to a gifted young actor who is not being rehired he says: 'Talent's important of course. Of primary importance. But talent's nothing without – well – ferocity.' Nobody does anything as well as Ivor played football without considerable confidence and strength of character. But if he did lack anything, it was the ferocity of which Blakemore's character spoke – the driving self-seeking egotism, the demand that *my* needs and objectives must be satisfied at any price, often seen in high achievers in any walk of life. Ivor was not driven to demand transfers or under-the-counter payments. If this is a failing, the world would be a better place with more fallibility, peopled with more likeable, rounded human beings.

The demand that sports heroes should also be 'role models' asks too much of them. It is unreasonable to expect that people who pursue a single activity with the obsessiveness necessary to reach the highest level and are then also subject to the consequences of abbreviated privacy, hero-worship and also vicious denigration, huge material rewards and insecurity about their continuation, will also be balanced human beings. A few will be, but most will not. Heroism is a strictly on-field activity, as I was reminded when, watching his hero performing below his normal standards in a baseball match in New York, my 6-year-old godson Jack asked 'What's wrong with him?' I evaded the answer, 'He's a drunk, a junkie, a wife-beater and a tax-evader', in favour of a more anodyne explanation about baseball being a very difficult game.

I was luckier. As well as being a wonderful footballer, Ivor was one of the good guys. Swansea's view of its 'Golden Boy' was reflected in the huge turnout at his funeral in 1997. There is perhaps one more thing it might do to perpetuate his memory. If all goes to plan Swansea City will shortly leave the Vetch Field, location for many of Ivor's greatest feats, for a new purpose-built stadium at Morfa. Such new stadia may make economic sense but they lack warmth and identity. There is little to differentiate them from other grounds, to create that feeling of 'home' so essential to fans. Swansea City cannot recreate the extraordinary atmosphere of the Vetch Field. But they can take something of the Vetch Field with them, stamping the Morfa as their own and commemorating the best memories of the old ground. The Detroit Tigers baseball club has understood this need to connect. The Tigers' spanking new stadium features a statue of old hero Al Kaline. The city of Newcastle has done it for Jackie Milburn, Cardiff for Gareth Edwards and Swansea itself for Dylan Thomas. There could be no clearer signal to Swans' fans that the Morfa is home than a statue of Ivor Allchurch at some strategic point, accessible to all visitors to the ground, in or outside the new stadium.

John Charles

Rob Hughes

The measure of William John Charles is that he implanted something that is forever Wales in the hearts of Italians who saw him at his best. We know him simply as John Charles, the elder of two renowned sporting brothers born in the 1930s in the Cwmdu area of Swansea. Italy remembers him by another name: *il buon gigante*, the gentle giant. To the Italians, he was a colossus of the football field, immense in defence, in midfield, and in attack as he wore the black and white stripes of the Turin club Juventus.

'La Juve' is more than a club. It is an institution, affectionately known as *la vecchia signora* (the old lady of Torino) and followed, estimates suggest, by some 10.6 million people the length and breadth of Italy. From the thigh to the heel of this boot-shaped land the *tifosi*, the fans, know of John Charles. Indeed, it was the affection of this mass and their curiosity as to the roots of this big, calm and gifted athlete that persuaded Luigi Scarambone, secretary of the Italian soccer league, to say in 1961: 'Wales should give Charles a medal. He has put it on the map. Nobody in Italy knew where or who it was before.' That might be a slight exaggeration. Offa left a landmark on the Principality, and the Romans, countrymen of Scarambone, visited Wales even sooner. But football folk see the world through their own eyes, and in the context in which the tribute was conveyed, John Charles almost certainly did bring Wales to the attentions of millions.

The Italians judged John Charles as a pivotal force in a team that won Italy's *Serie A* Championship three times and the Italian Cup twice in his five and a half seasons there. They revered his ninety-three goals in 150 games between 1957 and 1962, and this despite the fact that he was selected as a defender as often as a centre-forward in an Italian era when the fear of conceding goals bordered on the paranoid. Yet it was not just the size of John Charles, nor simply that he could constitute the difference between success and failure on the pitch that Italians so coveted; it was the very *manner* of the man.

To this day, those who played alongside Charles for Juventus think of him as the gentle giant who proved that the meek can inherit their turf. They recall a competitor so big he could crush like a hammer against the anvil any opponent who tried to test his mettle; and opponents did seek to goad him to see if this foreigner could be made to lose his temper. They never found out. He would hurt opponents with the ball, not through brute force. 'If I have to knock them down to play well,' Charles wrote in his autobiography, 'I don't want to play this game. Players have to realize that the public do not pay good money to see pettiness and childishness.' Decades on, we wonder. Which of us would cherish having our national characteristics associated with the turbulence of Roy Keane, the petulance of David Beckham, or dare I ask it, the only fleeting assertiveness of Ryan Giggs? The game has changed, become a millionaires' playground, with business ahead of sport. But John Charles, in his day, was the highest priced individual in football, the most lauded and pampered.

His subsequent fall from grace – his fallibility – always aroused deeper emotions around Turin than in his homeland. When he became a pub landlord, they could hardly credit it. When he went to prison for one night, the consequence of debt, Juventus at once sent emissaries to offer him a job. And when he fell gravely ill with cancer of the bowel in 1999, it felt in the household of the Agnellis, the family that owns Juventus, as if someone very close to them, someone who seemed next to indestructible, had been stricken. Perhaps in that way, those Italians who knew of Wales through Big John can appreciate that it is a land like any other, unprotected from hardships. I use the word 'appreciate' because it is one John Charles himself used when I first met him.

The setting was neither Swansea nor Turin. It was a ramshackle dressing-room at a spartan, windswept sportsground known as Throstle Nest at Pudsey, west of Leeds. I was there because, too young to have witnessed the prime of John Charles, I heard that he still played on a Sunday for the love of it, and for charitable causes. This was an opportunity to glimpse the giant in the flesh, to try to glean, to appreciate, what so many said he was. From that dressing-room came a distinct air of embrocation and whisky. Out on the playing fields, Big John Charles and Wee Bobby Collins, players of Leeds United past, began chasing around. This was 1977, Charles was 46 years old and measured 46 inches around the chest; he was some way over the fourteen stones that his 6ft 2½in. frame scaled at its peak. At the time, he and virtually the entire Leeds team of his youth met regularly to play on their memories, raising perhaps £150 a time towards the £4,000 required to equip the local hospital with artificial kidney machines. None of us sensed then the irony that Charles himself was destined to become dependent on such specialist medical science. Back then, he was relatively carefree, mine host at a Bradford public house shrugging off the years among former £20 per week maximum-wage footballers whose life-cycle had returned them to trades such as salesmen, office workers, bookies. Charity aside, their games were reunions, although some admitted to training twice a week to safeguard as much of their reputations as they could.

None had more to lose than John Charles. Stripped down among his contemporaries, he still looked a juggernaut of a man, still dwarfed the others. Softly spoken, and tending to speak only when spoken to, he conveyed a disarming humility. I arrived with a message for him, from Giampiero Boniperti, the idol of Juventus before Charles joined them. 'Boni' had gone on to riches, and to the presidency of Juve, and he wanted me to say to his friend John Charles that never, never did he enjoy a better partner in sport. 'Ah, I appreciate that, now,' replied Charles. I then offered a compliment of my own, that one could still see in him the pride and the pleasure, the anticipation with which he pulled on the kit. He appreciated that compliment too, although he added that, with age and cigarettes, 'I can't do it now. I run ten yards and then have to wait twenty minutes.' Ten yards from him might be worth ten miles from lesser players, from the journeymen whose main assets were physical fitness and obedience. 'Well,' he mused, 'you see, you can't go back. You want to, but the legs won't allow it. You do it in spasms, like . . . the legs boss you, y'know.' Then, it was time for action. A quick tipple, and the Leeds United Former Stars went out on that bumpy pitch to face an Italian XI. The way these charity matches worked was that each player in turn invited the opposition. Bobby Collins would bring down a team from Scotland, George Meek persuaded a local team from Walsall where he, after his years on the wing for Leeds, settled with a small tool-makers business. And Charles? After his life in another world, it had to be the old boys from Turin.

The Italians were skippered by Umberto Colombo, a pal from the Juventus days. There were younger, leaner Italians too, players who came to find out what it was like to meet John Charles in action, players who could tell their children, and then their children's children, how they once put the great man in his place. The moment I cherish, because I think it did give me some impression of what I had missed, was when two of these Juventus regulars jumped with all their might only to bounce to the ground off a white-clad figure who, with an enormous grin on his face, cushioned the ball on his forehead, swayed to his left, and volleyed the ball with a still awesome smack towards goal. Convinced that I had glimpsed the real John Charles, one of his spasms at the very least, I suggested that the charity game appeared to be played with a competitive edge. 'Has to be', Charles replied. 'We're mingling with people I haven't seen for eighteen years, and we like to win still. You'd appreciate that.'

In many respects, that meeting in Pudsey was the centre-point of the life and times of John Charles. He was able, in spasms, to indulge himself with play. The game was a game, no longer the living which had raised him from a schoolboy whom Leeds United took from Swansea Town for £10 to a performer for whom Juventus paid a world-record fee of £65,000 in 1957. It is no exaggeration to presume that in modern times, during which the Vatican has criticized transfer fees as obscene, a John Charles might fetch £50 *million* on the open market. After all here was a centre-forward guaranteed to score a goal every other game, a defender resolute in preventing goal-scoring, a wing-half who could interchange with the best on earth. A chameleon of a player, who seldom missed a game. A physical specimen intimidating by his presence, adaptable by nature, a player from a unique period in which the Allchurch brothers, the Charleses and the Joneses surely debunked the myth that the men of Harlech needed the ball to hand rather than to feet. Above and beyond the rest, John Charles also proved that soccer is a *lingua franca*, especially for a player whose predilection was to express himself in motion rather than words.

Between the high living on the Italian Riviera and his origins on Swansea Bay, the making of Charles was forged in Yorkshire. Leeds bought him for bulk, essentially for aerial dominance in defence and, when he was just eighteen, Wales blooded him at centre-half for the first of his thirty-eight caps, in 1949. And there he might have remained, anchored to the number-5 spot, a redoubtable defender through and through, had it not been for Major Frank Buckley, the Leeds United manager. It was Buckley who converted Big John to number 9. The trainer, for that is what they were called in the 1950s, spotted the burst of pace so unusual in a big and heavy athlete and spent countless afternoons on the training field until, in 1953, he unveiled his 'new' centre-forward. The legend was born. In that first season, Charles struck twenty-six goals in forty games, just the aperitif for a flow of forty-two goals from thirty-nine appearances in 1953/4. Where was he best, in attack or defence? It depended on the team need, and on who was handing out the jerseys (for the great Raich Carter had succeeded Buckley as manager). The player himself, agreeable to the point of subservience, simply did what was asked of him and played the game.

Had the Italians not come for him and made offers that both he and Leeds could not refuse, it is more than likely that John would have been content just to pick up his twenty quid from Leeds and to add to the occasions when he and his brother Mel played together for Wales – most notably in the 1958 World Cup in Sweden. Perhaps, had John not taken the *lire*, the *dolce vita* and the distractions and estrangement of being Britain's highest profile footballer abroad, he might have been able to resettle in south Wales as did Mel, the fishmonger, once his Swansea Town and Arsenal days were over. But once the course was set, the rise and decline of John Charles involved peaks of wealth and fame, and then some public humiliation, that are an object lesson for today's shooting-star pretenders who doubtless think that the good times will last forever.

It all began after John Charles netted his 150th goal for Leeds. For months, the club had been resisting the enticements of the dark stranger who appeared in reception talking *lire* in telephone number propor-tions. A real charmer, Gigi Peronace was an agent for the club rather than one of the multitude of players' agents who fill every corridor nowadays. He was also the emissary of Umberto Agnelli, the 22-year-old younger member of the family that controlled the Fiat company and owned Juventus. Sam Bolton, the Leeds United chairman, was as prag-matic as Yorkshiremen are supposed to be, but he was no match for the price and persuasion of the Agnellis, not only because of the world-record fee they would pay but because of the pledges Agnelli undertook towards Charles and his growing family of three (ultimately four) young boys. 'I make myself personally responsible to you . . . ' was the first line of the contract between Agnelli and Charles. And it ended, 'This document shall be legally enforceable against me to the fullest extent.' It was an agreement beyond the obligation between club and player, one that Agnelli was later to say he would only have committed to two players in the world – John Charles whom he got, and Tom Finney who never left his Preston roots. As you might expect, Charles himself was never likely to have bartered such a deal at the age of twenty-five; his advisers included his representative Terry Somerfield and the broadcaster Kenneth Wolstenholme.

Their negotiations brought Charles an £18 per week flat-rate Juventus wage, two pounds less than the English maximum. However, it was sweetened by the club paying his income tax and by bonuses which were commonly £15 for a home win, £25 for each away victory, and for special matches stretched as high as £500. 'That way,' Charles observed, 'you had to be a winner.' On top of that, he received £10,000 of the £65,000 transfer fee, paid in twenty-four monthly instalments as a signing-on sum. And there was a Fiat car of his choice, a rent-free family apartment, followed by a villa on the renowned Diano Marina Riviera, as well as gifts of clothing and jewellery from wealthy Juventus fans: all told, Charles once calculated, the club was meeting his bills of £240 a month. It was a *quid pro quo*. Juventus was sure that it had the world's greatest centre-forward, and Charles was told often enough that he would be the world's biggest idiot to give up his lifestyle.

Even so, he missed bacon. He became accustomed to lasagne verde, osso bucco and chianti, and grew to accept the Italian system of 'retiro', the regimented encampment that took players away from their families every week, home or away match, from Friday to Monday. He learned to tolerate the prying into his every move by the club, the press, the fans. And he appreciated the plush changing-rooms with their own hairdressing salon, the soothing tranquillity of the pre-match dressing-room in which budgerigars chirped. Yet, sometimes Charles knew he was trapped. The money was too much to reject, the life was a world away from Swansea where the Sabbath was for chapel, not the clamour of football. In Italy, church and sport are equal forces. While the results justified the outlay – and Juventus won the Italian championship, *lo scudetto*, three times in his first four seasons – the 'extras' by way of personal appearances were allowed. Charles, the quiet Welshman, sang on a record. He appeared, together with his inside-forward Juventus team-mate, the Argentinian Omar Sivori, in a film *Idoli Controluce* (Idols in Contrast).

There were also mixed fortunes abroad. Nothing compared to the acclaim when Juve became the first club to beat Real Madrid in a European Cup tie, in the Spanish champions' own Santiago Bernabeu stadium (a match in which, incidentally, the adaptable Mr Charles played right-half). And nothing was quite so frightening as the night in Vienna when he overheard doctors discussing whether to amputate his leg after an injury. Much of his time in Italy must have seemed almost surreal, a passage of time during which the goodies outweighed the sacrifices. But as Sivori and Boniperti, the two players with whom he was most associated, pointed out, none of them really knew what was going on inside the head of Charles. 'He was never a great talker,' observed Sivori, 'and if he had problems in Turin it was always his way to suffer in silence.'

A retreat into silence was to revisit Juventus in 1987 when, thirty years after Charles, the club again recruited a Welshman. Juventus had paid Liverpool £3.2m for Ian Rush in the hope that they had signed Charles the Second, but unlike Big John, Rush failed to integrate with his team-mates and the fans and failed to deliver. During this period, I attended a match at Stadio delle Alpi with Gianni Agnelli, the head of the family that owns the club, and whose influence and love of football exceeds even that of Umberto, his younger brother who had brought John Charles to Juventus. 'Why?' Agnelli senior asked repeatedly, 'why is Rush so quiet?' I suggested that it was just his nature and that Ian Rush expressed himself through scoring goals. 'Well,' retorted the Juventus paymaster, 'he's had little to say since joining Juventus!' The wit of the Italian, delivered in flawless English, spared Rush nothing. Rush was wealthy and stealthy, yet scored too seldom to transcend barriers of language and culture as Charles so powerfully did. A visitor could see why. Rush had no Boniperti, no Sivori at his side. He was isolated, and the fixation with the legend of Big John persuaded players to lump the ball high into the penalty box. Rush never professed to have Charles's aerial command, and the balls were wasted there rather than at his feet.

The relative failure of Rush heightened the nostalgia for Charles, and by bitter irony it brought to the fore the struggles that John Charles had endured since making what he admitted was the worst decision of his life. He chose to return to Leeds United, by then managed by Don Revie, who paid £53,000 to repatriate him in August 1962. By then, the magic of John Charles had waned. He was thirty, already losing his exhilarating burst of pace, and troubled in the soul. He had tasted the nectar of the *lire* billionaires, but while Juventus encamped its players in the weekly 'retiro', the families suffered. Several times his wife Peggy threatened to move the family back to Britain, a homing instinct that intensified as the boys Terence, Melvin and Peter neared school age. Extricating himself from the Agnellis proved less pleasant than the courtship that had taken him to Turin. The downward spiral was swift. He lost his edge, the impetus of his career, and he could not save his marriage either. He was to drown his sorrows in alcohol, was quickly sold again by Leeds to A.S. Roma, and just as rapidly moved down the scale to Cardiff City, then Hereford United. He was probably unsuited to management, but clubs were reluctant to find out. His reputation for meekness worked against him. How could this gentle 'king' of the European highroad adjust to the shoestring existence of the lower divisions where lesser mortals generally responded to rather coarser motivation?

Nor did he score as a businessman. Fame could not shield him, and his fortune was largely lost in a failed restaurant venture. For a time, he ran a sports shop trading on his name in Cardiff, and after that he became a genial, but ultimately poor, publican. Then, as now, the rule of thumb seemed to be that the higher a footballer reaches in fame, the less equipped he is to manage withdrawal from the game. Charles had a mild brush with the law in 1976 when he was fined £25 for handling leather jackets which turned out to be stolen, and in 1988 he spent a degrading evening in a police cell. He was not sent down because he was a criminal, but because he could not pay his way and his word could not buy him time. He owed £943 in taxes on a pub, and three women magistrates at Huddersfield were not convinced by this whispering giant who pleaded that friends in football had promised a testimonial game that would pay off his debts to society. The magistrates sentenced him to sixty days imprisonment – he did three hours before his second wife Glenda did what Charles himself would never do, begged and borrowed the money to bail out her man. They existed at the time on £70 a week social security income, and the kindly man who never refused a chance to play for the hospital charity, who donated his medals and memorabilia to worthy causes, almost gave up his liberty rather than ask for any charity in return.

He always said that he had the memories, and that it did not matter who had the medals. And from Turin, where the best of those memories were played out, Gianni Agnelli and Giampiero Boniperti reacted to his financial downfall. 'Juventus never forgets its great players,' the club announced. He was invited to come and discuss the possibility of a job, perhaps using his name to sell cars. 'John played in a great Juventus team, maybe the greatest of all time. He is still a famous figure in Italy. There are many who still call him the King.' The king of the playing fields, the uncrowned ambassador for Wales abroad, became inevitably just an ordinary man, coping with as much dignity as he could against the ordinariness of growing old. After he battled against cancer his other club, the one that paid a tenner for his youth, arranged two gala nights at Elland Road. The first, in February 2000, required him to kit out in black bow tie and dinner jacket and to stand proud among the greats of Leeds United past and present. The second, a month later, was a dinner in his honour. He heard Jack Charlton, who wore the Leeds number-5 shirt after Charles but could never have converted to the number-9, say: 'Whenever people ask who was the most effective British player of all time, they think of George Best or Our Kid [Sir Bobby Charlton]. But they forget John.' William John Charles just smiled, meekly. 'Only grandfathers', he once said, 'remember me now.' Because he performed before soccer's dominant television era, it is true that his witnesses are elderly. But legends outlive men. John Charles, *il buon gigante*, cannot erase himself or his mark from the annals of the game.

Medwin and Jones in the

'Greatest-Ever Side'

Peter Stead

The Tottenham Hotspur team that completed the Cup and League double in 1960/1 was dubbed 'soccer's greatest-ever side'. Aston Villa had last completed the double in 1897, but most experts thought that the modern dispensation of a twenty-two team First Division had made such a feat impossible. Nevertheless, in a season in which they were to be generally applauded for their attractive and attacking football, Spurs were to lose only seven of their forty-two League fixtures. One of those defeats came at Cardiff's Ninian Park on a remarkable Saturday evening in March. Unusually for those days the match kicked off at 7pm, which meant that many of those present had earlier taken the opportunity to watch the Welsh rugby team beat Ireland at the Arms Park. Strolling through the Canton twilight we could reflect on Spurs' terrific form. At one stage it had looked as if they were going to win every match, but in their twelfth game Manchester City held them to a draw and they finally succumbed in game seventeen at Hillsborough. When they came to Ninian Park they were twenty-one points ahead of Cardiff and they had won twenty-five and lost only three of their thirty-one games. Not many of us anticipated the completion of a Welsh double on that day, but we fully agreed with the programme editor who 'reckoned to see the best game of football so far this season at Ninian Park'.

The fact that a Welsh team had already played in Cardiff that day helped to give the evening soccer fixture the feel of an international match. Under the lights Spurs, in their white collarless shirts and dark blue shorts, looked like the England team and, of course, their highly publicized triumphs meant that every one of us could reel off their line-up – 'Brown, Baker, Henry . . .'. Making my way around to the bank I was fascinated and a little intimidated by the visitors' warm-up routine. Danny Blanchflower, looking even taller and more imperious in the flesh, was engaged in a fast and furious passing exercise with Mackay and White. It looked more skilful and purposeful than any pre-match activity I had ever seen; later I was to discover that American baseball players warmed up with the same intensity.

All 48,000 of us were thrilled to see Spurs that evening. A later generation of fans who boo and abuse visiting teams can little realize how much pleasure those of us who followed football in the post-war decades derived from the visits of famous old teams. We knew the history and lore of those sides, admired their colours and appreciated their stars; and, in particular, those of us who supported football in Wales took pride in the careers of any Welsh players who commanded a regular place in a fashionable or successful English club. Anticipating that evening in Cardiff we were in awe of what Spurs had achieved and delighted that the vastly entertaining football they had been playing owed much to two players who had grown up just a few streets from each other in the Sandfields area of Swansea. Terry Medwin and Cliff Jones were both very much Vetch Field products and they had both become stars at White Hart Lane.

The great North London rivalry between Arsenal and Spurs is a central tradition of the British game and, as Ken Morgan makes abundantly clear in this volume, there were many reasons why Welsh fans tended to support the Highbury team over the years. In my own case the question of where my loyalty should rest was forcibly explained by an uncle who had gone to London in the 1930s in search of work and subsequently found his passion for the Arsenal the most rewarding feature of those Depression years. He never lost the opportunity to remind me that 'they are a funny crowd at Spurs'. In the 1950s, however, I began to question his judgement, for a new image of Spurs was emerging. Nobody had told me about Eugene 'Taffy' O'Callaghan from Ebbw Vale, who played for Wales eleven times and scored ninety-four League goals for Spurs between 1926 and 1935. In contrast I knew everything about another Ebbw Vale man, Ron Burgess from Cwm, who loomed large in post-war British football.

When I first saw Burgess play for Wales in 1953, he was accepted as something of an institution: he looked older than his colleagues and we assumed that he had always played for Wales and always would. Ageing half-backs were not romantic figures and were not given the glory treatment, but it is now generally recognized that the former pit-boy from Cwm, who had gone straight from local football to Spurs in 1936 when he was eighteen, had developed into one of the most accomplished half-backs of his era, an era cruelly interrupted by the long war-time break. Having played in ten war-time internationals he went on to play in thirty-two official games for Wales as well as in a Great Britain team that took on the Rest of Europe. At Spurs he was a vital part of the team which was promoted from Division Two in 1950 and then went straight on to win the First Division Championship with real style. Under manager Arthur Rowe Spurs played an attacking game, un-imaginatively described as 'push-and-run' but widely acclaimed for having punctured the prevailing 'mania for defensive football'. As an attacking half-back and captain Burgess contributed significantly to the new club style and many commentators have made the point that, to the extent that the 'Double' team of 1961 attempted to replicate that of 1951, Danny Blanchflower was the natural heir to the man from Cwm. For club historian Ralph Finn 'the great-hearted indefatigable Ronnie Burgess' was 'surely one of the greatest half-backs of all time'.

Burgess played his last game for Spurs in 1953. In June 1954 he became player-coach at Swansea Town and, following the sudden death of Billy McCandless, he was appointed manager for the 1955/6 season. At the Vetch Ron Burgess first played alongside and then managed both Terry Medwin and Cliff Jones. None of Swansea's supporters could have realized at the time that they were watching the safeguarding and nurturing of the Spurs legacy at a club 200 miles distant from White Hart Lane. In fact, it was during Burgess's first season in charge that the Vetch Field came to the rescue of a troubled Spurs side: in April 1956 manager Jimmy Anderson dashed to Swansea to pay £18,000 for the 23-year-old Medwin who had already played three times for Wales and scored fifty-nine goals for the Swans. The departure of Medwin has always been recalled with a special sadness in Swansea for it was seen as the first breach in the dyke that was to eventually drain away so much of the town's homegrown talent. In early 1958, continuing with his policy of selling stars in order to buy a greater number of lesser players, Burgess sold Cliff Jones for a UK record fee of £35,000 to Jimmy Anderson, a Spurs manager who had successfully outbid several other clubs, including Chelsea. Jones had already won fifteen caps for Wales and scored forty-six goals for Swansea.

The year 1958 was one of the most dramatic in the history of British football for it witnessed both the Munich air disaster and the only World Cup Finals in which all four Home Nations competed. It was the year, too, in which Terry Medwin and Cliff Jones, together with Wales colleague Mel Hopkins who had been at Spurs since 1951, became caught up in a bewildering kaleidoscope of events in which disappointment and frustration went hand in hand with glory. All three players went to Sweden and contributed to that tantalizing chapter of near-fame. Both Hopkins and Jones played in all five games: the former was effective in a hard-working Welsh defence, whilst the latter by general consent took a few games to warm up. Medwin missed one match but overall was undoubtedly one of the Welsh success stories, flourishing in the freedom allowed him as a result of the heavy marking of his forward partner John Charles. In the vital play-off match against Hungary he scored the winning goal.

In that same summer of 1958 Bill Nicholson took over as manager at Spurs and with Blanchflower as captain, playmaker-in-chief and co-ordinator of on-field tactics, the club deliberately set out for greatness. Inevitably there were to be personal highs and lows. For Jones a disappointing summer ended disastrously, for in a training session at Cheshunt he broke a leg and was sidelined for four months. On his return, however, he quickly found a role, first on the left and then increasingly on the right flank where he could feed off the service of Blanchflower and White. But whether playing on the right or left he was licensed to roam, for it was appreciated that the fastest winger in the country was also an effective finisher with his head and both feet. He was at number 7 that evening in Cardiff and was poised to share in all the triumphs that lay ahead. He was to win League and Cup medals in 1961, a further Cup medal in 1962 and a European Cup Winners' Cup medal in 1963. In all he was to play 318 League games for Spurs scoring 134 goals.

Terry Medwin's years at Spurs were a little more chequered. Having scored two debut goals in 1956 he became a first-team regular either as a winger or inside-forward. Cruelly, he was struck down by a stomach bug in the autumn of 1960, and this allowed the diminutive and combative Terry Dyson to grab his chance. Disappointingly, Medwin was missing from the line-up at Ninian Park in 1961, but he had started the season in the first team and he returned to score vital goals at the season's end. His fourteen League appearances (scoring five goals) earned him a League winner's medal but he failed to make the Cup Final team. Once more fully fit he played regularly in the following season, and to our delight he was at number 7 and Cliff at number 11 when Spurs returned to Ninian Park in December 1962. That day 33,000 of us witnessed a 1–1 draw. Both wingers were also on duty at Wembley when Spurs retained the FA Cup. There was no double that season, although the acquisition of Jimmy Greaves had certainly made them a better side. For Medwin there was further drama to come, for in a 1963 close-season tour of South Africa he broke his leg. His final record for Spurs was 197 League games and sixty-five League goals. At White Hart Lane Cliff and Terry had experienced serious injury; and both of them express tremendous admiration and sympathy for Mel Hopkins who suffered a horrendous nose injury playing for Wales at Hampden Park in 1959, consequently losing his first-team place at Spurs. This very talented full-back, who never once complained, looked on as his colleagues collected their medals: for Wales, however, he remained first choice. In all he played 219 League games for Spurs including that 1962 draw at Ninian Park.

That Spurs side of the 1960s was generally regarded at the time as the best British team since the Second World War, not least because of its style and entertainment value. For John Cottrell, 'their greatness lay in their ability to produce the unexpected – the cheeky back-flick, the acutely-angled shot, the sudden switch of positions, the daring sally of a full-back into the attack'. With Spurs in mind Dave Bowler once argued that 'every great team has its own rhythm, its own pace, its own tempo', and in this respect it is worth recalling Jimmy Greaves's own judgement that the team he had joined in 1961 'purred along like a Rolls Royce'. He was to regard them as 'without any question the best team that (he) had ever played with and that takes into account England matches', admitting to getting 'goose pimples just thinking about some of the football we used to play'. Television coverage of European ties gave Spurs a wider audience as the decade went on, but there were always special memories for those of us who saw that team in the flesh. There is a particular pleasure in recalling that, at Ninian Park, they lost in 1961 and could only draw in 1962. Nevertheless, we never doubted that Spurs were great and thereafter a special magic clung to those players who had worn those white shirts.

In May 1999 the start of a vital League game at the Vetch was delayed as the referee inspected a very wet pitch. As the Centre Stand patrons were kept waiting in Glamorgan Street I bumped into Terry Medwin whom I had got to know when I was researching the life of Ivor Allchurch. Pointing to the small car-park adjacent to the prison Terry said 'that is where I grew up': his now demolished home had stood just twenty yards from a Vetch Field corner-flag. Terry and his six sisters were the children of an Isle of Wight man who had come to Swansea as a prison officer. Not surprisingly the young Terry was 'steeped in the Vetch', at first sneaking in to see games, later 'making a fortune' by selling as many as 200 programmes. On that day in 1999, and on other occasions, Terry stressed how much he had appreciated and benefited from the unique setting of his home between the Vetch on one side and Swansea Bay on the other. It was 'a brilliant upbringing' in which the sea itself and the sands ensured his youthful fitness and subsequently allowed a perfect training area for him and his fellow Swans. All the hard work and routine of jogging, sprinting and make-up games were more easily endured in this magnificent setting. With St Helen's just down the road it was hardly surprising that most of the Swans were good cricketers too, not least the defender Tom Kiley. Cricket was a passion that Terry would take with him to London; he would often travel from his home in Palmers Green to watch the big games at Lord's.

Now that he is living back on Swansea Bay Terry is keen to recall that golden childhood and youth which allowed him to flourish. He never particularly enjoyed working as a mechanic for Moorsmith Motors, especially as many of his colleagues were often absent at choir rehearsals with the Welsh National Opera, which just happened to be the main passion of his boss. In every other respect, however, his career was a pleasurable and uninterrupted progress. He was a brilliant school-boy player in a town which had produced more than 200 international players at that level and which justifiably regarded its schools football to be as good as any in the land. As he developed with the Swans reserves it was already apparent that, although his preference was for the right wing, his goal-scoring prowess often meant that he was used either as an inside- or centre-forward. This was a pattern that would continue throughout his career, and not least when playing for Wales. On the eve of his departure to Spurs he was generally regarded as 'one of the most skilful leaders in the Second Division'. He was scoring regularly, although one report pointed out that it was only 'his unselfishness' which prevented a doubling of his tally. Both Leicester City and Manchester

City had been looking at Medwin and one former England defender described him as 'one of the cleverest and most intelligent leaders he had faced'.

In his late sixties Terry Medwin remains a handsome man with a fresh appearance and an open and attractive personality. Many years ago at Lord's he was mistaken for Tommy Steele: he certainly has star quality but also an air of distinction which that confusion belied. It is a delight to talk to this articulate and thoughtful student of the game. He is clearly fascinated by the range of different personalities he had encountered in his career as a player, as a manager (at Cheshunt), as a coach (at Cardiff, Fulham and Norwich) and finally as assistant manager and chief coach at Swansea. He worked with individuals who were drinkers, smokers, jokers, loners and worriers. Perhaps it was the anxiety he experienced himself in later decades that was to give him considerable insights into the range of football types. He is genuinely proud of how little money meant to the players of his day; he rarely looked at his wage slips and was never particularly aware of any additional World Cup payments. His final wage as a player was £40 a week. He loved the way football allowed travel and he especially enjoyed Israel where he was the Welsh centre-forward in 1958. He is proud of his six children and a growing tribe of grand- and great-grand-children. With a son who is in business in Toronto he has become a supporter of the Blue Jays.

Terry has always been thoroughly appreciative of the football talent that came out of Swansea. On several occasions he has emphasized how great Mel Charles was in Sweden in 1958. After the World Cup Mel went to Arsenal but he had almost gone to White Hart Lane; one some-how feels that a fit Mel Charles would have contributed a formidable degree of skill and brio to that great Spurs side. For Ron Burgess, who is now eighty-three and living near Terry in Mumbles, he retains a special regard. Quite simply, Burgess was 'a genius' and was regarded as such by Bill Nicholson and everyone at Spurs. Billy Wright and Jimmy Dickinson are remembered as the great half-backs of those years but, says Terry, 'Ron was the better footballer'. Of his own generation at Spurs he picks out Dave Mackay as the star and suggests that one need only look up his incredible record of success under Bill Nicholson and then with Brian Clough at Derby. Mel Hopkins was 'a great leggy full-back' whom Stanley Matthews tried to avoid. They were always a great gang at Spurs; they all got on well, room-sharing was never a problem and life in Palmers Green and Southgate was good. The evidence for this is in the team photo of the Double side. Certainly Mackay looks a handful and Bobby Smith a tricky customer but, in general, they are a well-groomed and good-looking bunch with immaculate haircuts. While Danny Blanchflower was the prime minister, Terry Medwin was clearly the pin-up boy.

Neither geographically nor spiritually has Cliff Jones moved far from Spurs. He lives in a former farmhouse, a property he first noticed many years ago when commuting to the Spurs training-ground at Cheshunt. This part of Hertfordshire is a paradise for golfers but there are mixed memories in this respect, for quite near is the course where Cliff's great friend and room-mate, John White, was killed by lightning in 1963. Cliff is a frequent visitor to White Hart Lane and appreciates the way in which Terry Venables's Spurs Legends Club brings old friends together at selected matches. At his home he has a trophy-lined den packed with memorabilia that themselves constitute a history of the game. As much as his caps and his Spurs medals he values his PFA 100 League Legends medal and several items commemorating his friendship and charity work with Sir Stanley Matthews. Prominently placed is the Welsh Triple Crown medal won by his father: Ivor Jones himself is shown in his West Brom kit in an accompanying photograph. There is another photo of Ivor being presented with his old schoolboy cap which had turned up years later in Swansea's Pantygwydr Hotel. Cliff fully appreciates his father's legacy: Ivor was above all a ball-player as was his brother Bryn who, as one of the game's great passers, preceded his nephew as a North London hero, albeit at Highbury and not White Hart Lane.

Now in his mid-sixties Cliff Jones has changed little since I saw him play for the Swans in the 1950s. He would seem to be as fit and lean as ever, his golf and teaching ensuring a mental and physical alertness. He is fresh-faced and eagle-eyed and has about him something of the neatness of a jockey or of the groom that he once was in the Royal Horse Artillery. In some respects he looks like a rugby player and he is eager for historians to know that after soccer he played outside-half for the Scimitars, a Saracens reserve team. Above all, Cliff is an enthusiast who is deeply grateful for all the pleasure that football gave him.

Over the years he has helped many historians to tell the Spurs story. For Bill Nicholson, he explains, 'winning was never enough – things had to be done in style'. Bill was a manager who inculcated values. Unlike more recent trophy-winning managers he would never publicly berate a referee. 'Since when have players known the rules?', he would ask. At Spurs, success was based on the pattern of passing, with Dave Mackay, the engine-house, going 120 per cent and only wanting to win. Blanch-flower was the teetotal diplomat 'bridging the gap between bootroom and boardroom'. 'John White was a lovely character, all smiles and pranks'; together he and Cliff were 'just a couple of schoolboys'.

Cliff speaks eloquently about the Spurs side to which he contributed so much, but he is even better on his Welsh colleagues to whom he refers with awe and emotion. He feels strongly that history has not done them full justice. John Charles was 'the most complete footballer' he ever encountered, but Roy Paul was not far behind: the Rhondda man 'had everything'. Cliff loved Trevor Ford who was two-footed and 'laid the ball off cleverly'. In a tense Vienna in 1954 Walley Barnes, the Welsh manager, pleaded with Trevor to respect diplomatic niceties by not barging the goalkeeper. Within minutes of the match starting the goal-keeper was lying in the back of the net and mayhem ensued. 'I never touched him', was Trevor's half-time plea. On that trip full-back Alf Sherwood took on the Austrian army, with whom Wales were training, and beat all-comers at snooker, darts, table-tennis and ball-juggling. Alf was a 'natural sportsman and a total gentleman'. In Sweden 'Wales could have beaten Brazil with John Charles'; as it was, 'Mel Hopkins did not allow Garrincha to get a kick in'. To this day Cliff maintains that 'we were not aware of how good we were'. Wales had always produced good defenders: Ray Daniel 'was sheer class and a great character as well'. In a reserve match at the Vetch he was verbally challenged by Dyson of Spurs. 'Who are you?', asked Ray, 'The mascot?' For a time Cliff thought Mike England 'the best centre-half in Europe, possibly the world' and he was pleased to have played a part in bringing the Blackburn player to Spurs.

In his memories, vividly recalled and passionately expressed, there is a special place for the Vetch, 'that lovely old ground' where the Swans of his day were virtually unbeatable: of course, away games were another matter. At Swansea players were taught to play the ball to feet and to move into position for the return. For Dai Beynon, schoolteacher extra-ordinary, football was essentially a question of enjoyment and personality. It ought to be played 'with a smile on the face'; points won and trophies accrued were merely a bonus. Cliff is adamant that his 'happiest days were at the Vetch' and that if the directors had shown more ambition he would have stayed. The failure to replace the injured Tom Kiley in 1956 when promotion beckoned had been a portent, a dreadful moment of truth. His affection for the Swans ties in with feelings for family and neighbourhood. Cliff is essentially a Sandfields boy, eager to recall Bob Messer, his rugby-league-playing grandfather who ran the town's most famous fish-and-chip shop. Life was focused on Oxford and Beach Streets, apart from a war-time evacuation to Merthyr which cemented his links with the Jones dynasty. Central to these memories was his relationship with his brother Brin who had been a colleague at the Vetch. In Cliff's view the good-looking and fearless Brin could have been a great full-back but was used by the Swans and other clubs as a utility player; sadly, he died a few years ago.

Physically Cliff Jones may have changed little, but in other respects he has totally reinvented himself. In 1955 as a sheet-metal worker he had returned to Swansea's Prince of Wales Dock on a Monday morning after having scored the winning goal for Wales against England, only to be told by a foreman that it was time 'to pick up his tools'. When his football days were over (and after Spurs he played for Fulham and several non-League clubs) he once again picked up his tools and found work in a North London foundry; of one thing he was certain – he was not going to stay in the game. Football had always come naturally to him: he was an instinctive player and therefore management would have been a different proposition. His fitness and enthusiasm, however, made him an ideal teacher and having completed courses and met with Dr Rhodes Boyson he was all set to start a new career as a games and special skills instructor at Highbury Grove school. He was very much an all-rounder for he was a useful cricketer and, increasingly, a dedicated golfer.

One wonders how many of Cliff's students know what he has been. In 1961 Professor A. J. Ayer set out to determine how good was the Spurs side he supported; Blanchflower was the star but 'of the others only Jones, a wing-forward with the speed and swerve of a rugby three-quarter, could clearly command a place in a current World XI'. In 1984 former colleague Jimmy Greaves adjudged that 'at his peak Cliff Jones was without doubt one of the world's greatest wingers'. Greaves recalled how he would run 'with the pace, determination and bravery of a Welsh wing three-quarter', that he was 'brave to the point of madness in the penalty area' and how he 'would rise like a salmon at the far post to head spectacular goals'. In 1962 Cliff was included in Ivan Sharpe's all-time ten best British wingers; his action sprang 'from an electric spark that keeps on sparking' and he was 'the Principality's answer to Real Madrid's Gento'. For Ralph Finn, the historian of the Double team, Cliff Jones was 'the greatest winger in the game today'. Finn confessed that he derived 'more thrilling satisfaction out of a brilliant Jones display' than anything else in soccer: the Spurs winger was clearly 'the greatest entertainment' in football. For many writers Cliff was 'a whippet', for Brian Glanville he was 'a gazelle', but all were agreed that thrilling wing play was a hallmark of the new Spurs. If there was one shortcoming it was Cliff's tendency to run with the ball across the field. Only those who knew the dimensions of the Vetch could explain that flaw. How did that compact ground produce one of the fastest wingers ever?

Together the two Sandfields boys gave flair and edge to a great Spurs side. They did so by building on lessons that they had learnt at Swansea. It is the awareness of this heritage, taken with links of family and friendship, that forms the basis of their continued respect for the town and its football club. On twenty-two occasions they played together for Wales, more often than not on their respective wings. Their first match together for Wales had been in 1956 when, remarkably, all five Welsh forwards together with the goalkeeper and centre-half were Swansea born. One of their finest games for Wales was the 1958 victory against Hungary in Sweden when there were six Swansea-born players in the side. For a time the Spurs side for which they played was identified as truly great: a considerable part of Terry and Cliff's disarming charm and lack of affectation stems from their awareness that they had earlier learnt their football and their values in a town that was also great.

Mike England

Aled Eirug

Mike England was a world-class centre-half who ranks as one of the best central defenders ever to have played for Wales. It was in the 1960s and 1970s that he became a world-renowned centre-half and one of the earliest players to combine the role of the 'stopper' with skilful ball control and the ability to dribble the ball out of defence. For many of his contemporaries, both players and managers, England was the most skilled central defender of an era that included players of the calibre of Jack Charlton of Leeds United and England, Ron Yeats of Liverpool and Scotland, and Frank McLintock of Arsenal and Scotland. Mike England's international and club career in European competition showed that he could compete with, and outshine, the best forwards in the world. Nor were his talents confined to the playing field and, as manager of Wales, he created a team that was respected throughout the 1980s, bringing Wales to the brink of qualification for two major European and two World Cup finals. But, above all, his stature as a model professional, a loyal clubman and a staunch patriot marked him out as one of Wales's most effective soccer ambassadors.

England was born in Greenfield near Holywell in Flintshire on 2 December 1941. The early influences on him in Ysgol Dinas Basingwerk were Bill Beatty, an ex-player for Flint and Holywell, who was the PE master, and the headmaster, Gwynfor Jarvis. When a fire broke out some years later, the head's first thought was to run back into his study to save Mike's cap – the school's most treasured possession! He was also an extremely good cricketer who played as a number-three bat for Flintshire as well as his home clubs of Mostyn and Prestatyn. Both Lancashire and Glamorgan invited him for a trial before his father stepped in and forced him to choose his sport.

At the age of fifteen he was invited for trials with Everton and Blackburn Rovers. His father was an Evertonian who had played for Mostyn AFC, but Mike was influenced by two men to opt for Blackburn. Elfed Ellis was not only one of the Welsh FA's most prominent administrators, and a later president, but also a well-known scout in north Wales. Also crucial was an ex-Mostyn player who had gone on to Blackburn – Roy Vernon. Vernon, who himself was to play thirty-two games for Wales, was to act as a father figure to England when he arrived at the club as a sallow 5ft 7in. teenager with a reputation as a tricky inside-forward. At that time, there was little inkling that he would go on to become a formidable centre-half whose ball skills and heading ability would establish him as one of Britain's leading defenders.

England was fortunate to join Blackburn at a time when the club had a successful youth side. In May 1959 he was part of the team that won the FA Youth Cup, and which included future England players Fred Pickering and Keith Newton. In the semi-final against Manchester United, a crowd of 36,000 watched the first leg. Blackburn went on to beat West Ham 1–0 in the final, and in so doing gained an honour never before achieved by the club. It seemed a good foundation for the future development of the club as a whole.

When Mike England arrived in Blackburn in 1958, he had come to a town dominated by cotton mills and four breweries: 'People were very friendly – they were football daft.' He liked both the sense of humour and the dialect. He lodged with a Mrs Jones of Gorse Street, who was 'like a mother' to him. He was paid £5 a week, of which he spent 3s. 10d. on his weekly rent. It seems that Mrs Jones was under orders from the club to 'feed him up' with steaks and, within two years, England had shot up six inches in height. At the same time, his growing physique was complemented by a dedication and commitment to developing his defensive abilities. Jock Whiteman, one of Blackburn's trainers, had taken a liking to the enthusiastic teenager and he worked to develop England's dominance in the air. Every weekday afternoon, Whiteman would take him to a gym where he would suspend a ball from the ceiling for England to jump at and head. Gradually, he swung the ball from left to right or from right to left for England to meet as if he were heading a cross. That drill went on for an hour every afternoon for nine months until Whiteman said, 'I can't teach you any more.'

England's first-team debut came as a 17-year-old in the April of the 1958/9 season against Preston North End. The manager, John Carey, called him in on Friday, telling him, 'You've done very well. You're playing tomorrow at right full-back.' The youngster had a torrid time and Preston won 4–1, with the England forward Tom Finney scoring a hat-trick. As they came off the field, England said, 'Thank you Mr Finney.' Finney consoled the young defender – 'Don't you worry, you'll be all right.' Nevertheless it was another two and a half months before he was next selected for the first team. However, in the following season, England established himself as Blackburn's first-choice centre-half. By the time that he left the club in 1966, he had made 165 League appearances, scored twenty-one goals, and become an experienced and dominant centre-half – unbeatable in the air and skilled on the ground.

Towards the middle of his period at Blackburn, England made his debut for Wales against Northern Ireland in 1962. He was to play forty-four times for Wales, and in twenty-eight of those games he was captain. It says much that he was never dropped, but just as significant was the large number of games that he failed to play because of injury or club commitments at a time when club overrode the demands of country. It was a mark of the respect shown towards him that he was made captain after only eight appearances for Wales, and for the following eleven years he shared the captaincy with Terry Hennessey.

Amongst his most memorable matches was the South American tour in 1962. Wales had lost 3–1 to Brazil in Rio de Janeiro, and England was selected for the second game against Brazil at Sao Paolo in front of a crowd of 140,000: 'It was a great squad and included Jack Kelsey, Graham Williams from West Brom, John Charles and Ivor Allchurch.' His greatest thrill, as a youngster of nineteen, was to mark Pelé. The instruction from manager Jimmy Murphy was, 'Even if he goes off to go to the toilet, follow him.' For eighty minutes Wales competed well, but Pelé scored and Brazil again won 3–1. Nevertheless, this experience had boosted England's confidence and he was retained for the game against Mexico. He was one of the youngest players in the squad and his partner in defence, Terry Hennessey, was just as inexperienced. Hennessey shared a room with England and during the days leading up to the game both went to sunbathe. Unfortunately, Hennessey fell asleep and woke up 'as red as a lobster'. England had to treat him with camomile lotion for three days, and Hennessey failed to make the team.

England's time as an international player coincided with a Welsh side that, on the whole, performed disappointingly. His own record as captain reflected Wales's poor record; of the twenty-eight times that he captained his country, he was victorious on only five occasions, and lost seventeen times, with six draws. During this period, the team manager Dave Bowen was part-time, preparations for internationals were desultory or non-existent, and the nearest that Wales got to qualifying for a major championship was in 1973. In that year, a victory against Poland in Katowice would have enabled Wales to qualify for the 1974 World Cup Finals, but the game turned into a disaster. In an ill-tempered match, the Welsh midfielder Trevor Hockey was sent off, and Wales lost 3–0.

Nevertheless, throughout his time as an international player, England excelled against the top teams of the 1960s and early 1970s. He not only marked and outshone the best strikers in English football – Peter Osgood, Tony Hateley and Geoff Hurst, but some of the best forwards in the world including Italy's Riva and West Germany's Gerd Muller. Bill Nicholson, his manager at Spurs, considered that if he had been qualified for England, he would have been given much more inter-national recognition. Like others before and since, Mike England suffered from being an outstanding player in an ordinary team for most of his international career.

Meanwhile he was frustrated by what he perceived as Blackburn's lack of ambition: 'I wanted them to reach for the championship and FA Cup but they were too ready to sell their best players. We had a wonderful side – Peter Dobing, Brian Douglas, the England captain Ronnie Clayton, Fred Pickering – we wanted to achieve things in football, but they were all sold.' In his period in the first team, Blackburn sank from being a middle-of-the-table First Division team to the bottom position, and relegation at the end of the 1965/6 season. Blackburn's greatest success in the space of six years was to have reached the quarter-finals of the FA Cup.

Not surprisingly, England had become increasingly disillusioned with Blackburn Rovers and at the end of the 1965/6 season, after relegation, he put in a transfer request. Manchester United had initially shown interest in signing a player now clearly regarded as one of the best centre-halves in the country, and England was convinced that he would be signed by Matt Busby. One of his early mentors, Jimmy Murphy, the Wales manager, worked for the club and had brought his availability to the manager's attention. When those talks failed, Tottenham Hotspur expressed an interest and signed him.

Spurs had lost their centre-half, Maurice Norman with a broken leg, and the manager, Bill Nicholson, arranged to meet England in the Finsbury Park Hotel near the Arsenal ground. England's memory of the meeting was that 'they were desperate to replace big Maurice Norman'. At the time Spurs, had a great defence, with the teenager Pat Jennings in goal, and players like Cyril Knowles, Allan Mullery and Dave Mackay. Nicholson acknowledged that he had been particularly impressed by England during Blackburn's 7–2 win against Spurs in the 1963/4 season, when England scored a goal and created another. He went on to sign England for a British record transfer fee of £95,000. This was doubly impressive in that not only had the transfer fee record been broken, but that it had been broken by the purchase of a defender, which usually attracted lower transfer fees. Even today, Bill Nicholson's admiration of England remains undiminished and generous. 'He was very good . . . not cocky or too confident. He knew exactly what to do all the time. He was a great club man and strengthened the Tottenham team immensely.'

With Spurs, England was to play more than 400 games and score fourteen goals. In his first season, Spurs came third in the First Division but won the FA Cup. For the young England, it was a marvellous experience, and one of the footballing highlights of his life. 'I walked out through the tunnel onto Wembley and I remembered Kenneth Wolstenhome's words that "players hearts would be in their mouths". I thought – No – I'm enjoying this; it's a lovely feeling and it's what its all about.' Spurs beat Chelsea 2–1 and England gave an imperious display, marking Tony Hateley out of the game.

Tottenham went on to win the UEFA Cup in 1971/2 but, although they beat impressive sides in the run up to the final, he was disappointed to meet another English club, Wolves, in the final. He missed the League Cup win in 1971 after breaking an ankle in the semi-final against Bristol City, but played in the League Cup Final win against Norwich City in 1973. He also scored in the UEFA Cup Final in the 1973/4 season. In the first leg against Feyenoord, he headed home a free kick six minutes before half-time only for Feyenoord to score immediately before the break. Just after the hour, England's presence in the opposing penalty box caused a Feyenoord defender to slice into his own net, but four minutes from the end, the Dutch team scored an equalizer. Spurs then went on to lose the second leg 2–0.

During England's time at White Hart Lane, Spurs proved an excellent Cup team but failed to sustain consistency. However, there was no doubting the side's quality and ability. From the young Jennings in goal, through the two full-backs Cyril Knowles and Joe Kinnear, the wing-halves Allan Mullery and Dave Mackay, the classy midfielder Terry Venables, and the flair of Jimmy Greaves and Alan Gilzean, this was an extremely classy and competitive side. England's place as the lynchpin of the Spurs defence was unassailable. His background as a midfielder, before converting to centre-half at Blackburn, meant that he could control and pass accurately, and dribble the ball out of defence. His aerial ability was incomparable and his footballing abilities were recognized by his period as centre-forward in the 1969 season, and by his general success in scoring goals in the opposing penalty area. For such a big man, he was amongst the most skilful of defenders; he had the speed to recover should opposing forwards pass him, and he was extremely strong in the tackle.

Although Tottenham had appeared in four finals in three years, Nicholson became increasingly disillusioned. Spurs lost the first four matches of 1974/5 and Nicholson resigned to be replaced by Terry Neill, the former Arsenal captain and centre-half. It was not a popular decision with the supporters. How could a man be expected to show commitment to Spurs when he had played so recently for the arch-enemy at Highbury? By the time that Neill joined the club, England had been nine years at Spurs. Early in the season the new manager signed two new players, and meanwhile England had suffered a series of injuries, before the men met to discuss his future. 'I went to see Neill and I asked him about my testimonial which was due the following year. He told me that he couldn't guarantee me the testimonial and that I might not be in his plans.' Understandably, England was shocked by his attitude. Neill only lasted twenty months, before resigning in June 1976 and becoming Arsenal manager within two weeks. Mike England never played for Spurs again: 'My pride wouldn't let me. Not to be given a testimonial after all my efforts for the club that I loved was one of my greatest disappointments.'

The club's official line was that England was 'retiring'. Mike England, however, felt that he was being pushed out against his will. He played his last game for Spurs at Leicester City on 22 February 1975 and retired until he received a phone call from John Best, the manager of one of the sides which were part of the burgeoning North American soccer league. He enjoyed four months with Seattle Sounders, playing regularly in front of crowds of 30,000 and in the company of some of the best players from England who had gone to help establish – and exploit – the development of soccer in what could have been the most lucrative soccer league in the world. He was in the illustrious company of players such as Bobby Moore, Geoff Hurst, George Best and Pelé.

At the end of that summer, he was contacted by Cardiff City and offered a year's contract by the manager, Jimmy Andrews. At the time Cardiff City were in the Third Division and England joined – with Spurs's permission – as centre-half and captain. He turned down the offer of assistant manager at Southend to join the Welsh club: 'The reason I went to Cardiff was one, because as a Welshman, I wanted to do all I could to get them back into the Second Division. And secondly, because I honestly believed that at the end of the season when I intended to retire, I would get a job on staff.' England's contribution to Cardiff's success in the 1975/6 season was crucial as he captained the team back into the Second Division. But, to his intense disappointment, his contract was not renewed. According to England, he believed that he and his team-mate Doug Livermore would train the team and he bought a house in the Vale of Glamorgan on the basis that he would eventually be employed as a coach by the club. Looking back, England believes that he was perceived as a threat to the manager and that he was 'shaking in his shoes' at the thought of his staying there. On the day after Cardiff celebrated promotion following a win against Bury, the captain was packing his bags. It was a deeply angry, upset and disillusioned Mike England who reluctantly returned to North America in the first week of May 1976.

Characteristically, he made the most of his time with Seattle Sounders, with whom he played for three years. He also developed his strong business sense, which had led him to establish a timber company in Blackburn during his time there. He took 'real estate' exams, set up an antiques business and developed his coaching skills. It was while in Seattle that his father phoned him early in 1980 to tell him that the Welsh manager's post had become vacant following Mike Smith's resignation. England flew over for the interview to appear before the twenty-six members of the Council of the Football Association of Wales – a scene which reminded him of Botticelli's 'The Last Supper'. He remembers one member coming out of the interview and telling him what a 'crap' team Wales had. 'I told him we had some of the best players around, and that Wales can go places. We've got good youngsters but they need encouraging and we need a youth policy.'

Mike England defeated three other candidates for the job, including Jimmy Armfield, and accepted a three-year contract with a drastic cut in salary from $70,000 in Seattle to £15,000 a year, plus a car. A major factor in his appointment was that he could begin immediately. He appointed his former team-mate Doug Livermore as assistant manager. His reign as manager had a sensational start in May 1980, with a memorable 4–1 triumph over England at Wrexham. On the eve of his first game against England, the Wales team was surprised to hear its new manager address its first meeting in a Welsh-American accent and talk about 'defence' and 'offence'. He targeted specific weakness in the English team. In particular, one of Wales's most skilful players, Leighton James, was instructed to run directly at the centre-half Larry Lloyd at every opportunity, a tactic which caused much consternation in the English defence.

The manager had been angered by the media's dismissive attitude towards Wales. He was interviewed by the BBC's Barry Davies who suggested that the Welsh team must be shaking in their boots at the thought of playing against such a great English side. England gave a robust reply, and told Davies that they would talk about his view after the game. As he walked away from the interview at the side of the touch-line, he heard Davies refer to a very arrogant Mike England just back from the USA. The English team was well beaten, 4–1. Leighton James scored, as did Ian Walsh and Mickey Thomas, with an own goal by an England defender. The midfield trio of Flynn, Thomas and Yorath dominated the game and the team displayed Mike England's philosophy of management – to enjoy and to play positive, attractive football. England was then interviewed by Barry Davies after the game. 'I think we were quite confident beforehand that we had a good side,' said the successful manager, 'but it isn't good to be over-confident.'

England's enthusiasm and commitment to the cause of Wales brought him fantastic loyalty from his players. There was great respect towards him as an ex-professional. As Leighton James once said, England made it 'enjoyable' for him to play for his country. Terry Yorath, his successor, regarded him as always a fair, clear-cut and strong manager, and even when Mike England was to drop him after a run of bad form, Yorath still felt respect and admiration towards the manager. To his detractors, England was the 'nearly' man, who narrowly failed to get to the World Cup 1982 and 1986, and the European Championships in 1984 and 1988. But England's view is that, for the first time, Wales became a feared team and were shown respect. 'People had talked about Welsh rugby. They now had to talk about success in Welsh football and players like Rush and Hughes.'

His success was particularly impressive when compared to the fallow period of the 1960s and 1970s. In fifty-six games as manager, England won twenty-two, drew sixteen, and lost eighteen, with fifty-six goals for and fifty-one against, a success rate of 54 per cent. In contrast, his predecessor Mike Smith, and his successor achieved a success rate of less than 50 per cent. Leighton James who played for three managers – Dave Bowen, Mike England and Terry Yorath – is well qualified to compare their strengths: 'Smith was the most tactically aware but England had the most enthusiasm and desire to attack the opposition, in a period when we had been a very poor footballing nation.'

Mike England attempted to take Wales out of the group into which it was always placed whenever the draw for any championship was made. In his period as manager, Wales was a 'group three' nation so that of any group of which Wales was a part there were always two nations classed higher in the world rankings. It was not, therefore, a coincidence that Wales had difficult draws against more-fancied opposition. In group four, where Wales is at present, we always have three higher-ranked teams in the same group. Jack Charlton's success with the Republic of Ireland was partly to do with his success in qualifying for the major championships, for it meant that subsequent groups included less real competition from higher-seeded teams.

In 1981, Welsh fans had their hopes raised by their team's performances. Wales was unbeaten throughout the year with wins against Turkey, Czechoslovakia, Scotland and the Republic of Ireland. But Wales's qualification for the 1982 World Cup depended on winning against Iceland, at home, in Swansea, in October 1981. Mike England chose what some considered to be a recklessly attacking side, which included two recognized defenders and five recognized forwards. As Wales began to dominate the game with their unremitting attacking, the floodlights failed and the game was delayed for forty minutes. England still remembers the effect on both him and his players: 'Our players grew more frustrated and I hoped the game would be called off.' By the time that the game restarted, Iceland had had time to regroup and Wales had lost momentum. The game finished a 2–2 draw, with one of the Iceland goals a real gift, when the Welsh keeper Dai Davies allowed the ball to dribble into the goal between his legs. This disastrous result meant that Wales's only hope for qualifying was that Iceland would beat the Scots at home. England and Livermore travelled to Reykjavik to watch the game, where the unlikely result almost happened. However, Iceland missed a crucial penalty and Wales again missed out.

Two years later, Wales had to beat Yugoslavia to achieve qualification for the European Championships in 1984 but only managed a draw. They lost out again in November 1987, when the team had to beat Czechoslovakia – admittedly one of the best teams in Europe at the time – to go through to the 1988 European Championship but lost 2–0. However, the most fateful night for Welsh football occurred in September 1985 in Cardiff, when Wales had to beat Scotland to go through to the World Cup finals.

Both the manager and the team were unhappy to be playing in Cardiff. Wales had never lost a match at Wrexham under England's management, and the players had come to believe that they were invincible there. This was one of the biggest games ever for Wales, and Mike England thought that he had the FAW's agreement to play at Wrexham. 'I went to the FAW Council and asked them to agree to one thing. I'd been in charge since 1980 and both myself and the team thought we'd stand a better chance in Wrexham.' The Council agreed and England went away on holiday. When he returned, he found that the decision had been rescinded by Council officials because playing at Ninian Park was more lucrative. 'The Council thought they could raise £25,000 extra by playing in Ninian Park. But what they hadn't considered was that if Wales went through, they'd be raising £250,000. It was ridiculous.' On the night, Mark Hughes put Wales into an early lead, but with only seven minutes to go, the Welsh fans were totally silenced. The ball reared up in the penalty area and struck defender Dave Phillips's hand. Scotland scored from the resulting penalty, but even worse was to follow. The Scottish manager, Jock Stein, who had stood up from the bench for the penalty, collapsed and subsequently died on the way to hospital. Wales had failed yet again to qualify for a major competition, but England's thoughts at the time were with Stein: 'My thoughts were with him. I failed to go to the World Cup; he had lost his life.'

This game was, in England's opinion, 'the defining moment for Welsh football' in recent years. The end of the game was bedlam with journalists, cameramen and photographers jostling around the dressing-rooms. Understandably, the Scottish team was in a state of shock, caught between the elation of World Cup qualification and concern for their manager. The cameras also caught sight of a row between England and Alun Evans, the FAW secretary. They were seen on television arguing and England pushed past him. It was later reported that England had 'molested' Evans as he tried to stop England from entering the referee's dressing-room to complain. England still considers that Alun Evans over-reacted to his attempts to complain to the referee, and he recalls being restrained by the team's kitman, Harry Parsons, who 'brought an air of sanity to the place' at that tense time. He was also even more upset by Jock Stein's collapse. Stein had stood within yards of him throughout the game and England counted the Scottish manager as a personal friend. Within three months, England's contract was renewed but only on a part-time basis at a salary of £10,000.

His poor relationship with Evans became public again in December 1987 when Evans ridiculed the manager's record publicly in a football dinner. 'He's won the Bird's Custard Award for the Thickest Manager of the Year', for which he gave an unreserved written apology to England. Only months later Evans failed to notify England of a meeting with other nations to arrange fixture lists for the World Cup qualifying games. At the end of his period as manager, England spoke publicly about Evans's role: 'He did not help me one iota. In the five years he has been here, I think he spoke to me six times and one of those occasions was to say something derogatory. He's been a disaster as far as I'm concerned.' Mike England also found the FAW Council frustrating, cumbersome and bureaucratic. In his view, most of the Council members were full of themselves and concerned about what Wales would achieve for them. 'They've got everyday jobs making decisions about the future of Welsh football while people who know about soccer are not listened to.'

England's period as team manager ended in February 1988 after a meeting of the Council in Welshpool. He was called to meet representatives of the FAW in a hotel opposite the railway station in Chester. They crammed into a small room where he was told by the FAW president, Ivor Pursey, that because of the failure to proceed to the World Cup the Council felt that it had to dispense with England's services. England countered that the team had built up a good deal of respect. He recalls his feelings at the time: 'We were playing and getting results but at the end of the day someone had to pay, and that was it. They were expecting too much.' He told the FAW representatives: 'We now have a stronger squad than ever before, we have a youth policy. I've worked hard and done my best.' England then left to meet his wife. On their way home to Melidin, near Holywell, they stopped at a hotel and bought a bottle of champagne 'to celebrate eight good years'. He remembers the waiter asking whether they had anything to celebrate. 'No, only the sack!' England then took time to consider his future before his contract ended. He was offered managerial positions in Saudi Arabia, and at Athletic Bilbao. Several English clubs also expressed an interest in him but he eventually decided to develop his business interests and opened retirement homes in Rhyl and Colwyn Bay.

There is no doubt that Mike England was an exemplary professional who achieved respect and recognition as a world-class centre-half. He brought Wales to the brink of qualification to four major championships and built a national team that had gained respect in Europe by the time that he left his post in 1988. He embodied passion, drive and an ambition for success that gave new direction to Welsh football, and he created a team that played positively and was difficult to beat.

John Toshack

Huw Richards

It is a truth universally acknowledged, at least if one's universe starts west of Bridgend, that the single good thing to have come out of Cardiff is the road to Swansea. Our capital city was recently branded by Swansea's *South Wales Evening Post*, in a headline making up in pungent expression of local opinion what it lacked in linguistic elegance, as 'a greedy city with a big mouth'. Amid the immense range of fissures characterizing modern Wales and exposed most graphically in the referendum on the creation of the National Assembly for Wales – north v. south, east v. west, Welsh-speaking v. Anglophone, Objective One v. Not Quite So Poor – none is more ferocious than that conducted, ever since the two communities emerged out of industrialization as the polestars of south-east and south-west Wales, between Swansea and Cardiff. Part of this rivalry is rooted in differences in character. Swansea's fortunes were built on metal-bashing, its cosmopolitanism as a seaport leavened by the influence of a hinterland which is consciously Welsh and not infrequently Welsh speaking. Cardiff's *raison d'être* was its location as *entrepôt* to the Rhondda coalfields, its character informed by rapid late-nineteenth-century immigration which brought it not only West Countrymen but the black and Irish populations who have made such an immense contribution to its sporting culture. But the real roots of dislike are common to anywhere two cities of roughly comparable size jostle for leadership, and the prizes that it brings – Manchester v. Liverpool, Newcastle v. Sunderland and Southampton v. Portsmouth come to mind. This battle has been won conclusively by Cardiff, taking not only newly created baubles such as capital status and the series of government agencies that go with it, but also prizes which were once shared – international rugby in 1954 and county cricket in the later 1990s. If no one in Swansea ever truly believed that the city would get the National Assembly, the irony that Cardiff was this time awarded a prize against which it had voted added a further edge to the bitterness of rejection.

That rivalry is seen at its most visceral in sport, an outlet providing a notionally objective test of superiority. One reason why Glamorgan cricket did not fix a county headquarters at the time of its foundation in the 1880s was that matches between Swansea and Cardiff were noted for skulduggery and contested results, and the club had no desire to import the quarrel. Wilfred Wooller, an adopted Cardiffian, wrote of the utter fury of a Swansea crowd when he stole victory at St Helen's with a late drop-goal some time in the 1930s. In football, a tangible air of fear and loathing hangs like malignant ectoplasm over derby matches at Ninian Park and Vetch Field, with the day's battles liable to be worked out *ad nauseam* in the letter columns of the local press by the one-eyed and the brain-dead of both sides. The match also has an inexplicable charm for satellite television's match-schedulers who fail to recognize that the quality of the football, however good or bad the teams in their other matches, is almost invariably lamentable. Like certain sexual practices, Swansea City v. Cardiff City matches should be performed in private with participation confined to consenting adults. And the rivalry also spreads into other matches. If some apparently inoffensive opponent is singled out for non-stop hostility at the Vetch Field, the likeliest explanation is that he is a former inmate of Ninian Park.

Yet there has been considerable interchange between the clubs over the years. This was underlined, perhaps unconsciously, in 'Only Sixty-Four Years', the poet Dannie Abse's beautiful essay on his lifetime as a Cardiff fan, in *Perfect Pitch*. Abse described how he would while away hours of sleeplessness by summoning up the images of great Cardiff players: 'All wear the Bluebird shirt. Some announce their famous names: Trevor Ford, John Charles, Mel Charles, Ivor Allchurch, all of whom played for Cardiff City in their declining football years.' Cardiff fans will have reacted to that sentence by considering the counter-claims of such as Fred Keenor, Alf Sherwood and Phil Dwyer. No Swansea City fan can read it without instantly remarking that the four names Abse conjures from Cardiff memories dating back to the 1930s all came from Swansea, and all but John Charles first played for the Swans. This link was reconfirmed more recently at a book-signing session in a Cardiff shop for the club's centenary history. Representing Cardiff City were two current players – Andy Legg and Jason Bowen, both ex-Swans.

It has to be said that this is another exchange of which Cardiff has had the better. Swansea's contributions to them include the kings of Dannie Abse's subconscious, not to mention Alan Curtis and Robbie

James. The reverse traffic, in spite of the quality of ex-City players like Stan Richards, George Smith, Brian Attley and Jimmy Gilligan and Cardiffians like John Mahoney, is not nearly as good. To remember quite how desperate the Swans were in the mid-1980s it is necessary only to recall, although with names omitted to spare the guilty and the inadequate, some of the Ninian Park cast-offs recruited.

Managers, though, are a different matter. Some of the Swans' most effective post-war bosses have served time at Ninian Park before coming to the Vetch. Billy McCandless won promotion for Cardiff back to Division Two in the first post-war season, and then did the same for the Swans just two years later. Trevor Morris was Cardiff's club secretary before he took the Swans to the FA Cup semi-final in 1964. More recently the admirable Frankie Burrows mixed talent-spotting, astute management and a wild-eyed look that terrorized many innocent readers of his programme notes during a period at the Vetch which was bracketed by two with the Bluebirds.

Suitably enough the books are balanced by a player-manager – John Benjamin Toshack, as he is invariably called by Spanish journalists whose taste for full names is matched only by the rugby commentator Bill MacLaren. With the benefit of twenty years' hindsight a case might be made that Swansea's Toshack era was short lived, unsustainable and ultimately ruinous – the medium-term villain in the financial disaster that saw the club play the Boxing Day 1985 derby match at Ninian Park under a death sentence. Little matter. While the return journey was nightmarish in the extreme, Toshack's early years, featuring three promotions and a serious League title challenge in the space of five seasons, gave Swans' fans memories to sustain them through a lifetime of football watching. Bliss it was in that dawn to be alive.

It is incontestable fact that even as Toshack became a Messianic figure to *us*, he was and is one of *them*. Not just any one of *them* either, but the single most significant figure produced by Cardiff City in the second half of the twentieth century – their answer to the Allchurches and Charleses. His importance in Cardiff memory was shown by the club's centenary brochure. You might expect the 1927 FA Cup win and the 1924 League Championship near-miss to be treated as the outstanding moments, but Toshack's departure to Liverpool in November 1970 got as much space as the two earlier moments combined. This is probably not disproportionate. The story of Len Davies missing a final day spot-kick and so costing Cardiff City the Championship is one to tempt any Swans' fans to echo Oscar Wilde's verdict on Dickens's *Death of Little Nell*, 'that one would require a heart of stone not to laugh out loud at it'. To the neutral it is matched in poignancy only by the experience of one of Toshack's later clubs, Deportivo La Coruña, in losing the Spanish title on a missed penalty in the last minute of the season seventy years after Cardiff. Yet those Cardiff fans of the 1920s probably regarded that lost title as postponement of the inevitable. The club had only been in the League for four years and appeared inexorably upwardly mobile. They were to get to the Cup Final in the following season, and win it only two seasons after that. The wrath that was to visit them in the 1930s was as unforeseen as Swansea City's post-Toshack fate was in 1980.

Cardiff's loss of Toshack did end an era. They narrowly missed promotion that year, and every subsequent season in Division Two was dominated by the struggle to avoid leaving the division in the opposite direction. They were last in the top half of the League in 1985. If the club truly is the 'sleeping giant' it is frequently proclaimed, this must have been the point at which the anaesthetic was administered. The centenary brochure noted that it was not only Toshack's departure, but the delay in finding a replacement that cost Cardiff promotion that year. This failure, echoing those of the Swansea Town board in the 1950s, may just have lodged in Toshack's mind as well. While he has not been invariably successful in his transfer-dealings as a manager, he has rarely been indecisive.

By the time that Toshack arrived at the Vetch in early 1979, he was firmly identified with Liverpool. His spell at Anfield coincided with the first half of Liverpool's time as the dominant force in British and subsequently European football, putting together a record of sustained excellence that has still, for all the hyperbole about Manchester United's recent feats, to be equalled. This earlier side was more direct and traditionally British in style than the immensely sophisticated team developed in the 1980s under the influence first of Souness, Rush and Dalglish then subsequently Barnes, Aldridge and Beardsley. The Liverpool team in which Toshack played attacked vigorously down the flanks, making effective use of overlapping full-backs like Alec Lindsay, and made something of a habit of winning matches in the last few minutes as opponents succumbed to the cumulative battering on their goal and their psyches. As a target man who was never terribly mobile but was astute and perceptive, skilled enough to hold the ball up or flick it on to a team-mate with foot or head, Toshack was integral to the pattern, particularly in the period when the buzzingly persistent Kevin Keegan provided an ideal counterpoint. The target-man is a natural butt for opponents and critics alike – rarely the most elegant or skilled man in the side. Toshack was never elegant and a chronic thigh injury cost him both mobility and appearances, but he could play. And he had an impressive capacity for producing his best in big matches. His power in the air was decisive in Liverpool winning their first European trophy, beating Borussia Mönchengladbach to take the UEFA Cup in 1973, while he provided a headed pass for the first goal and scored the second when they came from behind to beat Wolves and snatch the Championship from Queens Park Rangers in 1976. While his record for Wales was relatively modest – twelve goals in forty matches – it included a fondly remembered hat-trick in Wales's 3–0 demolition of Scotand at Ninian Park in 1979.

The Liverpool connection overlaid media analysis of his success at Swansea – lazy journalism is always happier seeking out a connection with the big clubs rather than taking the trouble to find out what is really happening. Ian Callaghan and Tommy Smith did make useful, though comparatively short-lived, contributions to the rise and Alan Waddle became an authentic folk hero. Yet it was rarely pointed out that the Swans First Division team was stronger on ex-Evertonians than former Reds, and that five of the players who appeared for the club at the highest level – Robbie James, Alan Curtis, Jeremy Charles, Nigel Stevenson and Wyndham Evans – were local products inherited by Toshack from Harry Griffiths in 1978. What Toshack did bring from Liverpool was a capacity for delivering when it mattered. He scored the decisive goals in consecutive promotion seasons – a free-kick deflected off the defensive wall, which broke Halifax Town's resistance in the last game of the 1977/8 season, and a never-to-be-forgotten bullet of a header which beat Chesterfield a year later.

Just coaching a team would earn Graham Henry the 'Great Redeemer' tag from press and public two decades later. Imagine how

Henry would have appeared if he had also scored the winning tries in victories over France, England and South Africa and you have some idea of Toshack's status with Swans' fans during those early years. If Tosh had announced that the Swans intended to enter and win the Boat Race, the World Snooker Championships and the Emperor's Cup Sumo tournament, we would have believed him. Even if the inheritance was better than often believed, his feat of Fourth to First in four seasons – beating the previous record of five seasons by Wales 1958 World Cup captain Dave Bowen with Northampton Town – was extraordinary.

Toshack expanded the club's horizons. The Swans and their followers were fixated with regaining the Second Division place they regarded as their birthright on the basis of almost continuous occupation from 1925 to 1965. Joe Mercer's foreword to the 1976 club history by Brynley Matthews concluded with the wish that they would soon be 'back where they belong – in the Second Division'. Toshack saw no reason for stopping at the Second Division. The new club chairman or manager of a lower division club who has a master plan for 'Premiership football within five years' is a familiar, slightly pathetic, figure in football. Toshack not only believed that it was possible, but persuaded others that it could be done and then achieved it. There is little doubt that he owed much of his success to advice offered by Bill Shankly. Indeed, it was his admiration and affection for his old club and manager that prompted one of the few false moves of his Swansea career. The Swans were to visit Liverpool the week after Shankly's death. On that day Toshack wore a Liverpool shirt and, at the end of the match, he went to the Kop rather than acknowledge his own fans.

But if building an unprecedented winning run were that simple, ex-Liverpool players would have a better record in management than they do. While Shankly was a remarkable manager, he was not renowned for the tactical innovation that has been a consistent Toshack hallmark. Possibly the most remarkable element of his achievement is that it was as a player-manager – a hugely demanding role, not least because it is generally filled by players at a stage in their career where the simple business of staying fit becomes a burden. Toshack continued to play until the Swans won promotion in 1981, and his sixty appearances included a number in the unaccustomed role of centre-half after he lost faith in the abilities of Leighton Phillips. The last goal of the 238 he scored in senior football at a rate considerably better than one every two and a half games was scored at Ninian Park. On Boxing Day 1983, despairing of a Swans team already clearly destined to drop straight from the First to the Third, he picked himself for the first time in two and a half years. Living down to their dismal form, the Swans were beaten much more conclusively than 3–2 suggests, the gap narrowed when Toshack received the ball unmarked on halfway. Conservative estimates suggest that it took him eight minutes to reach the edge of the Cardiff area, but there was never any doubt what was going to happen, and the ball was duly despatched beyond the reach of the Cardiff keeper into the top corner.

He could not have scored on a more appropriate ground, the one which had seen his first goal, scored as a 16-year-old substitute against Leyton Orient more than eighteen years earlier. He paid for that last strike with a torrent of abuse from Cardiff's fans, never a reticent lot. It may have confirmed the extent to which he was now identified with Swansea rather than Cardiff, but Toshack has never ceased to be a Cardiffian. Anyone who doubts this needs only hear him conducting a post-match conference in Spain. His Spanish – recently displayed to British television viewers in the incongruous setting of the *They Think It's All Over* studio – is careful, clear and accurate, but there still resounds within it that distinctive 'A' sound which is the glory of the 'Kairdiff' accent.

But if you cannot take Cardiff out of the man, you can certainly take the man out of Cardiff. At the same time as being rooted in his native city, Toshack is as cosmopolitan a figure as the Welsh game has ever produced. The possibilities were evidently clear to him from early in his football life – his autobiography recalls that as a teenager with Cardiff City he was fascinated by John Charles's stories about playing in Italy. It says much about the extent to which serious sporting ambition can divert even the brightest from study that a man of his evident intelligence has only two O levels – as he pointed out 'two more than most footballers' – but it is worth noting that one of them is in French. Even if one disallows the claims of Kairdiff as a distinctive language, he can point to a good command of four – Portuguese and French on top of Spanish and English – plus a smattering in others including the formidably difficult Basque.

He has described himself as 'a bastard, but a lovable bastard'. That description might be contested by some – if he was revered by Swansea City's fans, he was not invariably loved by those who worked more closely with him. Toshack's career has been underpinned by formidable self-confidence. You need to be unusually secure about your status in a professional locker room to publish a book of poetry, however jokey, still more to give it a title which is so clear a hostage to fortune as *Gosh It's Tosh*, and then to follow up with a (rather decent) autobiography, eschewing the crutch which is normally supplied by a ghost-writer, titled simply *Tosh*. This goes along with a strikingly self-contained quality that has served him well in long periods away from home. While he is as much a citizen of the Basque Country as he ever was of Cardiff, Liverpool or Swansea, most of his appointments over the last fifteen years – a sequence running through Sporting Lisbon, Real Sociedad, Real Madrid, Real Sociedad again, Deportivo La Coruña, Besiktas and Real Madrid again – have involved a lonely period of adjustment to a new club, often a new culture. Spain's fiercely contested regional rivalries mean that, even in a country where he has coached for a decade and is firmly established, each new post requires considerable adjustment. To go from proudly Basque Real Sociedad to establishment club Real Madrid is as profound a shift as one between different countries. It has required great resilience in the face of high expectations – at Deportivo, desperate to break the hold of Madrid and Barcelona, he found that 'every weekend is a drama – you are expected to win all the time'. A coach comes under detailed and sometimes bizarre scrutiny. One controversy during his spell with Depor concerned his alleged preference for the *turron* of San Sebastian over that of the La Coruña district.

If fellow-Welshman Ian Rush's comment that Italy was 'like a foreign country' represents one extreme in British football's reaction to the concept of abroad, Toshack's exploits are the other. For many British coaches a spell abroad is a temporary arrangement between jobs in Britain. Toshack's memory of Howard Kendall's spell at Athletic Bilbao was that 'He was always talking about "home" and about the British games that had been on television the previous weekend.' Toshack, however, has assimilated so completely that while he adheres to the philosophy of 'never say never', it would be something of a surprise, for all the fevered speculation which occurs whenever there is a major British vacancy for which he is available, if he again took a post in Britain. His British managerial experience is after all confined to a single club getting on for twenty years ago, and his current reputation rests on his exploits in Spain. The record is not one of untrammelled success. He had an unhappy time with Deportivo, and his second spell with Real Madrid ended abruptly following poor results and a very public falling-out with his players. Real is a spectacularly ill-run club, cushioned from financial reality by its status as an institution – it would take a preternaturally brave bank manager to call in the overdraft of the Spanish establishment's team – afflicted by sky-high expectations and a destabilizing staff turnover. A man like Toshack, who refuses to own either a credit card or a mobile phone – the object club president Lorenzo Sanz was seen to have clamped to his ear at the moment when Real qualified for this year's European Cup Final – might be forgiven for regarding such an institution as grossly self-indulgent.

Yet his falling out with players – he memorably commented that while his instinct after a bad result was to drop the lot, by the end of the week you realized you were 'stuck with the same bastards as before' – perhaps indicated that at the age of fifty-one, the passage of time was finally catching up with him. It is thirty-five years since he started as a player, more than twenty since he became a manager. Distanced that far from his own playing days, one might expect him to become impatient with the demands and egotisms of highly paid youth.

But these comparative failures are more than outweighed by the success of two spells at Real Sociedad, divided by two seasons with Real Madrid. He has said that possibly his proudest achievement in football was Sociedad's Cup victory in 1987, only the second in the club's history, and the subsequent procession through the villages which form the club's hinterland showing off the trophy. He is equally proud that he was accepted for a second time at this fiercely parochial club after leaving to manage Real Madrid: 'They called me a traitor for leaving, but then they accepted me back.'

Spanish radio, with a wealth of local analytical talent at its disposal, chose to fly him from Wales to Madrid in order to comment on the 2000 European Cup semi-finals. In Spain he is highly regarded as a tactician, inventor of the 'sistema Toshack'. The first version of this was seen at

Swansea where Dzemal Hadziabdic and Gary Stanley were used as wing-backs – not a recognized position in the early 1980s – and the magnificent Yugoslav Ante Rajkovic as a sweeper alongside two centre-backs, Colin Irwin and either Max Thompson or Nigel Stevenson. Swansea being a long way from Manchester or London, his innovations received only limited media recognition, although the 2–0 win at Arsenal which was arguably the outstanding performance of Swansea's remarkable season in 1981/2 provoked an appreciative and perceptive analysis by Brian Glanville of *The Sunday Times* on the way sweepers, regarded as essentially negative in Britain, could be put to positive, creative use. At Real Sociedad he dropped conventional formations after a rocky start, and tactical innovation proved equally successful at Real Madrid: 'When we failed to score in our first couple of matches with one man up I was slaughtered in the press. We finished the season as champions with a record number of goals and Hugo Sanchez scored 38 of them.' Even though he could call on exceptional talents in his first spell at Real, these were still remarkable results.

Another consistent theme has been faith in the ability of young players, doubtless aided by memories of his own experiences of being able to cope with senior football at the age of sixteen. The Swansea City centre-back Dudley Lewis, whose considerable talent was eventually to be ground down in the club's decline, was trusted with key roles in a promotion push at the age of sixteen and a relegation battle when only two years older. Lewis coped brilliantly with both. Solicitude for his youngsters led, during the unhappy endpiece of his period at Swansea, to the extraordinary decision to split his squad between two dressing-rooms rather than allow them to be infected by what he saw as the cynicism and time-serving of older professionals. At La Coruña he complained that the Spanish Cup-winning squad he had inherited from the venerable Arsenio Iglesias was almost as aged as its sexagenarian creator: 'A castle in the air, the oldest squad in Europe with hardly a player under 28.'

One might think that being cosmopolitan, analytically intelligent and self-sufficient should have made Toshack an ideal national manager – such qualities being essential in a post which leaves more time for thinking than the intense day-to-day demands of club management. Yet his brief spell in charge of Wales, covering a 3–0 home defeat by

Norway, was a bizarre, bleakly comic episode which has yet to be explained fully and about which he is reluctant to talk. His side of the story will presumably have to wait for his memoirs. Given the extent of his experience in the British and European game and the literacy which allowed him to write *Tosh*, an interim volume in response to Swansea City's spectacular success between 1978 and 1982, they should be worth waiting for. A follow-up volume *Diario del 'Gales'*, a diary of his first two seasons at Real Sociedad, translated into Spanish by the British journalist Graham Turner, was a novelty in a country whose appetite for reading about sport is satisfied by daily newspapers rather than the autobiographies of players and coaches. The book of poetry and the interim autobiography provide a strong clue as to one likely element in the title. But we can be sure they will be tosh in name only rather than – like most football memoirs – in content.

Terry Yorath

Barrie Morgan

In August 1995 Lebanon languished at 144th in the FIFA world soccer rankings; just twenty-two months later, this small, divided country with 3 million inhabitants was eighty-seventh. This transformation in Lebanon's football fortunes was wrought by Terry Yorath, whose contract was not renewed by the Football Association of Wales (FAW) in December 1993, after the national team had narrowly failed to qualify for the World Cup Finals. Wales, managed by Yorath's successors, slumped from twenty-ninth in the world at the time of his departure to eighty-fifth, a mere two places above Lebanon in June 1997. Still the twenty-six members of the Council of the FAW could take some consolation that their numerous critics were denied the ultimate justification of a back-page headline: 'Yorath steers Lebanon above Wales in FIFA rankings.'

Terry Yorath has been no stranger to disappointment, both on the football field and on the touch-line. His years with Leeds, and with Wales both as a player and manager, provide a litany of near misses, culminating in losing the job that had been his lifelong ambition. However, the personal impact of tragedy has touched Yorath in ways which make the slings and arrows of football fortune pale into insignificance. He first came into close contact with human suffering as coach of Bradford City in the aftermath of the Valley Parade fire in May 1985, in which fifty-six supporters died as the blaze quickly engulfed the main, wooden grandstand. Seven years later in May 1992, he and his family suffered their own tragedy when his 15-year-old son Daniel collapsed and died in his arms of a rare heart disease, hypertrophic cardiomyopathy, during a garden kick-about at their Leeds home. Daniel had been following in his father's footsteps as an associate schoolboy with Leeds United.

In the spring of 1995 Terry Yorath's life was at a low ebb. Still trying to come to terms with his personal grief, for the first time in his life he did not have the outlet of soccer into which to channel his mind and energy. Fifteen months after being stripped of his position with Wales, he had resigned as manager and director of Cardiff City after the consortium of which he was a member failed in its attempt to buy the struggling Second Division club from Rick Wright, the Barry Island holiday-chalet owner who had stepped in as a temporary saviour. Many lesser men would have buckled under the pressure, wallowing in self-pity at home and relying financially on his wife's flourishing business interests. Yorath, his passion for football undimmed and with character-istic single-mindedness, chose to uproot himself from his family and Leeds home and travel more than 2,000 miles to settle in a bachelor apartment in Beirut in order to rebuild his managerial career.

The desolation of the war-torn city, with the boulevards and fine architecture of its once sophisticated cosmopolitan heart destroyed, was matched by Yorath's emptiness. Some 150,000 people had been killed during the civil war between the country's ethnic groups. As Yorath was to say 'the country and I shared a goal in putting our lives back together'. The city still echoed with the occasional sound of machine-gun fire and he needed a personal bodyguard. We Welsh are a nation with clannish tendencies, never more so than when discussing the relative merits of players from different locales on international day, but we are first and foremost fervently patriotic. The contrast that awaited Yorath in Beirut could not have been more stark. While it is common for the leading football teams in polarized societies to be ethnically based, these rivalries in Lebanon had reached a point where religion and club influenced national team selection. To succeed as national coach, Yorath had to persuade the country's footballers and administrators to set aside their differences. It is a measure of Yorath's determination to do the right thing, to field his best team in the face of sectarian bigotry, as well as his coaching skills, that Lebanon lost only seven of his forty-one games in charge.

Terence Charles Yorath was born in the Splott area of Cardiff on 27 March 1950. At the age of eleven, he became a pupil at Cathays High School, which like all Welsh grammar schools was a bastion of the oval ball. Readers who, like the young Yorath, were fervent soccer players in junior school will remember the shock of this transition; of trying to come to terms with a game in which brute strength and a capricious ball seemed the dominant elements. Yorath, however, like many natural ball players, quickly adapted to the new challenge and became a highly competent scrum-half who earned a final trial for Cardiff Schools rugby. He was fortuitously reclaimed by football when he went to watch his elder brother David, who subsequently played for Cardiff and

Crystal Palace, play for Cardiff Schoolboys against Rhondda School-boys. The team was a player short, and Terry Yorath stepped in. The following season he was asked to the trials, and was selected to represent Cardiff in his own right. Four Welsh schoolboy caps followed as an outside-right.

No Welsh grammar school sports master could take such a defection lightly; the health of Welsh rugby largely depended on the converted not lapsing and returning to their first love. Peter Stead and I had fallen under the benign influence of Haydn Morris, who is best remembered for his gazelle-like leap to secure Wales's last victory in Paris before the debut of the Pontypool front row, but Terry's teachers, Mr Watkins and 'Biffer' Harris, occupied the more fanatical end of the spectrum. He was treated as an outcast. Banned from playing rugby or even cricket again, and banished on sports day to the swimming pool, Yorath quickly became disenchanted with school life. At the age of fifteen, not waiting to sit his O-levels, he 'went north' to join Leeds United as an apprentice on the recommendation of Jack Pickard, the scout, who had previously recommended John Charles and Gary Sprake to the Yorkshire club. As he was to demonstrate time and again, nothing would be allowed to stand between Terry Yorath and football. He signed as a professional in April 1967, six months after I had joined the University of Leeds as a young assistant lecturer.

When Terry Yorath arrived as an apprentice at Leeds in 1965 Don Revie was three years into his thirteen-year reign as manager, during which time he metamorphosed a debt-ridden club heading for the Third Division into one of Europe's greatest club sides. This metamorphosis was founded on aggression, application, discipline and method, the foremost of which in the early years seemed to be aggression. Revie had been a constructive and stylish player, the fulcrum of Manchester City's 'Revie plan' which had introduced the deep-lying centre-forward to the English game. As a manager, however, only winning appeared to matter. The Second Division Championship season of 1963/4 saw Leeds earn eighteen cautions, more than any other club in the Football League that year, and earned the club a formal warning. Leeds's quest for the League and FA Cup double a year later was peppered with more bad-tempered, ugly encounters. In one, the match with Everton at Goodison Park, the referee was forced to take the teams off the pitch ten minutes before half-time to calm down.

It is difficult to judge how far the tenacious, tough-tackling and aggressive midfield player which Yorath became at Leeds was influenced by the pervading mores of the club. His subsequent comment that he thought 'that was what he had to do to make it' suggests the environment was significant. Certainly he must have learned much about the arts of coarse tackling when he was in digs with Norman 'bite your legs' Hunter, arguably the hardest of all defenders in a generation that included Tommy Smith, Ron Harris and Peter Storey. Replicating his club's troubles, Yorath's acrimonious hustling soon got him into trouble with referees. At the age of eighteen he was suspended for twenty-one days for kicking a Sheffield Wednesday player in a reserve fixture, and he continued throughout his career to test referees' writing abilities to the full.

One cannot help but wonder how Yorath and Leeds would have fared in the disciplinary climate of the modern game. I was a keen supporter of Barry Town and then Cardiff City from 1951, scarcely missing a home match, but only witnessed my first sending off when Billy Bremner was dismissed in a Leeds United game in the 1966/7 season. On 1 May 1999, I saw Rob Harris, one of the more card-happy of modern officials, send off three West Ham players, ironically in a match against Leeds United. Two-thirds of the way through the 1999/2000 season, Lee Bowyer, a true heir to the Leeds' midfield mantle, had personally accumulated fifteen yellow cards, only three less than the entire team in 1963/4. In the past, referees may have been too lenient on injury-threatening tackles and on the professional foul. However, the confetti of yellow cards which has littered matches in recent seasons, leading to potential dismissal for two slightly mistimed tackles, was in serious danger of short-changing spectators until some common sense seems to have returned with the dawn of the new millennium.

Just as the tag 'dirty Leeds' stuck when the team went on in the early 1970s to be one of the greatest club sides Britain has seen, so the popular image of Yorath is as the player who epitomized the harshness of Leeds, although he only began to break into the team when it was approaching its creative best. Between 1968 and 1974 Leeds won two League Championships, the FA Cup, the League Cup and the Inter-Cities Fairs Cup twice. The team, once it began to break free of the inhibitions brought on by Revie's near pathological caution and to show its abundant talent and ingenuity, became almost irresistible. While Geoffrey Green memorably wrote in *The Times* after a Liverpool game in the late 1960s of 'two sides as hard as a diamond but without that stone's brilliant flame', Hugh McIlvanney described, in 1972, white shirts flooding forward 'with the insistence of surf . . . their football breathless in its scope and fluency, alive with dazzling improvisations'.

This success was founded on what was arguably the best midfield in Europe: Johnny Giles, a master at creating time and space before delivering a long ball of piercing accuracy; Billy Bremner, the 5ft 5in. dynamo who was close to being the complete midfielder, and Norman Hunter. Terry Yorath was forced to serve a long apprenticeship to these masters, to the extent that he had played eleven times for Wales before he had played four full games for Leeds. In his fourteen starts for Leeds before the 1972/3 season he wore six shirts (2, 4, 5, 6, 8, 11). As his appearances became more frequent, he also played a bit part in some of Leeds's biggest disappointments. In May 1972, coming on for Allan Clarke, against Wolves at Molyneux, he had a shot headed off the line as Leeds fought in vain for the equalizer which would have given them a well-deserved League–Cup double. He came on as a substitute for Eddie Gray in the 1973 Cup Final, which Sunderland of the Second Division won 1–0 in one of the biggest of all Wembley shocks. Leeds so often fell at the last hurdle that commentators began to doubt that it was all bad luck (although even with the objectivity of nearly thirty years hindsight several vital games were lost through some poor refereeing decisions) and attribute it more to the complex paths of a brooding and over-anxious psyche.

Yorath began to establish himself in the side in the 1973/4 Championship season. With Gordon McQueen, Frank Gray and Joe Jordan also emerging as major forces, Andrew Mourant commented that 'the ageing and cantankerous side that so recently only seemed fit for the breaker's yard had metamorphosed into a rejuvenated team which looked as if it might only be halted by opponents resorting to grievous bodily harm'. The team went twenty-nine League matches without defeat until it lost to Stoke on 23 February; history does not record the police being asked to investigate the cause. Yorath played in eighteen of those matches, the last one as right-back.

It was generally, however, Yorath's huge misfortune to shoulder the burden of replacing Johnny Giles in the side. While Mourant's comment 'substituting a committed journeyman for a maestro was never a fair exchange' is a little hard in its description of Yorath, there is no doubt that he was really the natural successor to Hunter or Bremner (Revie used to describe him as the Welsh Bremner). The team became unbalanced, and Yorath the butt of the terrace's displeasure. Throughout his career he was the type of player who excited the passion of the crowd, but it falls to few to be loathed by both sets of supporters. By 1976 he was being jeered by the Elland Road faithful before he had touched the ball, and the new manager, Jimmy Armfield, left Terry out of the side for his own good. After repeated transfer requests, he joined Coventry City in September 1976.

Yorath was a more accomplished footballer than his reputation suggests. As much as he continued to develop, like Leeds he could not shake off his early image. My abiding memory is of a player with long flaxen hair matted with rain and sweat, seeking with abrasive tackles to create a midfield environment in which his side's more creative players could prosper. Although nature left him short of speed and his first touch sometimes let him down, he developed into a good, and at his best incisive, distributor of the ball with no mean shot. His emerging skills as an all-round midfielder were forced to develop at Coventry when Gordon Milne, the manager, adopted an attacking 4–2–4 formation. Despite being outnumbered, he and Barry Powell frequently dominated midfield in a side which finished seventh in the First Division in 1978. Finally at Tottenham, in the company of Hoddle, Ardiles and Villa, Keith Burkinshaw encouraged him to express himself on the pitch, and much of the latent skill that had been there all along flourished alongside the natural determination and discipline learned at Leeds. It is fascinating to speculate how Terry Yorath would be remembered if he had joined Spurs at the beginning rather than at the end of his career, had he been a product of Bill Nicholson rather than of Don Revie.

However, to discuss Terry Yorath in terms of his tackling, passing and shooting skills is to risk missing the essence of the footballer: his professionalism and his leadership. He was the ultimate professional who very rarely let his team down, in whatever position he was asked to play (he eventually played in all ten outfield positions for Leeds). In the words of Billy Bremner, Terry was 'one of the best pros I ever played with. He had his share of nightmares in the early days but however badly he was playing he never ducked it once. He was always there in support wanting the ball.' Yorath nicknamed himself the wall. 'They knocked the ball to me to get it back at the angle they needed.' Whenever he failed to get a game, he would return to Elland Road alone the next morning to work on his skills. One would describe his long apprenticeship at Leeds as character-forming except one suspects that the character was already formed. His wife Christine, paying tribute to his professionalism and contrasting it with some of today's superstars, tells the story of giving birth to Gabby, now the heart-throb of many football fans as a supremely professional football presenter. With only the baby's head visible, Terry left her in order not to miss the plane for a European fixture with Hadjuk Split. The club doctor both stayed to complete the birth and caught the same flight.

Above all, Terry Yorath was a natural leader on the football field. His potential was first recognized by Mike Smith who, shortly after his appointment as manager of Wales in 1974, in the search for a fresh face who would bring urgency and forceful leadership to the role made Yorath his captain. Many administrators and commentators were incredulous: 'too soon', 'not mature enough' and 'too wild' were common assessments. It proved, however, to be an inspired choice. No less a judge than Helmut Schoen, the legendary German manager, described him as an outstanding captain of Wales. Michael Boon who covered most of his forty-two matches as captain eulogized in the *Western Mail*, 'I have no hesitation in saying that he was the finest captain in any sport I have reported. He became the skipper to Wales that Bobby Moore had been to England.'

Yorath also proved to be a highly successful club captain. After a year leading Leeds, he immediately assumed the captaincy on signing for Coventry City. Rod Dean commented in a history of the club in 1991 that 'Yorath's time with City has tended to be mythologised . . . but he was a player who inspired those around him and was probably the finest first division captain Coventry have had'. His standing for club and country was not just down to his ability to inspire and motivate, or to the respect he commanded; he had a rare ability to read a game and a shrewd grasp of tactics which he was not slow to share with his team-mates.

Yorath and Smith never quite achieved the success they deserved together. Wales reached the quarter-final of the European Championships against Yugoslavia in 1976, but in those days it was a simple home-and-away two-leg fixture. One undoubted highlight was Wales's first victory against England at Wembley in 1977 during an unbeaten British Championship campaign. The seminal moment of the match was a hard but fair tackle on Brian Greenhoff from which Yorath emerged with the ball, after which the area he was patrolling in midfield seemed to become a no-go area for the home team. But there were disappointments, notably the infamous 'hand of Joe' incident in 1977 when Scotland went through to the World Cup Finals at Wales's expense. Joe Jordan, Scotland's centre-forward and godfather to Gaby, appeared to handle the ball, but Scotland were awarded a penalty which Masson converted. Yorath won the last of his fifty-nine caps against the Soviet Union in the qualifying groups for the 1982 World Cup. He had not developed the same rapport with Mike England, Smith's successor, possibly in part because he had moved on to play his football with Vancouver Whitecaps. But as Dai Davies the goalkeeper remarked, 'when Wales lost that unique Welshman, they lost the heart of the team'.

In retrospect, it appears inevitable that 'that unique Welshman' should return to serve his country with even more distinction as manager. Yorath served his managerial apprenticeship yo-yoing between Bradford City, where he later returned as assistant manager, and Swansea City. He joined Bradford City as player-coach in December 1982 and helped Trevor Cherry, a former Leeds colleague, build the Bantams into one of the most improved sides in the country. In May 1986, Yorath was appointed manager of near-bankrupt Swansea City, which had plummeted from the first division to the basement of the fourth. He steered the club to promotion via the play-offs in 1988 but walked out, with his side challenging for promotion again and with six months of his contract remaining, to manage Bradford City. This move sparked a long-running dispute between the two clubs over compensation, and left many Swans fans to this day ambivalent about his achievements. The second spell at Bradford did not work out, and within days, in March 1990, he returned to manage Swansea for a second time. One should never go back: in the wake of a run of poor results, he was sacked for the second time in a year.

Yorath became part-time manager of Wales in July 1988 during his first spell with Swansea. From the outset, members of the FAW Council seemed to harbour serious doubts about the wisdom of employing an inspirational young Welshman with a burning passion for his country, hankering instead after a big-name manager like Brian Clough. He was initially appointed as a caretaker for three friendly games, and after that only awarded a one-year contract. Living on a salary of £15,000 after he left club management, he had to plead for his job to be made full-time. Wales's first ever victory against Germany in the European Championship, after which the FAW banked £750,000, forced the Council's hand in June 1991. In May 1992, however, he was effectively put back on trial with a seventeen-month contract.

To be fair, Yorath made an inauspicious start in international management. Wales did not register a win in his first ten matches, or against Germany, Holland and Finland in the qualifying group for the 1990 World Cup. However, Yorath's tactical astuteness was beginning to shine through and Wales put in their best performance in an away match for years in losing 2–1 to Germany in Cologne. There followed a much more successful European Championship campaign which went to the wire before Germany prevailed. With Luxembourg as usual there to make up the numbers, Belgium (3–1) as well as Germany (1–0) departed Cardiff with their tails between their legs, and an away draw (1–1) was earned in Belgium. Before the disappointment of losing 4–1 in the away match with Germany, Brazil were sent packing after a 1–0 defeat. Wales entered the qualifying round for the World Cup, in a group with three strong teams, in an optimistic frame of mind. However, thirty-four minutes after kick-off in the first match of the campaign in Bucharest, Terry Yorath's charges were 5–0 down as Gheorge Hagi ripped them apart. Slowly they clawed their way back into contention in the group, with a 2–0 victory over Belgium and a draw (2–2) with the Czech and Slovak Republics in Cardiff, to the point that they entered that fateful last game with Romania needing a 2–0 victory to ensure a place in America '94.

Yorath had moulded a very successful team from a mixture of bricks and straw. When he took over, Hughes, Rush, Southall, and Ratcliffe were world-class players; Ryan Giggs came through during his tenure. But the choice elsewhere was limited. In November 1989 there were only eighty-three Welshmen playing professional football in the United Kingdom. This meant effectively a pool of thirty potential players who might be considered for international duty, little more than half of whom played regularly in the First Division. Overblown as the expectation might have been, it is to his overwhelming credit that he took Wales to the brink of the success that the Welsh public craved: qualification for a major championship. Like Don Revie before him, Yorath the manager belied Yorath the player. While developing a superb team spirit, he eschewed both the long ball and kicking people in order to make up for the gap in class in favour of creativity and the measured build up. Perceptive and intelligent, he started employing the sweeper system after losing to Finland in his first championship campaign, and developed the likes of Eric Young, Kit Symons and Paul Bodin, not necessarily the most promising material, into a defensive unit which made Wales hard to beat. Such was his success that, for a period culminating in the match against Romania, he and his team carried on their shoulders the sporting hopes of a nation seeking deliverance from repeated humiliations in the fifteen-man game.

That November evening in Cardiff, which marked Yorath's century of matches with Wales, is burnished on the memory of all Welsh football lovers. Unable to travel to Cardiff, I followed it as best I could in Bromley, Kent. One could write a chapter on the frustration of trying to follow Welsh sporting events in London, of a radio pressed to the ear trying to pick up the faintest signal from Radio Wales. On this occasion, I was reduced to score flashes as the BBC chose to screen England v. San Marino from Bologna, notwithstanding that England's interest in the World Cup under Graham Taylor had died in the Netherlands the previous month. With ten or so minutes to go in Cardiff, and England on the verge of a meaningless six-goal victory, coverage was switched to the National Stadium as Paul Bodin placed the ball on the penalty spot with the score at 1–1. The ball struck the bar; Romania soon after broke away and scored a second. Wales had failed again, and Yorath carried the can. The public were far more appreciative. Their reaction to the FAW's failure to renew his contract was captured by a cartoon in the *South Wales Echo* showing FAW headquarters with two post boxes, one marked 'mail' and the other 'hate mail'. Realistically, given the poverty of the country's playing resources, a Welsh manager is nearly always going to be judged by the adjective applied to failure. Yorath has been Wales's best manager during my lifetime. His was a glorious failure.

Players with the personal qualities of Terry Yorath are rare. Short of that ultimate touch of class, he succeeded by force of character and will-power in improving his game to hold his own with the best. He was eventually so successful as a player that, when Leeds tried to re-sign him from Tottenham in 1981, his financial demands (a £40,000 signing-on fee and £600 a week) led Manny Cussins, the Leeds chairman, to suggest that inflated transfer fees and wages were threatening the game's survival. Whether an 18-year-old Terry Yorath would now have the same opportunities, with the top Premiership sides flooded with foreign imports, the majority of whom would not cross the Channel for less than £20,000 per week, is perhaps doubtful. He and his like, who contribute so much more than they take, are the bedrock of football. The game in general, and the Welsh national team in particular, will be immeasurably weakened if his successors do not have the same opportunity to develop at the top level.

This chapter is dedicated to the memory of my mother, Hilda Morgan, who died as it was nearing completion.

Ian Rush

John Williams

Ian Rush, possibly the greatest post-war British football striker, was lost to the English and claimed forever by the Welsh on 20 October 1961, the year of the lifting of the maximum wage in English football. Eventually, Rush would earn more money from football than any other British player of his generation, enough to keep himself and his family for the rest of his life – though he would have to travel, briefly and unhappily, to Italy to do so.

Ian Rush was a 'border' baby, which means that he *should* have been born in England at the Chester Maternity Hospital, which is barely a dozen miles from the Rush family home, a three-bedroomed council house in Woodfield Avenue, Flint. But his father, Francis, a steelworker at the nearby Shotton works, a staunch Catholic and a Welshman to the tips of his workboots, would not countenance any of his children being born among English stock. So, off went Doris Rush on the by now familiar trek to the hospital at St Asaph in north Wales. It was not possible to know then, of course, that Ian, their ninth child and the bonniest of all of Francis and Doris Rush's ten offspring, would become St Asaph's best-known and favourite sporting son.

The new arrival joined an already large and competitive brood in the Rush family home. Young Ian shared a bedroom with his five brothers and, like the rest of them, he shaped his sleeping patterns as best he could around the shift work of his older, already employed, siblings. His childhood memories of his father are mainly of a keen worker and caring provider for his children, a man without real political commit-ment save his strong national sentiments which were mostly played out via his sporting interests, especially in rugby and football. His mother, perhaps unsurprisingly, produces quite different memories. 'She seemed to spend her whole day cooking, cleaning, washing and ironing', recalled Rush later.

At five years of age Ian contracted meningitis, and by all accounts he was fortunate to survive a coma in an oxygen tent at the nearby Cottage Hospital, Flint. He attributes, almost certainly wrongly, his later wiry build to the weight he lost from his chubby frame during this early illness. After his recovery, it was back to the familiar routine of hand-me-down clothes and clinging on to his older brothers' bootstraps. He eventually got his first pair of football boots as a six-year-old, marvelling at the stylish Puma green-dyed sole and the real rubber studs which had reasonably survived their time with at least two of his older brothers. 'Rushie's' *real* life was about to begin.

Like a lot of professional footballers in Britain, the young Rush benefited from an early age from playing 'pick-up' football with *older* local lads, in his case friends of his brother, Stephen, most of whom were at least three years older than Ian. He survived in this company because he was a reasonable size for his age, he could play, he didn't moan, and he was tough. These rough twenty-a-side contests, dawn-till-dusk events in the summer, are the kind of grounding whose loss is now bemoaned by older football coaches and players in Britain, especially as open green field sites have increasingly been swallowed up, and television and computer games have conspired to drag kids in off the streets. The younger Rush would have learned how to survive against much bigger and stronger kids and even how to deal with the physical intimidation that all professional players must later learn to face. It showed. At seven years of age he played for the local primary school team, St Mary's, when all the other players were already aged ten. In his last year of primary education, and by now playing pick-up football routinely with 'hard' local teenagers, it was clear that, when playing against opponents his *own* age, young Ian was already a frightening prospect. As a ten-year-old, he famously broke the Deeside Schools goal-scoring record, notching seventy-two goals in just thirty-three games. His record survived for some twenty years, before succumbing to another promising local young forward, a tiny Michael Owen.

At St Richard Gwyn High School, and now playing in midfield, the 14-year-old Rush played for Flintshire and Deeside Schools, and he was also scouted at this age for Liverpool but, a costly mistake this, no further contact was made by the club with his parents. Rush seems originally to have been a Spurs' fan, but he sometimes attended matches at Everton where his boyhood hero had been the chunky Blues centre-forward, Bob Latchford. Famously, Rush became one of the 'turncoat' Evertonians – Fowler, Owen and McManaman are others – signed, damagingly for Goodison hopes, by near neighbours Liverpool. He would return to haunt Everton many times. Later the young Rush also

170

played, very proudly, for the Welsh Schools Under-15s, firstly against the other home countries, and then (his first time abroad) against Germany and against France in 1977 at the Parc des Princes in front of 20,000 spectators; a 'nerve-wracking experience' he recalled later.

In his early teens Ian's precocious extra-curricular childhood experiences looked at one stage as if they might also draw him into serious bother. He seems, in actual fact, to have been like a lot of young men of his age and background in England and Wales: lacking in real depth and self-assurance, and sometimes reckless. The period between thirteen and fifteen years of age he describes as his 'wild years', when he was involved in 'countless' punch-ups and even spent a night in the police cells at Rhyl, and later in court, after a schoolboy shop-lifting expedition. Already something of a pub regular by fourteen, Ian and older brother Stephen must have been quite a handful in a large family where discipline was sometimes stretched. Despite his generally calm football persona later, the young Rush was surprisingly noted then for his short fuse and his willingness to join with other school 'hard cases' in gang fights with 'similar nutters' from local rivals, Flint High School. The rows were serious: 'Vicious they were', he recalls, probably with a little bravado. 'I've had a few good hidings in my time, been beaten up, had the boot put into me. I've had a few black eyes and I've dished a few out. You had to in order to survive.'

Rush later admitted that his wilful resistance to formal schooling and his general hanging out with the bad guys meant that his wife, Tracy, an O-levelled bank clerk, was the brains in their relationship. But he left school with a 'respectable' five CSEs, pretty much just before school 'left' him. By this time Rush was often playing football up to four or five times a week, including for the Welsh Schools Under-18s and the British Catholic Schools. But even later, as an apprentice at Chester, 'Rushie' still sometimes longed for a little weekend street action: 'We'd have a few quid in our pockets, my mates and I, and we'd blow it on a good drink – and often as not a good fight to end the night. I suppose I was still a bit of a wild lad in that first year at Chester.'

Rush's growing football prowess had drawn the attention not only of his local club but also keen interest from both Wrexham and Burnley. He rejected the Clarets because of their regimented, overly organized style; not enough laughs. Wrexham, in contrast, was shambolic; not enough shape. Chester seemed just right; only a couple of schoolboys signed on, and they trained right away with the first team. A later bid for Ian by Manchester United, who offered apprentice terms, and also some under-the-table money from a 'Midlands' club, were both rejected by Francis Rush, clearly a man of some principles: Chester had been promised, and Chester is where the young Rush would go. Francis also probably knew his own son well. The painfully shy and inexperienced Ian Rush was unlikely to have taken easily to either of these larger clubs, despite their late and attractive offers.

In 1978 the 16-year-old Rush signed as an apprentice at Chester, for what seemed like the grand sum of £16 a week. When pre-season began the new apprentices pounded out the miles with the pros, did the weights and the sprints which followed, played a full-scale practice match in the afternoon, *and* cleaned up the ground in the evening ready for another day's work. This, plus the Dickensian cleaning of the old pros' boots, which often produced an unscheduled spell in the shower for work badly done, meant long and exhausting days. Time for fighting and larking about – if not for drinking – gradually dried up as Rush also began to make real football progress at Chester. He just might, Rush allowed himself to think, he just *might* yet make a professional player at this level.

In his first season, playing for Chester's youth and reserve teams under the experienced eye of Cliff Sears, Rush faced the usual mix of young kids and gnarled old professionals; the latter tried to kick him up in the air or else muttered their dark threats. His 'retaliation' was scoring goals; they came slowly at first, but Sears was soon telling the local press – and anyone else in earshot – about his rising new star. In the last game of the 1978/9 season, away at Sheffield Wednesday in the old Third Division, Rush got his first first-team start in midfield. A 2–2 draw was a reasonable return, but on the coach home, too much celebratory cold lager put the young debutant in bed for a number of days, much to the amusement of the club's senior players.

At the start of the 1979/80 season the 17-year-old striker was pushing for a first-team place. He scored his first senior goal against Gillingham, and then, when club top scorer Ian Edwards was sold by the wily Alan Oakes to local rivals Wrexham, Rush was promoted into the club's number-9 shirt. He never let go. In thirty-eight first-team games in his first and only full season at Sealand Road he scored seventeen goals. His wages went up to £50, with a £250 bonus for a spirited Chester FA Cup run. Friday night was no longer spent out with 'the lads', looking for trouble. He was now down to the local chippie at 8pm and then back home to bed. Saturday was disco night, and it was around this time that the young Rush first met his wife-to-be, Tracy. For this local boy with few other prospects, it was hard to better this. Regular football, a nice girlfriend, a decent wage, and even some interest from the Welsh Under-21s. Then, distressingly, out of the blue Liverpool's Bob Paisley came knocking.

When Liverpool first came in for Rush at the end of 1979/80, he had no hesitation in turning them down. He was a small town boy, more than content with his progress at Chester. 'I'm not good enough', he told manager Oakes. 'I want to stay here.' But Bob Paisley, a seasoned assessor of young football talent had seen in Rush something he liked – and wanted. A few weeks later Liverpool called by again, and this time Ian and his dad got the full tour of Melwood and lunch at Anfield with Paisley and his staff. The works. Francis was a Liverpool fan; to see his son play at Anfield was a dream. No worries there. But Rush, himself, was hesitant. Big club; small town boy. The cash helped to swing it, despite his own serious misgivings: Liverpool was willing to pay him £300 a week, six times his Chester wage. His club was offered £300,000, a record British fee for a teenager. Rush signed.

Kenny Dalglish remarked later that: 'If anyone ever walked into the Liverpool dressing room determined to be the whipping boy, the butt of all the jokes and wisecracks, they could not have done better than Rushie did on that first meeting.' Liverpool, the dominant club in the country – and in Europe – was known inside the British game for three things: the mythical 'boot room' coaching set-up established by Bill Shankly, and taken on by Paisley and his staff; the sheer *quality* of the footballers signed by the club; and, finally, for the 'no superstars' fierceness of the club's dressing-room 'canteen' culture. Even by English football's formidable standards in the 1980s, Dalglish, Lawrenson, Hansen, McMahon and the rest were merciless in their cruel humour, wind-ups and pranks. This was, of course, the source of the unquenchable team spirit for which Liverpool was rightly famous. Add this sort of spirit to real quality, and the mix was nigh unbeatable. Into this bearpit came this gangly big-money kid from nowhere, with his hicksville tee-shirt and jeans. Had he arrived to do the plumbing? Dalglish asked him if he had come from a jumble sale. The dressing-room shop stewards at Liverpool began calling Rush 'Omar' (after Omar Sharif, a guy who really *could* dress well). When they later saw his weak heading they decided on 'Tosh' (after Liverpool and Welsh ace Toshack, a demon in the air). Rush, slinked into a corner. He *hated* them.

He hated Liverpool. Rush played a few reserve team games in 1979/80, but he was still achingly self-contained and lacking in confidence. He refused to speak to these braying stars – his new team-mates – even when coming back in 1980/1. He was frightened of being late to work, so he was ragged by the rest for always being early. Also, he lived with his mum in a backwater, Flint, so he seldom socialized with the rest, who lived north of Liverpool in the affluent golf-course belt around Southport. Rush later described Liverpool as a 'restless' club, meaning that first-teamers were feted, while everyone else seemed to be waiting to move on – or, simply, hardly to exist at all.

Rush also felt envied by the club's younger players in the reserves, having arrived on a fat fee, effectively, to step on their toes. He had a 'miserable' first season, by his own account: 'I wasn't playing well, the goals had dried up, and, all in all, I was ploughing through a real depression.' The Welshman's one pre-Christmas first-team start came at Ipswich on 12 December, replacing one of his dressing-room tormentors, the great Dalglish. It was a respectable 1–1 draw, but Rush then went back into the reserves. His break finally came with an injury to David Johnson before Liverpool's League Cup Final replay against West Ham in April 1981. Rush did well, and Liverpool won, so he played another six League games before the season's end, plus a European Cup semi-final tie against Bayern Munich. He had no goals yet, but at least he was beginning to speak. He had also even started to dress reasonably enough to satisfy the Liverpool fashion police. The teasing no longer hurt quite so bad. His confidence was rising and Paisley promised him a place in the European Cup Final squad for 1981. Things, suddenly, looked much better. Of course, it couldn't last.

Rush was left out of the 1981 Liverpool squad for Paris and was hurt by this apparent betrayal, one which Paisley failed to explain. The ageing manager may even have forgotten the pledge. The next season, Paisley offered Rush a 10 per cent pay rise. Egged on, perhaps maliciously, by some senior players, a puffed-up Rush asked for £100 – a 33 per cent rise, which Paisley flatly refused. An interesting and vehement row ensued between the two, essentially over the playing philosophy Rush was being taught at Anfield. Paisley wanted more responsibility, much more *selfishness* for his money from his putative young goal-scorer: he wanted *goals*. Rush claimed Anfield was teaching him the *opposite* of this: the importance, above all else, of teamwork and passing.

By now, his dander up, Rush was even looking to *leave* Liverpool, but he did take this new 'selfish' approach back into the reserves – and goals soon came. Paisley remained annoyingly silent, however, about the obvious improvement but, at Christmas, with Rush now a fixture in the first team, he offered the striker his £100 rise. Rush, typically, asked for the £100 *plus* the original 10 per cent. A deal was eventually done. It was good business. For five years Ian Rush and Kenny Dalglish were to become the best striking partnership in the English game. Some good judges claim it was the best British forward partnership *ever*.

In his first 'full' season at Liverpool, 1981/2, Rush scored thirty goals in all, seventeen in the League. He was already very good, but he was still a novice compared to what he *could* do. In 1983/4 he rattled up forty-nine in the season, an astonishing achievement, and including two for Wales. His career goal tally easily exceeded that of all his partners and most of his rivals. In all, he scored a record 346 goals in 658 appearances in two spells at Liverpool, a quite phenomenal tally. He also became record goal-scorer for Wales, with twenty-eight goals, and sometimes perilously little in the way of support around him.

His goal-scoring 'secret' was difficult to explain. His technique was certainly far from flawless and he lacked the forensic six-yard box precision of, say, a Gary Lineker or a Robbie Fowler. Welsh manager, Terry Yorath, admired his ability to relax – to 'switch off' during matches. Alan Hansen thought Rush excelled at looking along the line of a back four in order to stay onside. Dalglish pointed to the exquisite timing and direction of his partner's runs. The Scotsman's strength and guile and Rush's angled darts and lethal finishing were, indeed, a potent mix. Rush, himself, like a lot of great strikers, pointed simply to the 'instinctive' nature of what he did. He also recommended, however, that young strikers master the basic skills of the game with hard practice, learn the value of good timing and, *pace* his row with Bob Paisley, become single-minded to the point of selfishness. The rest, as it often is with great goal-scorers, remained something of a mystery. In any case, Liverpool did not want him *thinking* too much about what he was already doing so well. He once said: 'I don't see myself remaining in football as a coach once my playing days are over. I'd be the worst coach in the game. If I don't know how I do certain things how could I possibly coach someone else to do them?'

Most serious observers agree that, apart from his deceptive pace, real courage and an unerring eye for goal, Rush's other great quality at Liverpool was his incredible, ego-free, work-rate. The Welshman prowled along the line of defenders in search of mistakes, while the wily Dalglish waited just behind to pick up the pieces. It often worked. 'Defend from the front' became the credo at Liverpool in the 1980s: Ian Rush led the line fearlessly and he hunted the ball incessantly.

Ironically, having spent so much time initially on the 'outside' of affairs at Liverpool, Rush was initially astonished – and then delighted – by the sheer pace of the 'social' side of the Liverpool machine, something which tends to put recent Merseyside 'spice boys' stories into some perspective. When appropriate, a night 'on the bevvy'– as it was at many top English clubs at the time – was an important part of the forcing-house of the Liverpool approach. 'There were no strict rules and regulations regarding players having a drink', Rush commented later. 'You're never told what nights to stay in, there are never any deadlines put on us. If you went out on Friday night and got legless, that's up to you. Not a word would be said. But if it shows in your play – boy, you're out!'

The 'best' Liverpool social sessions were held once the serious football action was deemed to be over, but they still could be impressive affairs. In 1982, for example, Liverpool travelled on the day to relegated Middlesbrough for a final Tuesday night fixture, the League title already secured. Incredibly, by the middle of the afternoon Rush and his senior colleagues were in a Teeside pub, downing lager. 'It was the first of quite a few pints I sank in the next couple of hours. And the rest of the lads were enjoying themselves too.' The squad stumbled back to their hotel rooms for coach, Ronnie Moran's, 4pm room check. The match ended in a disjointed 0–0 draw. 'Apparently the Middlesbrough players had got wind of our afternoon session', reported Rush. 'They were half embarrassed at playing us.'

After the last match of the next, 1982/3, season Liverpool left on a short tour of Israel. In Tel Aviv, the night *before* the first tour game, a group of the younger Liverpool players got badly drunk. Rush fell over in a bar and a 'free fight' broke out *between* the players over who had 'pushed' him. The next morning, equipped with shiners and facial gashes, a group of Liverpool players, including the tyro Rush, were up before a stern Bob Paisley, but no further action was taken. In fact, Rush's final game for Liverpool, before moving to Italy in 1987, was also a washout, again in Israel: 'We'd all had a bit to drink and we didn't do ourselves anything near justice.' The game, before a large local crowd, was ignominiously lost, 3–0. This was the last time for a while, however, that Rush would spend any real leisure time with his team-mates. In Italy, things would be very different.

As early as the beginning of 1984, when Rush was just twenty-two, the Italian club, Napoli, had come in with a huge transfer bid (some £4.5 million) for the striker, waving massive wages to match. Rush, by now with extended horizons, was happy to take the money, but Liverpool refused to let him leave. Napoli signed the peerless Diego Maradona instead, and Rush 'blanked' Liverpool chairman, John Smith for months afterwards. Two years later, new Liverpool manager, Kenny Dalglish, informed Rush of more Italian interest, this time from Juventus. The deal now suited Liverpool: it brought in cash to cover some of the losses produced by the Heysel ban, and it also helped in a small way to heal the still open wounds with Juve. Again, the money was good, so Rush and his advisers decided the time was right. Because of restrictions on the number of foreign players in Italy, Liverpool could keep Rush for a year, even though he had already 'signed' for Juventus.

Some fans on Merseyside organized a 'Rush must stay' campaign, but Liverpool had no hope of matching the Juventus offer, and most supporters in the city, in any case, sympathized with his 'for the sake of my family' line and wished him good luck. Moving to another British club would have been sacrilege; moving to distant Italy, where the wages were delivered in wheelbarrows, well, anyone would be crazy to turn it down. In his final Liverpool season before the move, when his mind might, justifiably, already have been elsewhere, he scored *just* forty goals in fifty-seven matches, for his English 'loan' club.

The nature of the deal also allowed a full year of preparation for the move to Italy. But, while Tracy got on with her Italian classes, Ian mused over the potential loss of his favourite eggs and beans diet. The portents were not great. When the couple first arrived in Italy, Rush was asked by the Italian press pack about all things English, from the Falklands and Shakespeare to Charles and Di. But hadn't he come here to play *football*? On this front, Juve liked a 'defensive' counter-attacking game, but their great midfielder, Platini, had just retired, while Michael Laudrup was having a poor time. Who would supply Rush in this period of transition? And where would the *craic* come from among these stylish aesthetes who were now his new team- mates? There were plenty of questions, but with few signs of convincing answers.

After a decent start, with goals in early friendlies, the depth – and the cleverness and cynicism – of *Serie A* defending meant goals were much harder to come by at senior level. He managed just seven. Rush's lack of Italian also isolated him inside the dressing-room and brought back grim memories of early Stalag Anfield. Expensive new foreign signings in Italy were expected to be sometimes highly strung, certainly domin-eering, personalities. They would have been slaughtered, of course, back at Liverpool. Life at Juve was *meant* to be part sporting epic, part showbiz extravaganza, part soap opera. It just was not Rushie's style. Even decent victories produced none of the cherished collective celebra-tions that had so bonded the lads back at Anfield. Here, the players went home to their families.

Club owner, Agnelli, nicknamed, *il avvocato*, the lawyer, tried to be supportive, but club president, Boniperti, was only evasive, while the Juve manager, Marchesi, was weak and ever under pressure. Rush was soon left lonely and demoralized. He began to fear his telephone was bugged. When Liverpool sensed that new foreign signings might squeeze Rush out at Juventus, they enquired about a possible quick return for their striker. He jumped at the chance, even with his wages halved. He returned to Liverpool in 1988 playing almost all his old tunes. In the 'Hillsborough' Cup Final of 1989 the Everton staff were relieved to see their dreaded adversary, reduced by injury, sitting on the substitutes' bench. No matter: he came on to score twice to win the trophy again for Liverpool.

Ironically, the highlight of Rush's stay in Italy was playing for Wales in a violent international against the *Azzurri* in Brescia in June 1988. The visitors, famously, won 1–0. Rush, inevitably, scored the goal, something, at least, to show his many doubters in Italy. He had always loved playing for Wales, though as a north Walian, with strong 'scouse' connections, he was certainly not one for banging out the anthem: he didn't know the words. From his debut at Hampden in May 1980, until a falling out with the hapless Welsh manager, Bobby Gould, in 1996, he boasted of missing only one international when he was fit, a friendly against Spain in Valencia in 1982. Paisley had urged him not to play: he was quite exhausted after a punishing campaign with Liverpool. His Welshness was important to Rush. When he won the PFA award for player of the season for 1983/4, his usual nerves in public venues were stilled by the prospect of receiving the award from another proud patriot, Neil Kinnock: 'He's a Welshman through and through', commented Rush, approvingly. 'More like the leader of Plaid Cymru than the Labour Party!'

Rush wrote in his first autobiography about the emotional and physical 'biffs' of playing for his country, which he did a record seventy-three times. Even winning championships and cups galore for Liverpool, clearly, never really came close to compensating for Wales missing out on qualification for all the major finals during Rush's era. 'Three million Welshman who will feel some pride if we win', he liked to remind the scoffers. 'You can't get a bigger incentive than that.'

Things were undoubtedly made harder at international level by the routine ineptitude of the Welsh FA. Rush had little time for the committee men, who flew first class while the players went economy. Some of them even got wrong the names of Welsh players they had helped to select. Joey Jones had christened the Welsh national squad 'Ragass Rovers' when they trained in ill-fitting kit before a crucial World Cup qualifier in Scotland in 1986. The Scottish *youth* squad had better gear, but this kind of neglect also fired up Rush and his men to show their detractors that, whilst playing for Wales may lack some of the football glamour of other nations, 'Nothing', as Rush put it, 'can surpass the pride and pleasure of pulling on a Welsh jersey.'

Apart from the satisfying winner in Brescia, a lightning strike by Rush also secured a famous European Championship qualifying win in 1991 in Cardiff against the world champions, West Germany. A win against England, at Wrexham in 1984, was also a special moment, as was a 1–0 triumph over Brazil in 1991. When Terry Yorath first offered him the Welsh captaincy, against Malta in a friendly in Valetta in June 1988, Rush described it as, 'One of the proudest moments of my life. I felt fit to burst with pride.'

Mostly, however, it was bitter disappointment with Wales. In November 1993, a victory at Cardiff against the wobbling Romanians would have taken the Welsh to the USA for the 1994 World Cup finals, a fitting reward for Rush's loyalty and his whole-hearted commitment to the cause. Instead, it was another demoralizing defeat. Despite all this, Rush was almost unswervingly supportive of his international managers throughout his Welsh career and threatened, with other senior players, to 'strike' when first Mike England, and then Terry Yorath, were threatened with the sack by the Welsh FA. His patience was finally breached when Englishman, Gould, left Rush out of a Welsh squad to play Holland in 1996. Wales, disgraced, lost, 7–1. Rush, uncharacteristically, blasted Gould in the press. He never played for his country again.

In 1995, Liverpool signed the very un-Rush-like Stan Collymore for a record £8.5 million. In 1996, when Rush rejected a new one-year deal, Liverpool offered the Welshman a free transfer. Even at thirty-three, and commanding a signing-on fee of £500,000 and wages of £8,000 a week, some fourteen clubs came in for him. He eventually went to Leeds United, but soon found the new Leeds manager, George Graham's methods negative and uninspiring. Scoring was also becoming increasingly difficult: Rush managed only three goals for Leeds in thirty-six games. In 1997 he moved on, briefly, to Newcastle United, and then on loan to Sheffield United, but by this time some of the spark – if not the enthusiasm – had, understandably, gone from his game.

Declining to 'leave at the top' and perhaps wanting to contribute something specifically to the *Welsh* game, Rush next rejected overtures from Japan to join his old Welsh colleagues, Joey Jones and Brian Flynn, at Wrexham as a player-coach. He still had problems, though, articulating his thoughts about the game: he was nervous even when talking to awe-inspired youngsters in the Wrexham youth team. On the field, he could not buy a goal for his new club and he gradually moved back into midfield. In 1999, at thirty-seven, it was clear it was time to pull the curtain down. Playing was no longer an option: coaching in a professional club seemed unsuited to his character and to his real talents as a player.

In a career spanning almost two decades Rush had won every major domestic title with Liverpool, including five League Championships. He had also finally secured a European Cup winner's medal in 1984. After a brief stint in Australia he set up the Ian Rush Finishing School for young strikers, which now travels the land offering tips to young players. One can already feel the hairs rising on the backs of the necks of defenders charged with curbing young Rush graduates. Rush was described by *The Guardian*'s Stephen Bierley in 1994 as having, 'Not an ounce of puffed up pride or self importance. He remains the nicest and most approachable of men.' When 'Rushie', as he was known universally throughout the game here, addressed the crowd at Anfield before his testimonial match against Celtic in the same year he said, with typical grace: 'I'd like to say thank you for the fourteen years you've looked after me. You've been magnificent and I will love you always.'

Did Rushie score a goal against Celtic? Well, what do you think?

I would like to thank Sam Neatrour for some of the original research done for this chapter.

Neville Southall

Rob Steen

Tony: Who's in goal for East Cheam, anyway?
Sid (checking paper): Um . . . Chalky White.
Tony: Chalky White. Oh well, we've had it. We won't get a draw with him
between the sticks. Biggest score in history. Ninety minutes of kick-offs and
goals. He's useless, that man. Not only can't he see them coming – he has a
job finding them once they're in. Wandering about the back of the net
poking around here and there. . . he kicked his hat out twice last week.

(Hancock's Half Hour, 1959)

For those with short attention spans, there are two things crucial to an understanding of Neville Southall's refreshingly reticent place in our cultural constellation. The first is that Pat Jennings once exalted the man hailed by the *Daily Mail* as 'the game's last working-class hero' as a goalkeeper 'without a weakness', which is a bit like Alexander the Great composing Napoléon Bonaparte's epitaph. That the compliment was duly repaid virtually verbatim – 'there was not a single weakness in [Jennings's] game' – suggests either an acute sense of politesse or a mutual appreciation society without equal in the entire history of Celtic relations. In the spring of 1986, as fate would have it, Big Pat came out of retirement to serve as cover for Big Nev. One can only guess at the lovey-doveying that ensued.

The other essential factoid is that when David Farr's play *Neville Southall's Washbag* transferred to London's West End, the title was changed, for disreputably commercial reasons, to *Elton John's Glasses*. When the stage show honouring England's most reputable crisp promoter graduated from the fringe, who would have had the gall to propose that Gary Lineker's name be substituted by that of, say, David Bowie? Granted, there may well be those who sincerely believe that the Pasha of Pinner has contributed more to civilization than the Laird of Llandudno, but even among such blinkered dolts this was surely a cause for regret. It was not as if the old Crocodile Rocker was in dire need of the royalties, let alone a reminder of his shortcomings in the optical and taste departments. Then again, if ever a figure with a high public profile derived pleasure from the shadows, it was Southall.

In an age when every Tom, Dick and 'Pretty Boy' Shaw is availing the world of his dreary and misbegotten ways, it is a salient fact that Southall is the most celebrated sportsman never to have lent his name to an autobiography. The closest approximation, ironically, was *Everton Blues*, a largely monodimensional diary of the 1996/7 season, which began with his 700th League appearance but soon descended into the least pleasant of his career (in December he was hailed by his manager, Joe Royle, as the Premiership's best; by the end of January he had been dropped for the first time in fifteen years). For that alone, he warrants a lofty plinth in the pantheon.

The movie would be a hoot. Gene Hackman as Southall, endlessly whingeing or snarling, indomitable yet self-effacing, doing it his way while observing the key laws of the jungle: the craggy maverick as team man. And who better for the key role of the hard-drinking Howard Kendall, the boss who flogged him hardest but understood him best – 'It became my greatest ambition', said Southall, 'to give [Kendall] nothing to criticize' – than Robert Duvall? The part, after all, would be a fusion of Colonel Kilgore, the napalm-loving anti-hero of *Apocalypse Now*, and Tom Hagen, the squeaky-clean *consigliere* whose extra-marital affair provides much the most shocking moment in *The Godfather.*

Given his impeccable track record for depicting the quirks and struggles of the athlete as a backdrop to making broader points about the nature of existence – and provided, of course, that he can shelve the middle-aged Statesider's antipathy for 'sahh-ker' – Ron Shelton would be the ideal director. As the only man to concoct more than one truly memorable piece of celluloid about sport (*Bull Durham* and *Cobb*, plus the only marginally less terrific *White Men Can't Jump* and *Tin Cup*), not to mention the only one with a convincing feel for dressing-room dialogue, he would certainly relish the prospect of ferreting out and unravelling the clues. *Llandudno Men Can't Smile*, anyone?

'Celebrity', Shelton told me recently, exuding compassion, 'is a sickness.' All the signs are that Southall sussed that out early. In the immediate aftermath of his £150,000 transfer from Bury to Everton he would repeatedly reflect on his non-League experiences with Llandudno Swifts, Bangor City, Conway United and Winsford United, of labouring on a building site or collecting dustbins while completing the less than negligible transition from centre-back to keeper. It was a mantra, a way of maintaining perspective.

Not that it was an entirely meteoric rise. Turning professional with Bury in 1981 initially proved less lucrative than schlepping that hod around; he and his wife were forced to sell furniture to pay a heating bill. Roundly rubbished in his second season following a 5–0 roasting in the Merseyside derby, he was briefly shipped to Port Vale on loan. By the time he finally secured the freehold to Everton's number-1 shirt he was already in his mid-twenties. As reputation and confidence grew, so the need to humour the fourth estate receded. One reporter recalls 'the deadpan face' and unslakeable thirst for 'piss-taking'. The latter would be in particularly mischievous evidence prior to an international. 'That was when the English press naturally gravitated to him. "We've got better in Everton reserves than Van Basten" he'd say. You could picture him chuckling as he read the papers. Once he said, "I think I'll manage England!" It took us two years to cotton on! Then he stopped. But he still tried to perpetuate the old "keepers are mental" cliché.'

Can there be any more nauseating adage than the one which attests that the more efficient a keeper is, the less confident he must therefore be about the whereabouts of his marbles? Here, surely, is the ultimate one-man show, just the ticket for individualists with a penchant for exhibitionism. Besides, coping with the attendant stresses demands a mental acuity and discipline far beyond the vast majority. Pat Jennings summed up the unfairness of it all. 'Goals are always someone's mistake. It's impossible to have a goal without the manager being able to point at someone. Very often the obvious one is the goalie. One mistake and that's it. You can't redeem it, the way a forward can. He can miss five and then score one and everyone's pleased. Everybody sees a goalie's mistakes. That's the way it is.'

Southall once co-owned an antique clock emporium. An Everton follower recollects meeting him at Llandudno Town Hall while his hero was immersed in one of those gratuitously over-the-top American extravaganzas that so expertly mock the noble fraternity of Greco-Roman wrestlers. Whether either of these peccadilloes renders him sufficiently touched to qualify as a 'typical keeper' is open to considerable doubt. Set beside John 'Budgie' Burridge, indeed, he is nothing if not yawn-worthy. One evening in 1996, Burridge agreed to sign for his twenty-first club, Queen of the South, then – as was his wont – retired to bed in his goalkeeping gloves. So driven had he once been to emulate Peter Shilton that he took a photo of him to his barber and demanded the same perm, poodle curl for poodle curl. During his formative years in Workington, he was regularly beaten by his father, 'a rough, hard-drinking man' who became a casualty of the pits when his son was fifteen, saddling him with responsibilities before he was equipped, much less ready. 'I'm forty-four going on seventeen', he proclaimed with a puppy-like grin and nary a trace of embarrassment. Some will stop at nothing to reclaim the youth they never had. Or, in Southall's case, the hope he never had.

If the seeds of inspiration were embedded in less traumatized soil, Southall's flowering was also enhanced by a dedication bordering on the obsessive, not to say a tolerant spouse. At Everton the training ritual was set in stone: first in the changing-room, last to shower. Even in five-a-sides his competitiveness was palpable. Delighting in putting one over the specialists, he would taunt Andy Gray and Graeme Sharp whenever he bulged more nets than they. That zeal to succeed, to transcend past incarnations – though never decry or diminish – was fuelled by a pursuit of perfectionism. 'You sense', pondered Peter Johnson in the *Mail*, 'that all his life has been driven by the late-starter's fear that one moment of relaxation would put him back on the bins.' How the failure of others to meet his standards must have niggled. Another reason to stay in coaching, to pass on that expertise (for all that, when Mark Hughes became Wales manager he strangely had no desire for the acting player-coach's services). Management is for those able to comprehend imperfection.

The 1984 FA Cup final, scene of his first significant winner's medal, saw Southall get one over the piano player, Everton defeating Elton John's Watford 2–0, thanks in no small part to Andy Gray heading the ball from Steve Sherwood's grasp in a creditable impression of Nat Lofthouse's equally dubious (and decisive) barge on Harry Gregg at Wembley twenty-six Mays previously. You could no more picture Southall allowing himself to be so intimidated than Sylvester Stallone playing the lead in *Gandhi*. Gray, indeed, contended that sheer strength made Southall 'almost intimidating', the qualification decidedly curious.

'I worked a lot on intimidation', Southall once confessed. 'Not so much physically as mentally dominating the box so that it forced players to think – something most of them couldn't do.' In the estimation of Kevin Ratcliffe, so often the penultimate line of Southall's defences for club and country, Everton gave away precious few penalties during their pomp 'because we didn't have to'. Why bother bringing opponents down when the chap at the back was a better-than-even bet to prevail in any mano-a-mano collisions?

The greatest irony about Big Nev, of course, is that he has never remotely justified his *nom de plume*, at least not literally. Amid the hallowed ranks of colossal custodians, that wimpish 6ft 1in., after all, leaves him far behind the likes of 'Fatty' Foulke and 'Mighty Joe' Corrigan. The moniker, surely, refers to that metaphysical aura. How many strikers, the night before tackling him, have dreamed of a beast lurking somewhere between John Lennon's Walrus and Fungus the Bogeyman?

Inasmuch as it captures that disdain for surface gloss, the alternate alias, 'Baggy', seems more apt. As understatements go, to say that Southall has never been the apogee of dapperhood is a bit like declaring that Debussy deployed chords and crotchets with a pleasing ear for order. Nor has age withered that passion for anti-fashion statements. A survey of Liverpool fans as late as the mid-1990s – taken shortly after a post-match interview for which he had removed his jersey to uncover a cut-off T-shirt festooned with irrefutable evidence of his toils – saw 'Bin Man' romp away with the coveted 'Scruffiest Player Ever' award. He polled sixteen votes, more than three times as many as George Best, the runner-up.

It often struck me, I must admit, as an act. When a chap habitually wears the collar of his undershirt half outside his jersey, and shin pads outside socks, it goes beyond the lax. Was he lulling the opposition into equating sloppy attire with carelessness? Had somebody secretly advised him that *al fresco* shin-pads afforded better protection? Or was he simply trying to live up to all that working-class-hero schtick? If nothing else, the indifference to outside perception seems plain. The Volvo he brought to training during his Goodison days, according to one regular observer, perpetually groaned with 'junk and dogs'. Southall, he added, 'always seemed happy to be a slob'.

But what a slob. If the *Rothmans Book of Football Records* is to be trusted, Wales boasts 16,000 registered footballers. The same as

Vietnam, a tad above Tahiti, Armenia and Macedonia, fewer than Tunisia, Iceland or Egypt. Consider the conspicuous dearth of household names to have emerged from Cairo and Saigon, and the memory of a Welshman soaring to the summit of his trade gains in improbability. That his pre-sporting life saw him cook, carry a hod and collect refuse merely adds to the seductive charm (a phrase, admittedly, that sits a mite uncomfortably when applied to a bloke whom one strongly suspects would sooner sell life insurance to a tortoise than sell himself).

It hardly requires a newly qualified Celt (all right, a Londoner transplanted to Cornwall) to point out that Wales has done appreciably more than its bit for the furtherance of athletic appreciation across the planet. Wilde and Winstone, Meredith and Charles, Reardon and Jackson, Gareth and Barry, JPR and Merv: all have elevated standards and raised spirits. Yet in terms of sustained quality, a measure of greatness that defies both exactitude and contradiction, none can touch Big Nev. As of June 1999, according to the Recreational Sport Soccer Statistics Foundation, he held the distinction of being comfortably the best-known of the half-dozen shot-stoppers who possess their country's record number of caps – the others, in case you question such bumptious presumptiousness, being Borislav Mikhailov (Bulgaria), Drazen Ladic (Croatia), Peter Rufai (Nigeria), Roberto Fernandez (Paraguay) and Rodolfo Rodriguez (Uruguay). Even so, those ninety-two matching items of tassled headwear represent but the tip of an imperious iceberg.

From 1988/9 to 1991/2 he appeared in all 156 of Everton's engagements in the world's most rigorous and punishing league (which is not quite the same as the best, as Wapping and Canary Wharf seldom tire of asserting). Come the end of the 1995/6 campaign, now pushing thirty-eight, he had missed only three such dates in eight seasons. Not bad for a fellow obliged to put his head at the mercy of onrushing boots on a weekly basis. Those record 751 stints as a Toffeeman, moreover, constitute almost twice the tally of Ted Sagar, the man whose mark he erased. In 1994/5, his thirty-seventh year, that fortress remained impregnable for seven consecutive games, a sequence unparalleled in Premier League annals: a single goal, a lone error, in four of those matches would have meant relegation. Between 15 November and 11 May in the title-winning season of 1986/7, to take an even purpler patch, he permitted just fourteen goals in twenty-seven League outings. On seventeen occasions during that run he kept a pristine sheet (a feat he managed on 272 occasions for Everton alone); only twice did he concede more than one in a match. He made the staggering common-place.

'In 1985 he made this save against Tottenham, from Mark Falco', recounts Mark Tallentire, an Everton follower for thirty years and counting, the incredulity still fresh. 'Five yards out and he still got up to the top corner! He said it was his finest, I think. Well, he did that once a month!' Mark, incidentally, claims to be one of only 7,914 people to have seen Southall score a senior goal (Full Members Cup quarter-final v. Charlton, Goodison Park, 3 March 1987: a firmly thwacked contribution to a penalty shootout that went awry). 'We loved him, but we saw him wane before our eyes. He was mortal by 1992.'

The plunder has been suitably extensive: two League championships, two FA Cups, a European Cup Winners' Cup, plus a Footballer of the Year award (the first Evertonian recipient). Yet how many more might there have been but for the banning of England's finest and fittest from European competition in the wake of the Heysel tragedy? The 1984/5 season, after all, was the most productive in Goodison history, the Toffees usurping Liverpool with a vengeance, relieving them of their domestic title by a record margin of thirteen points, then sauntering past Hans Krankl and Rapid Vienna in Rotterdam to secure the club's only continental honour to date. The sole disappointment came at Wembley two days later, when Southall had the misfortune to fall foul of Norman Whiteside's astonishing curler, ensuring lasting fame as the poor soul on the receiving end of the most audacious shot to win an FA Cup.

All of which begs one question. For all the eerie anticipation, uncanny reflexes and implausible agility that enabled this heavy-footed, cumbersome-looking individual to dive two different ways to block the same shot (witness the double save from Manchester United's Paul Scholes that resolved the 1995 FA Cup final), for all Franz Beckenbauer's famous insistence that 'Wales always have a chance because they've got the best goalkeeper in the world', why does 'the last working-class hero' appear to be so unloved? Being a mere stopper of shots cannot help. Nor that his derring-do occurred mostly on the wrong side of Stanley Park. 'No other ground has songsters to compare – / Except for

Goodison across the park!' acknowledged Peter Maloney in 'Ode to the Kop', but such largesse is rare, even from those without an emotional stake in the debate. 'For the joy of the game, / Yes the great red heart of the great red game,' asserted Adrian Mitchell in his post-Hillsborough poem 'By the Waters of Liverpool', reinforcing a now-ancient verity. By the Mersey, as by the Manchester Ship Canal, red, not blue, is the colour.

Evertonians point to an incident at half-time on the opening day of the 1990/1 season, an episode so bizarre that a decade has done nothing to dilute its magnificence. There they were, drawing breath and comparing tans, when out, well ahead of schedule, ambled a sheepish-looking Southall in his Jackson-Pollock-meets-Mondrian jersey. Initially, eyebrows steadfastly refused to arch; the notion of such a zealot opting for mid-match practice was not that far-fetched. Whereupon he sat down, back to a goalpost, silently fuming. 'Southall in sit-down strike', roared the tabloids. Manchester United had apparently made an offer for his services, whereupon the Everton board had blocked the deal, hence the militant action. He was fined a week's wages. The next home game saw a pointed banner fluttering in the breeze: 'Once a binman, always a binman.'

As with so many aspects of Southall's career – and much of the credit goes to that scampish attitude towards the media – distilling fact from the whirlpool of rumour, innuendo and accepted wisdom is a task beset by bluff and blind alleys. The alternative version, as duly apprised to a few journalists, was more rugged: a dressing-room row had reached such a pitch that the fiery Southall had been sent back out to cool off lest he did something he (or, more likely, a team-mate) would regret. 'Nev ended up feeling a bit foolish that day', recalls one correspondent. 'He was forever saying he could move to a bigger and better club, but he never did because, at heart, he was perfectly happy.'

Not that he was shy when the cause demanded. After Wales's elimination from the 1998 World Cup, he waded in with both feet: '[The Wales FA] need to get off their backsides and make a ten-year plan. I hope it reaches crisis point. Someone has to wake up at two in the morning and realise that we're in the shit.' In *Everton Blues*, meanwhile, came a withering treatise on what it apparently took to fulfil his next ambition, namely to enter management (ideally at Goodison). 'People say you need experience, but experience of what?' he wondered bitterly towards the end of the season, shortly before Royle resigned. 'I'd rather be experienced as a winner than a loser. I can't see the point of employing someone who was a loser at his last place. It's fantastic – it must be the only sport in the world where you can flop but still get another job next week. People have made a career out of being failures.'

And, in Southall's case, being stubborn. 'You didn't argue with Neville,' stressed Ian Rush, like Ratcliffe a companion on endless commutes from Wales to Merseyside. 'What he said was right, even if everybody else knew it was wrong.' Southall accepts that he seldom aimed to please. 'I've never been a conformist,' he assured the *Mail*. As his romantic liasions, dangerous and highly unorthodox, bore out.

Eryl met Neville on a blind date in Llandudno. He was eighteen, bumbling along in the refuse business and keeping for Bangor City at weekends. They married in 1980, initially enjoying what she later described to the *News of the World* as 'a loving relationship . . . we went for long walks with our dog Broody. There were no hints at him being interested in other women. Then one morning he came out of the bathroom without the black bushy moustache I liked so much.' It transpired that whenever hubbie had a fling he would shave to avoid recognition. 'It was if he was trying to tell me something,' said Eryl, 'like a naughty schoolboy wanting to be found out but not having the guts to tell the truth.' The first time she forgave him. And the second. Whereupon he made an exceedingly public, if entirely misconstrued, response, lifting his jersey during the 1985 Charity Shield to reveal a vest bearing the inscription, 'I love my wife.' So far as Joe and Joanne Public were concerned, this was little more than cringe-inducing confirmation that Southall was that oddest of oddballs: the superstar who, rather than booze with the lads/cavort with the lasses, cannot wait to get home to the missus.

Not that this signified a reformation. News of a six-year affair with a waitress broke in 1997, shattering that carefully cultivated image of wholesomeness. That it took more than a decade for reality to reach the popular prints testifies to the loyalty of Southall's colleagues as well as to the inordinate depth of Eryl's patience (which ultimately, understandably, expired). On second thoughts, perhaps he is simply more lovable than he seems? And still (as I write) he remains firmly, proudly smitten. A free transfer from Everton having led to stints at Southend, Stoke, Doncaster and then Torquay, there he was at the outset of a new century, forty-one years young, still toting that washbag. How could you not marvel at his working week? Commuting 1,000 miles a week in a Vauxhall between Llandudno and coaching assignments in Huddersfield, Tranmere and Bradford, flying south-west for match days only, squeezing in the odd word of encouragement for Eifion Williams, a callow striker from Carmarthen. Cue a midweek mayday from an injury-beset Bradford City club stretching every sturdy sinew and limited resource to prove its manhood in the Premiership. The selfsame club for whom Chris Waddle had converted a 40-yard chip to put Everton out of the Cup a few years earlier, embarrassing Southall and hastening his exit from Goodison. Wes Saunders, Torquay's manager, eschewed sensitivity: he had let Southall go because he had recently cost the side a couple of points. If Southall was hurt, he disguised it well, confining his comments to the occasional razor-edged aside. 'I still believe in my ability,' he pronounced, 'and obviously somebody in the Premiership believes it too. But to be honest, I would rather still be at Torquay.'

The sentiment persisted. 'I wish I'd been at Torquay', he reiterated to *Wales on Sunday* after what may prove to be one of the more synchronicitous Saturdays in Welsh footballing lore. While that similarly durable boyo 'Deano' Saunders was scoring the winner for Bradford against Arsenal, there was Big Nev, backside adjusting to life on the bench, attention diverted by a more pressing matter some 400 miles distant. Was Ryan Northmore, his 19-year-old Plainmoor protégé, keeping a clean sheet? He was. Better still, Torquay, to Southall's transparent delight, thrashed Halifax 4–0, with young Eifion notching a hat-trick on debut. All guilt trips should be defused so efficiently.

He also informed *Wales on Sunday* that his 'dream' was to finish his career in the ailing League of Wales. Could we detect a mellowing? Not according to the evidence of a recent outing for Hednesford United. The visitors were leading when the ball went behind for a goal kick, whereupon Southall pursued it with about as much urgency as a snail chasing a chef. Condemnation from the terraces was swift and unequivocal yet the offender remained oblivious, pausing only to emit a mild snarl. The late starter never knows when he is finished.

Ryan Giggs

David Eastwood

On 14 April 1999 Manchester United faced Arsenal in a FA Cup semi-final replay at Villa Park. United's season was on a knife edge: they were still in the UEFA Champions' League and chasing the Premiership, but now were reduced to ten men and fighting to stay in the FA Cup. In extra time a pulsating game seemed to be heading towards the synthetic climax of a penalty shootout, when suddenly the match reached its apotheosis with a goal of transcendent quality. Ryan Giggs picked up the ball fifteen yards inside the United half. In a mesmerizing run he beat defender after defender and then scored with a thunderous shot into the roof of the net. Football is sometimes a game devalued by hyperbole, but when Alex Ferguson described this as a 'historic' goal, no one demurred. When he hailed it as 'one of the best goals ever scored in major football', few disagreed. Many footballers can score fine goals, only the greatest score goals as such as this.

This one goal symbolized Giggs's career and footballing greatness: mesmeric ball control, the ability to float past defenders, pace and balance, courage and commitment, and sheer exuberance in scoring. His goal opened the road to Manchester United's unique treble of winning the Premiership, FA Cup, and European Champions' League. United had been beguiled by the dream of 'the treble' throughout the later 1990s; since 1968 the club had desperately sought to repeat its single triumph in the European Cup. Two Championships had been lost by a single point, in 1997/8 United won nothing, and the greatest prize, the UEFA Champions' League, had eluded them year after year. Fans were fearful that history would repeat itself with a tragic inevitability. Arsène Wenger's Arsenal, double winners the previous season, was a team of genuine quality. Often teams comfort themselves with clichéd solace – defeat in one competition would enable them to concentrate on another. United supporters knew better. With defeat in one competition, the whole dream might again fade. In 1999 such anxieties were assuaged in Giggs's moment of transformation. Within a month the treble had been won. In the great arena of the Nou Camp, United defeated Bayern Munich with two goals in injury time. After this most extraordinary victory Ryan Giggs was the first player to embrace Alex

Ferguson. At twenty-five he was the longest serving player in Ferguson's all-conquering side.

Although Manchester United is a club that inspires enthusiasm and hatred in a uniquely passionate way, although rival supporters constantly urge one another to 'stand up if you hate Man. U', Giggs's goal, like Giggs's talent, stood outside this passionate antipathy. Everyone applauded; everyone who loved the game hailed this as a moment of consummate beauty in the beautiful game. Ryan Giggs was a player who compelled admiration and escaped the polarizing mixture of envy and criticism that defined the popular reputation of so many stars.

His semi-final goal also recalled a former United number 11, George Best. That comparison had been made early in Giggs's career and continued to be made thereafter. They both had the same close control, the same cruel ability to devastate defenders by their pace or turn them with an almost balletic sense of balance. They both had the same eye for goal. They also had similarly striking looks, and both had complex and rich ethnic identities: Best as a Northern Irish Protestant, Giggs as a Welshman with mixed ancestry. These parallels could be and were overplayed. Best was an even more complete player: genuinely two-footed, and a wonderful header of the ball. Indeed to many who saw him Best lingers in the memory as a unique talent. He was also, notoriously, a victim of his talent, and his ended as a career corroded rather than crowned by stardom. By contrast Giggs's personality managed to comprehend his talent. He lived life to the full, but not to overflowing. He carefully policed the borderlines between his public career and his private life and, long after fame beckoned, he retained strong commitments to family and friends. His manager, Alex Ferguson, relates one incident where he was informed that the young Ryan Giggs, Lee Sharpe, and other young professionals were partying loudly between two important games. Ferguson arrived and ordered them home, cuffing each errant player on the back of the head. Giggs, according to Ferguson, never transgressed again. He was, Ferguson believed, 'a fine young man' and 'a credit to his mother'. Many careers were destroyed by excess. Giggs saw and rejected such excess, and in so doing gave his talent full rein and earned respect throughout his sport.

Ryan Giggs was born Ryan Wilson, in Cardiff, on 29 November 1973. He lived in the Welsh capital until he was seven: long enough to acquire a Welsh accent, the words of the Welsh anthem, and a sense of actually being Welsh. Throughout his later career, when people bemoaned his being Welsh and thus confined to playing on the margins of international football, Giggs would reply simply that he was Welsh, and was 'proud to be Welsh'. After leaving Cardiff he would return regularly for weekends and summer holidays. His father, Danny Wilson, signed for Swinton Rugby League Club after making a handful of appearances at fly-half for Cardiff. Ryan moved north reluctantly. He attended Grosvenor Road Primary School in Swinton, shed his Welsh accent because he was teased for it by other kids, and shone as a footballer. From early days he was a natural athlete, with pace, balance and a passion for the game. He played everywhere, was a capable goalkeeper, but gravitated naturally to the left wing. A destiny was emerging.

By all accounts Ryan was a quiet child, respectful towards his teachers, but with a passion for football. A reputation soon spread. Although he played rugby league on Sundays – predictably as stand-off – no one seems to have doubted that football was his natural game. He soon progressed to Salford juniors and made a mark in Lancashire junior football. Like all Mancunians, he had to make a choice between United and City. Ryan chose United, saw his first game when he was eight or nine, and remembers only Mickey Thomas, 'because he was Welsh'. In so far as a quiet demeanour allowed, Ryan became a passionate Stretford-ender. Sometimes he chanted, but most of the time he just watched. Mark Hughes and Bryan Robson adorned his bedroom. He loved Hughes 'for his spectacular goals and, of course, for the fact that he was Welsh'. In the way that it only can for those who live nearby, Manchester United was entering his blood.

Then an odd thing happened. Dennis Schofield, a devoted City supporter and scout, recommended Ryan to the Manchester City School of Excellence. He trained there from the age of nine to fourteen. United knew about him and were tracking him. Ryan would arrive in United colours, but City wanted to keep hold of the lad. Things may have worked out differently had Alex Ferguson not arrived at United in 1986. Manchester United's scouting system had been poorly managed and its youth policy in disarray. Harold Wood alerted Ferguson to Ryan. Joe Brown was instructed to watch him, and Ferguson gave Ryan a trial. For Ferguson this first sight of Ryan was 'one of those rare and priceless moments . . . A gold miner who has searched every part of river or mountain and then suddenly finds himself staring at a nugget could not feel more exhilaration than I did watching Giggs that day'. On the evening of his fourteenth birthday, Ferguson arrived at Ryan's house, talked with the lad and his mother, and signed him on schoolboy forms. The short march to United stardom had begun.

Already there were signs that Giggs was unusually self-possessed and focused. His parents had separated and Ryan was being brought up by his mother. As a statement of identity, affection and commitment, Ryan took his mother Lynn's surname and Ryan Wilson became Ryan Giggs. Having joined United shortly after Ferguson's arrival, he also witnessed Ferguson's remarkable reconstruction of the club and was one of the first of Ferguson's own protégés to make his mark at the highest levels. There were others in this first generation of Ferguson youngsters, but they fell by the way for a variety of reasons. Lee Sharpe and Ferguson's own son Darren both made the first team before Giggs, but Giggs's temperament honed his talent whilst Sharpe squandered his, and Darren Ferguson never had Giggs's exquisite skills. At the age of sixteen Giggs left school and became a full-time apprentice professional on £29.50 per week plus £10 expenses.

From then on, Giggs's career was carefully managed. A prodigious talent was nurtured and a young man shielded from premature celebrity. He made his full debut on 4 May 1991, fittingly against Manchester City. United won 1–0, the winning goal emerging from a goalmouth scramble. The ball hit Giggs and others on the way in. Typically Ferguson credited the debutant with the goal, made him the toast of red Manchester, and did not play him for the remainder of the season. The following season he became a regular, scored four times, and won the Rumbelows Cup. In 1992 and 1993 he became the first player to win the Professional Footballers' Association 'Young Player of the Year' award twice. The press started to clamour for interviews. Ferguson, however, ruthlessly shielded the young Giggs from interviews and prying television cameras. Ferguson's relations with the press may have suffered grievously through such fastidiousness, but the careers of youngsters such as Giggs, and later David Beckham, Nicky Butt, the Neville brothers, and Paul Scholes, were thus nurtured to maturity.

Giggs, a United supporter before he was a United player, felt the pain of failure more than most. In 1991/2 he was part of the team which agonizingly finished second to Leeds United in the final Division One League Championship. But Giggs and United now stood on the verge of success without parallel in the club's history. The next eight seasons would see United winning the Premier League six times, the FA Cup three times, the double twice, and the UEFA Champions' League once. By the time United won the Champions' League, Giggs has played 375 times for the club and scored seventy-nine goals. From his first full season onwards, Giggs's talent was beyond question. For a while he vied with Lee Sharpe on the left, but soon claimed the left wing as his by right with Sharpe dropping back. The young Giggs sometimes mesmerized even himself. He tried to take on one too many defenders. His eye for goal shut out team-mates in space. Defenders would try to make him cut in and shoot on his weaker right foot.

Yet Giggs's was not just a precocious talent, it was a developing talent. His game became more mature. His vision became wider, his movement bolder, his flexibility much greater. When opposing teams put two men on Giggs, he saw this as a challenge, allowed the rest of the team to exploit the space thus created and tracked back as necessary. In the Champions' League victory against Bayern Munich in 1999, with a midfield decimated by the suspension of Roy Keane and Paul Scholes, Ferguson initially played Giggs on the right. The critics roared disapproval as Ferguson lauded Giggs. 'The strain Ryan put on them', Ferguson later commented, 'was one of the factors that steadily drained them in the second half.' In mid career Giggs, the natural left-winger, was also hugely flexible. Regularly he could switch with Andy Cole or Dwight Yorke, moving to inside-forward to pull defensive strategies out of shape. He was not the world's most natural tackler, but his pace and fitness enabled him to cover effectively. Throughout a match his head would remain high and his appetite and work-rate unrelenting. As his club and international managers averred, Giggs was a professionals' professional.

Indeed, there was a time when Giggs's virtue threatened to overwhelm his natural talent. He worked so hard to develop his vision, his awareness of space and his passing game, that for a time he ran at defences less. Ferguson has commented that Giggs's 'inner struggle to become the complete player has frequently inhibited the expression of

[his] amazing talent'. For Ferguson it was Giggs's 'speed, balance, touch and courage' that put him in the 'tiny elite of the world's most penetrative front players'. Injury may have compounded Giggs's quest to become a truly rounded player, and certainly few players feel more strongly a sense of obligation to the team. The goal on 14 April 1999 reminded everyone, including Giggs, of his ferocious natural talent. The following season was probably his best yet.

Giggs approaches his sport as an athlete. He has recognized that his game rests on pace, close control, crossing under pressure and an explosive left foot. Talent like his may be ineffable, but inspiration only flows from perspiration. Like any artist, Giggs has worked at his craft. Training is basic, and something to be enjoyed and not endured. He noticed that Eric Cantona would generally remain behind to work on aspects of his game, and the young Giggs saw the point. He has also recognized that players of flair and pace have a responsibility for escaping injuries. He may be able to rely on referees for some protection, but frustrated defenders will kick out just as slower defenders will tackle late. Giggs has always maintained that players like him have a responsibility to ride tackles and to look after themselves. Throughout the 1990s he escaped serious injuries, although he did suffer periodic hamstring problems, a peril of his explosive pace. His niggling hamstring problems in the 1997/8 season played their part in United's losing the title by one point to Arsenal. Though Ferguson had cover for Giggs, he never had a replacement.

Throughout the 1990s Giggs graced United teams of breathtaking accomplishment. Paradoxically, this limited aspects of his game. By the end of the 1990s many fans had forgotten what a fine striker of a dead ball Giggs was. Proprietary rights over free kicks and corners now belonged to David Beckham, the finest striker of a dead ball in the world. Occasionally one would see Giggs lingering longingly behind a free kick outside the penalty areas. Still, team player that he was, he would defer to Beckham. In any other team such scoring opportunities would probably have been Giggs's by right. By the end of the decade the career of David Beckham was a remarkable counterpoint to that of Giggs. Beckham played on the right although, even more than Giggs, he was hugely effective in a more central midfield role. Beckham's crossing was even more mercilessly accurate than that of Giggs, although Beckham lacked Giggs's remarkable pace and ability to beat men and turn defences. Off the pitch, too, the contrasts were profound. Whilst Beckham lived in the full glare of publicity, relishing superstardom at its most forthrightly self-asserting, and marrying a still more famous pop-singer; Giggs remained an intensely private person, retaining old friendships in Manchester, welcoming moments of anonymity when he could find them, having but not parading girlfriends, and remaining close to his mother's family. By mid career he would frequently be interviewed, but always talked about the match and the club and rarely about himself. He handled the press adroitly and more articulately than most players of his generation. His seemed to be a comfortable accommodation with fame.

Giggs's international debut came against West Germany on 16 October 1991, making him the youngest ever Welsh international. From the start his international career was surrounded by controversy. Alex Ferguson, who was carefully cultivating the young Giggs, urged the then Wales manager Terry Yorath not to play him too soon or too often. There were rumours that Terry Venables had bemoaned that Giggs, who had captained England Schoolboys, had been allowed to slip through England's net. Giggs, however, remained steadfastly Welsh. He made his way into one of the better Welsh international sides, which included Mark Hughes, Ian Rush and Neville Southall, then players of genuinely international class. There were hopes, dashed always at the eleventh hour, that Wales might somehow make it to the last stages of the World Cup or European Championships.

Captaining Wales in 1993 was, Giggs repeatedly says, his 'proudest moment'. Critics who bemoan his frequent absences from friendly internationals, should remember this. Like all international players, the demands faced by Giggs from the mid-1990s were awesome. True he often reported unfit and many in Wales scoffed at another of 'Ferguson's hamstrings'. True, Ferguson did think that all his players' first loyalty was to their club, and that friendly internationals mattered less than club games. The energy and capacity, even of natural athletes such as Giggs, is not limitless. Choices have to be made, and those choices were never as easy as 'club versus country'. Giggs has always sought to play in competitive internationals. Friendly internationals stand in the same relationship to qualifying internationals for major competitions as do League Cup matches to United's other fixtures: and Giggs has been as likely to miss a League Cup match as a friendly international.

In all sorts of ways Giggs's experience as a Welsh international has been in stark contrast to his experience as a Manchester United player. At United he has encountered almost limitless success, for Wales he has known some glorious triumphs and much recurrent frustration. United has been a settled club under inspired management. Wales in the 1990s went through periods of frequent, and sometimes seemingly mindless, upheaval. Giggs thought Terry Yorath was shabbily treated in 1993 when he asked for a better contract, and Giggs seems genuinely to have been angered by Yorath's treatment. He also witnessed the brief reign of John Toshack, which was ill-considered on all sides. Wales could not have produced a first-rate international side in the 1990s, but they could have produced a more settled structure and a more coherent approach. The start of 2000 perhaps heralded a new beginning. The Millennium Stadium provided a new and inspiring stage; cheaper tickets and Giggs's presence filled it. His old friend Mark Hughes, now Wales manager, confirmed that 'Everyone in the squad is lifted when he [Giggs] is around.'

In an age where many leading footballers have been unquiet souls – driven by money, agents and uncritical adulation; and unsettled by the pressures of stardom, the cruel scrutiny of the media and the evanescence of their excellence – Giggs has been a more serene figure. True there have been celebrity girlfriends, fast cars, big houses and stupendous wealth, but he has retained a sense of perspective. Money, he suggested, mattered less when you had more of it. Friendships and family affections are not something to be paraded occasionally for the press, but to be lived and nurtured. In an era when many leading players seemed to regard football as a branch of show business, for Giggs it has remained a sport in the truest sense. He is a professional athlete, and the demands of the game come first. Life is to be lived, but not in ways which compromise his performance on the field. He noticed that Eric Cantona did not drink for four days before a match, and took note. He recognized that natural talent made training more important not less. He knew and said he was 'a flair player', but flair and talent simply gave him a decisive advantage as a professional athlete. Where some, such as Paul Gascoigne, abused natural talent, and others, George Best most notably, were ultimately overwhelmed by it, Giggs was content to hone his skills, preserve his pace and recognize that exquisite skills imposed responsibilities to deliver match-winning moments for the team and entertainment for the fans.

Behind all this lies a more complex and more mature personality than many of his peers. Here, perhaps, Giggs's richer sense of identity was important. Here, perhaps, his Welshness mattered. For many footballers nationality matters relatively little. It is there, inherited, assumed: it does not have to be lived. Giggs's Welshness was different. Different because some people thought it was a negotiable identity; different because he was a Welshman in Manchester; and different because sometimes his commitment to Wales and the Welsh side was questioned. Giggs often referred to himself as 'a local lad', by which, of course, he meant a Manchester lad, a Stretford-ender, a graduate of Greater Manchester schoolboy football. His primary cultural identity was and is Mancunian, and it is this that informs his powerful identification with United as a club and as an institution. United, by now the largest club in world football, casts its spell on most who play for it. For those like Giggs who grew up in its shadow and felt its history, that sense of identification with the club is still more profound.

And yet Giggs has remained persistently and publicly Welsh. His greatest moment of personal pride was in captaining his country. Nothing, he thought, 'would top captaining Wales'. Wales was 'where I was born', Manchester where he grew up, and United which made him a star. As we have already seen, much has been made of Giggs's missing so many friendly matches for Wales. On both sides of the border this has been read as betraying a lukewarm commitment to his country, and as suggesting a sense of regret that his talent was confined on the international stage to representing a minor footballing nation. This is to misread Giggs's motives and to misunderstand his professionalism. The English may have a particular reason for doing this. They, almost to a person, have wished that Giggs had been English. He had captained England Schoolboys, so he could, they thought, have played for England. This sense of loss was misplaced. Giggs is Welsh, wished to represent his country, and was wanted by his country. Nevertheless, this sense of loss was all the more piquant for English supporters and commentators because, throughout Giggs's career, the English have lacked a gifted left-sided forward, and never even glimpsed an English left-winger of Giggs's speed and touch. An English Giggs, the argument went, would have transformed England. Moreover, the English national side would have showcased Giggs's talent in a way nothing else could

This argument was mistaken on many counts. England throughout the 1990s was a moderate team managed, with the exception of Terry Venables, by men of very moderate abilities. Playing for England Giggs would have won nothing, though he would have played in the final stages of the World and European Championships. Crucially, though, it would not have changed the evaluation of his quality either by contemporaries or by posterity. Giggs, the Welsh international of the 1990s, was in a different position from, say, George Best the Northern Ireland international of the 1960s. Best played in a British First Division in which he dazzled, and in a declining Manchester United team with which he did win once in Europe. Some still suggest that Best was not tested frequently enough at the highest level. For those who saw Best the argument is wilful and his genius beyond question. Still it has been made and parallels have been drawn with Giggs.

Yet Giggs's case is quite different. He has played the bulk of his career in an international Premier League. By the mid-1990s the English Premier League, awash with television money and advertising revenue, was truly an international league. Manchester United despite numerous foreign stars was, in fact, the most British of the leading clubs of the later 1990s and, week in, week out, played against teams expensively assembled through lavish chequebooks from among the world's best players. At the turn of the century, Chelsea often fielded no British players, Arsenal transcended their reputation for remorselessly efficient defensive play by constructing a sparkling team compromising predominantly imported players, and even Liverpool followed suit. Giggs thus played international football every week. He plays for what most critics, at the turn of the century, regard as not only the finest club side in Britain but also probably the best club side in Europe. Certainly United has been a vastly better side than the Welsh teams which Giggs graced, but then they have also been a vastly better side than any England team fielded in the same period. There can be no doubting Giggs's standing on the international stage: he has graced that stage week by week. More than that, his talent has shone against all kinds of opposition. He is a flair player: he has had some moderate games, but even then the threat is always there. In a moment he can, and does, turn a game. The exquisite skills of the natural winger are the most striking aspects of Giggs's game, but to those who have watched closely, and above all to those who have managed and coached him, he has remained throughout a model professional. His work-rate is prodigious, he destroys defences, he delights crowds, and he has repaid his manager's faith onehundredfold. Performing regularly at this level has been powerful confirmation of his ability and achievement. In the modern game few have displayed a better temperament and more consummate professionalism, and goals such as that against Arsenal in the 1999 FA Cup semi-final are goals of pure genius. Such moments, shimmering in a career of constant achievement at the highest level, are why Ryan Giggs may come to be remembered as the greatest of all Welsh footballers.

Mark Hughes

Peter Stead

Newspaper editors are well aware of the power of sports photographs and the extent to which they can reflect the joys and agonies of particular occasions as well as help to sustain loyalties and identities. In March 2000 a widely circulated press photograph proclaimed the arrival of an era of confident expectation for Welsh football. What was shown was an empty stadium with one man, dressed immaculately in grey suit, blue shirt, a tastefully subdued tie and highly polished black shoes, cleverly keeping a football in the air. The setting was Cardiff's magnificent new Millennium Stadium and the man was Mark Hughes, who had recently been confirmed as the manager of the Welsh team. Apparently he had requested personally that his first home game in charge should be played not at Ninian Park but rather at this home of Welsh rugby. Already it was known that the game against Finland would be a 66,500 sell-out, a record for a football match in Wales, and this in itself was generally interpreted as being a vote of confidence in the new manager. 'The public are backing him all the way', reported Swansea's *Evening Post*, and clearly the man in the photograph had the class, distinction and authority that invited respect and support. One would not have been surprised to read that he had bought the stadium.

In the event Wales played indifferently, especially in the first half, and lost 2–1. The occasion, however, had been more important than the match itself. Welsh football had rediscovered its audience, had put down roots in a comfortable and stylish new home and had generally given notice that important things were about to happen. 'At last we have a football ground to be proud of', said the *Evening Post*; 'we are now in the big time, potentially at least'. The Swansea paper was in no doubt that the new manager's decision to play at the Millennium Stadium represented 'the rebirth of Welsh soccer'. As the months of uncertainty had dragged on Welsh football fans had yearned for his appointment as full-time manager to be confirmed. The game in Wales was crying out for authoritative leadership and intelligent judgement. Once in post Hughes had immediately displayed these qualities. Initially the manager took his team to Qatar, where after only a couple of days' preparation he opted for a formation involving a back-line of five and only one man up front; they secured a 1–0 victory. 'So Hughes has made his stance', commented the *Post*; 'he's unlikely to be swayed and buffetted by critical and public opinion as others have been in the past' for 'the days of public debate are gone in the new hard-nosed Hughes era'.

After Finland it was Brazil's turn to come to town and this time an even bigger and younger crowd filled the stadium. Again 'the new hard-nosed Hughes era' was in evidence, and Stephen Wood of *The Times* was very struck by the mix of 'the courteous and curmudgeonly' in the manager's approach as he used his news conference in the John Charles Suite at Ninian Park to make clear his ambitions for his team. Some had thought the Brazil fixture a mistake but Hughes had wanted it. He was confident that Wales could repeat their victory of 1991; he had played in that match on an evening when, he recalled, 'the samba had given way to Welsh hymns'. Moreover, he thought of Brazil's return as extremely useful preparation for the forthcoming World Cup games. As it happened, Wales were to lose to Brazil but their manager's wish that every game at Cardiff should be fought all the way was fulfilled throughout. It was an evening, said Stephen Wood, when 'humiliation was never on the agenda'. The Welsh team had caught the mood of their boss, who had made his own determination clear by ordering the groundsman to narrow the pitch and let the grass grow: if Brazil were going to play 'the beautiful game' they would have to do so on his terms.

As never before, Welsh football followers in the year 2000 knew that they were being led. They accepted this new authority not only because it was born out of what the *Evening Post* described as 'the knowing and understanding' of a long and uniquely successful playing career but because it came in the person of a man who had always been first and foremost a fans' player. The hallmark of his career had been his sheer professionalism: he had simply got on with playing the game and he had done that in a way which had given him a very special place in the affections of regular supporters at every club at which he had played. Reporters often had occasion to comment on the fact that, unusually, he was welcomed back by the crowd when he returned as an opponent to play against an old club. He belonged to his fans because he 'did the business' on the field; there was no mediation. Hughes had never been a creation of the tabloid editors, style and marketing consultants or the television studios. He was known to be a man of few words, 'singularly undemonstrative' in Jim White's phrase, and it was precisely that eschewal of gossip, whingeing and false drama that clinched both his professionalism and his place in the affections of those who are professional in their following of the game. He is, said Dennis Wise, a former colleague at Chelsea, 'what I would call a proper man'.

Remarkably, the man in the grey suit, the new manager of Wales, was, at the age of thirty-six, still playing Premiership football. In fact, having spent all week in Cardiff for the Finland match he returned to Everton to play against Watford in a 4–2 victory where he scored the first goal and set up two others. His move to Everton earlier in the year had given special pleasure. He had joined a famous old club whose historic ground with its high stands and surrounding terraced streets still stood as a monument to earlier decades, when football was classically the passion of the working classes and when Liverpool dockers had made their club the best supported in the land. In every respect Goodison Park was a more appropriate stage for Mark Hughes than the suburban Dell at Southampton, not least, of course, because there is always a Welsh dimension at Everton. Wales is only sixteen miles across the water and, over the years, many Welsh fans have gone to Goodison to cheer on heroes like the great Tommy Jones, Kevin Ratcliffe and Neville Southall. In a way Mark Hughes had come home, for his native Ruabon was only fifty miles to the south and even closer was his subsequent base in Cheshire.

But there was more to his being at Goodison than sentiment, for his boss there, Walter Smith, opted to play him up front. For a couple of seasons at Southampton he had grafted away in midfield, a role thought altogether appropriate for an ageing star who had never really had much speed and whose famous legs, 'crafted from steel' in Jim White's view, were thought to be going. Caution and survival had been the watchwords in Hampshire, but on Merseyside Everton were having one of their better seasons and were going for a place in Europe. It was hoped that the Welshman would not only relish the opportunity to score goals again but would inspire his front-running colleagues. What was soon clear was that Mark Hughes still gloried in the physical challenge of taking on defenders. Dennis Wise had spoken of how 'defenders hate him', and it was now time for a new generation of young Premiership defenders to experience bad times. The *Evening Post* suggested that 'he was arguably the most abrasive striker in the top flight', while his colleague, John Collins, had no doubt that 'until he stops playing he will always be the same: every game is a challenge, every tackle is a challenge'. Famously, Sir Alex Ferguson has described Hughes as 'a warrior you could trust with your life'.

In another judgement Sir Alex has given the most fitting summing up of what Mark Hughes has achieved in football. For Ferguson, Hughes was 'the best big game player I have ever known'. Almost without the media noticing, the Hughes trophy room had become well and truly cluttered as the souvenirs accumulated from big games he had helped win. Suddenly it was appreciated that he was the only player in the twentieth century with four Cup Final winners' medals and they, of course, had to be put alongside two Championship medals, a European Cup Winners' Cup medal and a League Cup medal. Twice he had been the PFA's Player of the Year and once their Young Player of the Year. In the time-honoured language of programme editors 'he has won almost every honour in the game'. It is now almost impossible to remember a time when Mark Hughes was not in the thick of top-level football, battling away for honours. He has played at the highest level of British League football since 1984, and it was in that year that he won the first of his seventy-two Welsh caps. At every stage in this remarkable career it seemed as if there were things to be proved, a drama to be sustained, trophies to be won. Throughout his career, too, the pattern of his involvement, the nature of his play, were consistent. There was the ceaseless and relentlessly physical task of gathering and retaining the ball as defenders crashed into him from behind; not surprisingly all this body contact would occasionally lead to flare-ups, especially when the aptly nicknamed 'Sparky' made it clear that he was not going to be intimidated. Every now and then, and particularly if the match was a big one, there would be a spectacular Hughes goal. In the words of the *Daily Telegraph*, 'he never scores a dull goal'.

I caught a definitive Hughes performance at Sheffield's Bramall Lane in January 1994. This was a classic FA Cup third round tie with defences well on top, the main focus of attention being an intensely physical battle between Manchester United's Hughes and the Sheffield United defender David Tuttle. We were all beginning to think 'goal-less draw' until, in the sixty-second minute, Hughes was involved in a passing movement down the middle. When the ball came back to him he took it wide to the left-hand side of the six-yard box, far too wide it seemed, but then at the last possible moment he slid it past the diving Alan Kelly to score what was immediately assumed to be a tie-killing goal. There were indeed no more goals, but in the dying moments of the game Hughes crashed into Tuttle and was ordered off by referee Gerald Ashby. Initially Alex Ferguson condemned the victimization of his forward whom he thought had been assaulted throughout the afternoon. Later the video evidence indicated to everyone, Ferguson included, that Mr Ashby had really had no option. We left Bramall Lane loving the delicate skills of 'Hughesie' but astonished by the sheer ferocity of physical commitment that seemed to be generated in this kind of English fixture. I kept the press photos as a souvenir of the occasion. In them Hughes is wearing the yellow and green colours that United had opted for on that day: in the first his concentration is complete as he anxiously wills his shot into the net; in the second, in which he is described as being 'on his way', he is realigning his shirt and looking back over his shoulder with a sarcastic look of contempt at an official who had failed to realize the pressures of being a Premiership striker. In this second shot Eric Cantona's features are blurred but one can almost hear him say 'there by the grace of God' or words to that effect.

That day in Sheffield when Hughes wore yellow and green (the original colours of Newton Heath someone suggested) was the last time I was to see him in a Manchester United shirt. He had made his first-team debut eleven years earlier and had actually been on their books since he was fourteen: for two years before that, the story has it, Christmas cards from Old Trafford had been arriving at his Ruabon home. He was an essential part of the woof and warp of United, a key figure in their re-emergence as a glamour club and then in the early stages of their transformation into a super club. He was moulded by some of the big names in British football. It was Dave Sexton who had arranged for the Wrexham Schoolboys player to become an apprentice at Old Trafford, and then it was youth coach Syd Owen who suggested that the hitherto midfielder should try playing up front. It was 'Big Ron' Atkinson who put him in the first team and who saw that he had found a partner and subsequent replacement for his chief striker, Norman Whiteside. It was Atkinson, too, who decided to sell Hughes, who had scored thirty-three League goals for him in two seasons, to Barcelona for £2.5m. Playing for Terry Venables the Welshman, dubbed 'El Toro' by locals, was not a success; at the Nou Camp he was somewhat off-message both on and off the field. After a successful loan spell at Bayern Munich it was Alex Ferguson who took him back to Manchester where for a couple of seasons he and Eric Cantona were to form one of the most skilful, enchanting and successful forward partnerships in the recent history of British League football.

Between 1984 and 1994 it was the fans of Manchester United who backed the judgement of successive managers and coaches by identifying 'Sparky' not only as a hero but also as an all-time great. The London-based press and, more especially, the television commentators were slow to see beyond the purely physical dimension of his game. Meanwhile he had become the people's player, the punter's choice, and he was soon taking his place in various fantasy teams of the decade and even of all time. With every justification Old Trafford historian Stephen F. Kelly identifies him as 'one of the all-time United favourites' with, he adds, 'a habit of scoring sensational goals'. Those goals were the icing on the cake, a way of saying thank you to his army of followers. His shot, says Kelly, was 'ferocious', his volleys 'as spectacular as Old Trafford has ever seen'. In David Lacey's famous dictum in *The Guardian* in 1998 that Hughes was 'a scorer of great goals, not a great goalscorer', only the first phrase will survive. Of his 'great goals' for United two stand out. In 1991, in what *The Times* described as 'the most delicious of ironies', Hughes scored twice as United beat his old team Barcelona to win the European Cup Winners' Cup in Rotterdam. The first was a simple tap-in, the second came after he had escaped a marker and gone wide; from the widest angle he truly 'thumped' it in. But surely his most famous and 'miraculous' United goal came at Wembley in the FA Cup semi-final of 1994. He was to develop a habit of scoring at Wembley but none of his Cup Final goals were as dramatic as the last-minute equalizer against Oldham to ensure the replay that United were to win. 'Brian McClair', explained Hughes, 'chipped a great ball over the heads of the Oldham defenders and as it dropped over my shoulder I smashed it into the back of the net for a life-saving goal.' In his autobiography, written with David Meek, Hughes analysed this goal and explained that on the training ground he specifically practised volleys to compensate for the fact that 'for a centre-forward, I'm lousy with headers on goal'. That volley against Oldham eventually allowed United to return to Wembley for a final in which they defeated Chelsea.

In the summer of 1995 Hughes was at the end of his contract with Old Trafford and, suddenly, the fans were flabbergasted by the news that for £1.5m the player had signed not only for another club, but for a southern, London club and in particular for Chelsea. For Stretford Enders this was the sickest of bad jokes, but for those of us who for decades had longed for Chelsea to embrace their destiny this was glorious news. The story broke just as the London club was parading its other new signing, Ruud Gullit. Manager Glenn Hoddle had decided to rebuild his team around these two thirty-something superstars; there were jokes about 'Chelsea pensioners' but clearly the club was aiming to play 'quality football'. A new era was beginning in British football as Sky took over, stadiums were redesigned and foreign stars arrived to look for homes. Living in an under-achieving south Wales I tried to keep in touch with these developments both on television and in the flesh. I had been a Chelsea supporter since postgraduate days in London and subsequent occasional (and expensive) visits to Stamford Bridge were my way of keeping up to date. It was time to take stock of the foreign influx so I went to the

Bridge to see the Arsenal game. All the press speculation had centred on the Gullit–Dennis Bergkamp confrontation and, in truth, my chief memory of the game was of the formidable Gullit. His was the most impressive physical presence I had seen on a football field since John Charles. He controlled the game from the back, lording it over all and sundry. I rarely took my eyes off Gullit, but at one point in the second half the ball fell to Hughes in a crowded penalty area and he fired the ball past Seaman for what, once again, was to be the only goal of the game. The scorer's delight was obvious, and in my records I have a marvellous photo of him jumping higher than I have ever seen him in a match; the arms are raised, the fists clenched and he looks as pleased as punch. He had won the match, stolen the headlines, inspired a whole new section of the population to chant 'Hughsie, Hughsie' and made my season.

Meanwhile, this veritable hero and quintessential champion of the Premiership was battling away for his country as well. Hughes had scored in his first ever match for United, repeated the feat on his League debut, and therefore it was no real surprise when he marked his international debut by scoring the only goal of the game against England at Wrexham in 1984. From the start of his international career Hughes operated in tandem with Ian Rush, a player who had grown up only some twenty-five miles away from him but who was two years older and already a veteran of four seasons in the Welsh side. It was soon apparent that Welsh manager Mike England had at his disposal what he was to describe as 'one of the best attacking partnerships in world football' and, remarkably, they were to play 'sixteen or seventeen' matches together before experiencing defeat. Hughes always thought of Rush as 'a fair player', 'a player's player' who worked hard for the team, going back to tackle as he was often forced to for Wales. One particular comment Hughes made about Rush would seem to indicate that the former has all the psychological insights necessary to manage Wales, for he pointed out that the Liverpool striker could 'get quite frustrated at times because he expects such a lot, but his commitment to Welsh football cannot be questioned'.

In some respects the high-water mark of the Rush–Hughes pairing came early on. In the qualifying rounds of the 1986 World

Cup, which was to be held in Mexico, Wales were placed in the same group as Spain, Scotland and Iceland, with only one team guaranteed a place in the finals. Wales began disastrously by losing in Iceland and Spain, but eventually Mike England's strike force struck and, in so doing, gave Welsh fans some of their best ever memories. The match at Hampden Park was described beforehand by the *Western Mail* as 'arguably the most imortant in the history of Welsh football'. On thirty visits to Glasgow Wales had managed only three wins, the last being thirty-four years earlier when Ivor Allchurch had headed a last-minute winner to silence the Hampden roar. This time it was Rush whose dramatic shot silenced not only the crowd but also the Scottish television commentator whose chatter until that point had been incessant. His sudden and prolonged silence made me think that sound had been lost. This was one of the national side's best-ever performances and the whole team had responded to the lead given by Rush and Hughes. A month later Spain were beaten 3–0 at Wrexham in what *The Times* described as a 'hard fought, bruising clash'. Ian Rush opened the scoring just before the break and then in the second half 'the strength of the lively Hughes began to stretch the Spanish defence'. It was Hughes who scored the second when, with 'a supreme piece of skill', he executed a 'spectacular scissors kick'. Near the end he put Rush through for the third, but it was that second goal which provided one of the golden moments of Welsh football history. Historian Rob Humphreys was there that night and he described this to me as 'perhaps the finest goal ever scored by a Welshman at international level'; it was a volley 'which confirmed that Hughes inhabited that parallel universe which is the preserve of world-class players only'.

When Scotland came to Ninian Park in September there was everything to play for. For most of the match those of us there thought it was going to be Sparky's evening. In the words of the *Daily Telegraph* he had 'stamped his class on the match by scoring on the turn from a low cross by Peter Nicholas'. It was a goal that deserved to take Wales to Mexico, but it was not to be enough: in the eightieth minute defender Dave Phillips was harshly adjudged to have handled the ball and a stunned crowd watched substitute Dave Cooper score the penalty. Wales were effectively out: Spain qualified automatically and Scotland made it to the finals after play-off games against Australia. The pain of that evening had to be somehow suppressed, for tragically the Scottish manager Jock Stein, much loved in Wales after his spell as a centre-half at Llanelli, collapsed during the game and died. The photograph of his touch-line collapse with an anxious Alex Ferguson looking on provides one of football's most poignant momentos. There were to be other tournaments and other disappointments, many of them recalled in this volume, but for Welsh fans 10 September 1985 will remain as the blackest day. The match in which Jock Stein died was one which effectively denied the massively in-form Rush and Hughes their place on the world stage.

For season after season the chief pleasure of supporting Wales was the opportunity of watching Rush and Hughes at work. The Barcelona interlude meant that Mark was often unavailable and when he did appear it tended to be in midfield. In *Hughsie* he was to explain that it was all very well for Wales to have world-class strikers but who was there to give them the vital through balls? Increasingly, both players had to do their own foraging, and necessity dictated that the powerfully built, strong-thighed and hard-tackling Hughes should be the midfield workhorse. Denied their trip to Mexico both players operated disappointingly on the European stage, Hughes at Barcelona and Rush at Juventus. For Welsh fans, however, they remained talismanic, a joy to watch and enduring proof of Wales being a significant football nation. They had much in common: both came from small north Wales industrial communities and both established their identities as heroes with club sides in major English cities, with both the clubs and cities having strong Welsh connections. Every Saturday evening *Match of the Day* would highlight their exploits, Rush for Liverpool and Hughes for Manchester United, and frequently there would be glimpses of the Welsh national flag draped on the fences or hanging from the stands. When interviewed both men came across as reluctant personalities: they were shy men who clearly believed that everything that needed saying had been expressed on the pitch. They were content to be ordinary blokes who just happened to be utterly professional and, as it happened, brilliant footballers.

Of course, one always wanted more than that and in the case of Mark Hughes the promise seemed to be there. Ian Rush could have been the product of any urban culture where soccer skills were rated highly; one can see him as a great striker for a local club in Milan, Rio or Buenos Aires. But surely Mark Hughes could only be Welsh. His disarmingly courteous, softly spoken and somewhat deferential manner suggests a Welsh upbringing in which he was warned to be always on his best behaviour. And those curly locks could only belong to someone who was made to eat every crust. The face, which is at the same time smooth and craggy, strong and innocent, is unmistakeably Welsh. What makes him such a fitting Welsh icon is that he has the look of the farmer-poet who has just been chaired at the National Eisteddfod or even of the thoughtful young Baptist minister about to be inducted at the chapel down the road. The older Hughes has become more gaunt and more photogenic. There are wonderful shots of him scoring goals and then celebrating; often he turns with quiet dignity to acknowledge the crowd with a look which says 'trust me, I'll do the job'. Ultimately, what impresses is his instinctive understanding of what is important: he has no interest in the silly, trivial or flash.

He is, of course, Ruabon's greatest son. Most Welsh guide-books are forced to conclude that the town's chief advantage is its location. I think of it as being fortuitously placed at a right-angle bend which forms a dramatic cultural divide. To the west is the beautiful Vale of Llangollen, and the aqueduct at Froncysyllte, the town of Llangollen and the abbey at Valle Crucis are all nearby. To the north, towards Wrexham, there was once coal, steel, male choirs and all the attractions of modern urban civilization. This mix of the pastoral and industrial, the past and the present and of things Welsh and cosmopolitan would seem to offer the perfect place for a balanced childhood. In his autobiography Hughes strongly identifies with his Denbighshire roots and he talks of a Welsh-speaking grandmother and playing the violin at school. It is obvious where he learned his values.

As a dedicated admirer I have over the years looked for clues that would confirm Hughsie's place in my mythology and in my own personal pantheon. Once in Barcelona I was grilling my taxi driver on the current form of Barça and, in particular, of their foreign imports. 'Lineker', he shouted, 'Wonderful. Hughes. No good.' My heart sank, my whole trip was ruined. But then he turned; his analysis was not finished. 'But Mrs Hughes', he added, 'Fantastic!' and at this point he kissed his fingers. Some weeks later I was watching Wales at the Racecourse and understandably I spent more time looking for the wives in the stand than at the Welsh forwards and their tussle with the Czech defence. I had to make do with the wedding photographs in the papers. As far as the Hughes family was concerned the taxi driver had got it half right. I thought then what I even more firmly know now: the Hughes boy from Ruabon is a class act. At the start of a new century Welsh soccer is luckier than it has any right to be.

Hope Springs Eternal

Huw Richards

It is perhaps an Australian who has best captured the psychological reality of being a Welsh football fan. We identify Australians with teams who expect to win and do. But the academic and writer Brian Matthews knows from a lifetime of watching Australian Rules football what it is like to support a team that does not win that often. 'Following the St Kilda Football Club for so long taught one a great deal about the meaning of life – which was struggle, defeat and hope springing eternal'. Substitute Swansea, Cardiff, Wrexham or Wales for St Kilda and that is our state of mind, of hope winning out over experience. Experience means being realistic in our expectations, and treating newly installed club chairmen who promise Premiership football within five years with the scepticism accorded to government spin-doctors. Hope means never giving up the belief that things will get better, and deriving fresh optimism from any sign of progress, however limited.

Such signs do, indeed, exist in mid-2000. Bitter experience may warn against automatically assuming that there is light at the end of the tunnel, for far too often that light turns out to be flames. Yet there are definite reasons to be cheerful, even if this has to be heavily qualified by a historical perspective. Let us remember that twenty years ago Swansea were in the First Division, Cardiff and Wrexham were members in good standing of the Second and Newport County were pressing to join them. If FIFA rankings for national teams had been invented, we were not then aware of them. Today, when your national team is rated 101st in the world, it is not hard to believe that the only way is up and, thankfully, signs of Welsh revival go beyond widespread relief that Bobby Gould finally quit the managership – in many eyes a fair exchange for a 4–0 hammering by Italy.

The end-of-season meeting with Brazil was ludicrously over-hyped – claims that it was 'the biggest match in Welsh football history' must have come as a surprise to survivors of the 1958 World Cup quarter-finalists – and will be remembered as a pleasant occasion highlighted by a richly deserved, long overdue international debut for Roger Freestone. But the game against Brazil was not even the most important match of that season. Surely that must have been the earlier meeting with

Finland. This was not because of any excellence in the performance – Finland were even better value for a 2–1 win than Brazil were for their 3–0 stroll – but because of the size of the crowd. Brazil is after all the most charismatic team in the world, whereas Finland is nobody's idea of a glamour team. Yet more than 65,000 people, attracted by the chance to watch the national team play at the Millennium Stadium at rock-bottom prices, came to see them in a mid-season mid-week friendly. The price-cutting was attributed to new national coach Mark Hughes, which suggests that, whatever his performance as a coach, there is a future for him in sports marketing. The lesson here was the one demonstrated in the mid-1990s by Glamorgan County Cricket Club, but still to be understood by the slow learners at the Welsh Rugby Union, is that if you reduce the prices enough you will be rewarded with decent crowds.

Capacity crowds will not make the Millennium Stadium into a fortress. You need better players than we have to achieve that. Nevertheless, if the youngsters who packed the stadium for the Finland and Brazil matches can be kept excited by Welsh football there will be serious long-term benefits for the game. It is particularly important that this message is remembered for Wales's World Cup qualifiers. Like Finland they offer the worst of all possible worlds – opposition of no great glamour, but highly competent. Wales will need all the help it can get – and a 50,000 crowd who have paid £5 apiece will be a lot more help, and in the long run more profitable, than 15,000 who have paid £20. Maybe the best that we can hope for is restored respectability and self-respect. Even if we had a gaggle of outstanding youngsters poised to make an impact internationally it would be hard to make a case for Wales qualifying for the 2002 World Cup. Losses have outweighed gains in recent years, and this is likely to continue for the moment. The outstanding generation of attackers to which Hughes belongs is at an end – only Dean Saunders is still a candidate for selection. Neville Southall has gone, and chronic creative deficiencies remain.

The Finland match was also significant for the sight of Ryan Giggs turning out in a friendly. This is not because Giggs is capable single-handedly of transforming the fortunes of the team – claims before the Brazil match that he is a better player than Rivaldo were welcome proof that we have not lost the national gift for satire – but because of his talismanic significance as the one Welsh player of genuine international renown. It was this that made his extraordinary sequence of withdrawals from friendly match national squads so damaging and anger-inducing.

The Welsh team is seriously short of players who hold down a regular Premiership place. Ability to do so in that rather over-inflated competition does not in itself confer international status – the recent, painful memory of Vinnie Jones's grotesque international efforts is a reminder of that. But to have a group of players proven, and regularly tested, at the highest domestic level would undoubtedly help. As it is the Wales team, if entered in the Football League, would probably find its level around halfway in the First Division – roughly where Fulham's twin pursuits of stockpiling every Welsh centre-back and recreating the Swansea City back four of the late 1980s have landed them. Prime youthful talent is not obviously plentiful. Craig Bellamy, the best of the rising generation, has lost a year to injury. Swansea City's current clutch of youngsters contains several players with every reason to hope for good League careers at a decent level, but scarcely compares with the Charles-Curtis-James group of the 1970s. Cardiff City's bright group of a couple of seasons ago has disappeared almost without trace, with the implosion of Lee Jarman's career a particular disappointment. In 2000 Cardiff reached the English Schools Shield final for the first time in more than eighty years, but it will be several years before any potential saviour emerges from that group.

What would undoubtedly encourage Mark Hughes would be signs of a serious revival by the Welsh clubs. No Welsh club has played in the top two divisions of the League since 1985. Of our somewhat woebegone trio undoubtedly the greatest failure has been Cardiff City, whom the otherwise eminently sane football correspondent of *Wales on Sunday* persists in labelling 'Wales's premier football club' in face of the fact that it is twelve years since they were last the best-placed Welsh club. Cardiff City, not so much sleeping giant as persistently vegetative, has been hamstrung by uncertainty over ownership of the club. Full of optimism at the start of the 1999/2000 season after winning promotion to the Second Division, they fell away completely after a lively start, lost the shrewd Frank Burrows amid boardroom infighting and collapsed back into the Third. It is not so very long since a survey by *When Saturday Comes* fanzine found that Cardiff was one of the clubs most admired by fans of other clubs. That was during the chairmanship of the erratic but often inspired Rick Wright. He may have had three bad ideas for every good one, but at least he had ideas and gave the club a buzz and momentum it has never recaptured. The only leagues Cardiff are likely to top nowadays in supporter surveys are those asking whose fans are the greatest menace to the maintenance of public order.

Swansea City has similar crowd problems, with particular worries over an ugly upsurge in racism. The sound of 'No Surrender to the IRA' – not in itself a racist song, but a well-established mating call – was one of the stranger, nastier memories of the 1999/2000 season, a year inevitably clouded by the death of fan Terry Coles, by all accounts the personification of the innocent bystander, under the feet of a police horse in the final Championship-deciding match at Rotherham. In the mean time, the Swans showed themselves to be that authentic rarity – a team whose most dedicated fans felt they were not really as good as their results. My memories of twenty-two matches point to a hugely convincing victory over Halifax, a memorable first-half in the promotion decider at home to Exeter and what proved to be the crucial forty-five minutes of the season, a truly remarkable comeback from 2–0 down to win 3–2 in the first game of the new year at Peterborough. The rest seemed oddly unconvincing.

Swansea rose on their remarkable ability to preserve a lead, never losing a match once they were ahead and only being pegged back four times, all away. No team has ever won a division championship with as few as fifty-one goals before – a great tribute to the organizational skills of John Hollins and Alan Curtis and a defence built round the understanding between the admirable Freestone and his centre-backs Matthew Bound and Jason Smith. Results against teams from higher divisions in Cup-ties suggest that they should adjust to the Second Division, with the extra time and space suiting a rather deliberate style of play. Medium-term prospects are harder to assess. The club's owners have tied their fortunes very firmly to the planned new Morfa Stadium, seen by the city council as a means of regenerating the lower Swansea Valley. If the move works, the Swans' commercial potential will be greatly increased, but things will have to go extremely well to convince many fans that the sacrifice of the battered and cramped but greatly loved Vetch Field has been worth it.

Wrexham kept their supporters on edge throughout the season, without ever quite sliding into real jeopardy at the bottom of the table. This was their second such season in a row, following on three when they just missed out on the play-offs. With moods in football so dependent on expectation, this is inevitably not enough to satisfy fans. But unlike the southern duo, Wrexham are at least playing at, or above, their traditional historical level – and have been Wales's top club for the last five seasons. That the smallest community with a Football League club should have established itself as a member of the Second Division – it is now seven years since they were promoted together with Cardiff City – is a considerable achievement. But that achievement also points to their major difficulty. The Wrexham club may be better run than the other two, but it is seriously limited by its small catchment area. Crewe Alexandra and Walsall have shown that extremely well-managed small clubs can make it into Division One, but that they are likely to struggle once they get there.

Further down the food chain Wales arguably lost half a league club when border-straddling Chester was relegated, while Newport and Merthyr marked time. But there was unequivocally better news from the Welsh League, with TNS taking the title. This is not to decry Barry Town's achievement in dominating the league over several years, but even my Barry-born co-editor agrees that any competition loses its attraction if it becomes too predictable.

So what prospect is there of a significant improvement in the fortunes of Welsh football over the next decade or so? This raises questions of to what we should aspire, and what we might reasonably expect – two very different things. Welsh fans should dream that their clubs might play in and win the Premiership and FA Cup final, that the national side might one day qualify for and win the European Championship and World Cup. This is Matthews's 'hope springing eternal', an essential backdrop to being a supporter. To take dreams away, to make the unlikely into the impossible – as both codes of rugby are increasingly doing – is to damage seriously the attraction of the game.

Swansea and Cardiff must also face the reality that football's underachieving communities tend also to be rugby towns. Hull, Bristol and until very recently Bradford are good examples. They know that some proportion of the community's collective talent, emotional energy and capital will go into rugby. The Swans and the Bluebirds will have to rise a long way up the league before they look like a more attractive investment than their neighbouring rugby clubs – among the strongest in Britain and likely to provide annual serious European competition. Even so it is not unreasonable that our clubs might aspire to the standards set by, say, Norwich City and Barnsley – well-run clubs playing in decent stadia who can sustain a place in the First Division and hope in good years to push for the Premiership. It will not be easy. Any serious advance is an uphill struggle, with growing inequalities increasing the gradient. However, difficult is not the same as impossible. The sports media are prone to fatalism, to confusing the likely with the certain. One of the joys of sport is that it does not invariably follow strict financial logic. If it did, Deportivo La Coruña would not have won the Spanish championship, Leicester City would not have won the League Cup and Kidderminster Harriers would not now be playing in the Football League. The start of the 2000/1 season sees Cardiff under new ownership, the Swans determined to make their mark in the Second Division, and Barry Town pioneering new links with a Premiership side: once again there would seem to be grounds for some not entirely illogical optimism.

The national team has to be run with a similar eye to aspiration and reality. Of course Wales should aspire to qualify for major competitions. At Euro 2000 Slovenia, with roughly Wales's population, contributed some decent football and infectious joy at simply being there. We have been close enough ourselves to believe in the possibility. But we also have to accept that such triumphs will be the exception, and that failure is not a sacking offence. The FAW's failure to recognize this led to the non-renewal of Terry Yorath's contract and the catastrophic appointment of Bobby Gould. They also forget the basic rule of importing when applied to national teams in any sport – the import has to be better than local alternatives and patently up to the job. We can supply our own incompetents.

Mark Hughes must be given proper backing, not least in further experiments like the price-cutting for the Finland and Brazil friendlies. The FAW also needs to accept that, for better, for worse, our football has been connected to England for more than a hundred years. It was perfectly reasonable to want a decent domestic competition, but not to persecute those who preferred to stay outside. Participation in the Football League gives our clubs the chance, in theory at least, to reach the highest level in one of the strongest competitions in Europe – success that can only benefit the game in Wales. To force the three League teams and others still in the English ladder to leave it would lower standards massively in the short term, with no promise whatever of any long-term recovery.

The task for Welsh football is to accept the reality of that conjuction of struggle, defeat and hope. Life will be an uphill struggle, but the consequence is that the rare occasions when it is not become yet more relishable. We cannot expect to win, or perhaps even qualify for, the World Cup or the Premiership, but it is important that we are good enough to dream.

SELECT BIBLIOGRAPHY

Contributors found the following works particularly useful and relevant. Martin Johnes has a Bibliography of Association Football in Wales on http://www.cf.ac.uk/suon/postgrad/walbib/wbib2.html

WALES

Dannie Abse, 'Only Sixty Four Years' in Simon Kuper (ed.), *Perfect Pitch No 1, Home Ground* (London: Headline, 1997).

Walley Barnes, *Captain of Wales* (London: Stanley Paul, 1953).

Ron Burgess, *Football – My Life* (London: Souvenir Press, 1952).

John Burgum, *Swansea City FC* (Manchester: Archive Publications, 1988).

John Charles, *King of Soccer* (London: Stanley Paul, 1957).

John Charles, *The Gentle Giant* (London: Stanley Paul, 1962).

Richard Coombes, *King John: The True Story of John Charles* (Leeds: Leeds United Publishing, 2000).

Peter Corrigan, *100 Years of Welsh Soccer* (Cardiff: Welsh Brewers, 1976).

John Crooks, *Cardiff City Chronology 1920–1986* (Cardiff: 1986).

John Crooks, *The Bluebirds: A Who's Who of Cardiff City Football League Players* (Cardiff: 1986).

John Crooks, *Cardiff City Football Club: The Official History of the Bluebirds* (Harfield: Yore Publications, 1992).

Gareth M. Davies and Ian Garland, *Who's Who of Welsh International Soccer Players* (Wrexham: Bridge Books, 1991).

Gareth M. Davies, *From Adams to Youlds: A Who's Who of Wrexham FC* (1999).

David Farmer, *Swansea City: 1912–1982* (London: Pelham Books, 1982).

David Farmer and Peter Stead, *Ivor Allchurch MBE* (Swansea: Christopher Davies, 1998).

Trevor Ford, *I Lead the Attack* (London: Stanley Paul, 1957).

Ryan Giggs, *My Story* (Manchester: Manchester United and Virgin, 1994).

John Harding, *Football Wizard: The Story of Billy Meredith* (Derby: Breedon Books, 1985).

Mark Hughes, *Sparky – Barcelona, Bayern and Back* (London: Cockerel Books, 1989).

Mark Hughes (with David Meek), *Hughesie: The Red Dragon* (Edinburgh: Mainstream, 1994).

Geraint H. Jenkins, *Cewri'r Bêl-droed yng Nghymru* (Llandysul: Gomer Press, 1977).

Martin Johnes, 'That Other Game: A Social History of Soccer in South Wales, 1906–1939' (University of Wales PhD 1998).

Martin Johnes, 'Fred Keenor: A Welsh Soccer Hero', *The Sports Historian*, 18(1) (May 1998).

A. Jones, *The Official History of Wrexham AFC* (Shrewsbury: Temple Publicity, 1974).

Cliff Jones, *Forward with Spurs* (London: Stanley Paul, 1962).

Peter Jones, *Wrexham: A Complete Record 1873–1992* (Derby: Breedon Books, 1992).

Jack Kelsey, *Over the Bar* (London: Stanley Paul, 1958).

G. G. Lerry, *Association Football in Wales 1870–1924* (Oswestry, 1924).

G. G. Lerry, *The Football Association of Wales: 75th Anniversary, 1876–1951* (Wrexham: 1952).

Brian Lile and David Farmer, 'The Early Days of Association Football in Wales 1890–1906', *Transactions of the Honourable Society of Cymmrodorion*, 1984.

Grahame Lloyd, *C'mon City: A Hundred Years of The Bluebirds* (Bridgend: Seren, 1999).

Bryn Matthews, *The Swans: A History of Swansea City Football Club* (Swansea: Uplands Bookshop, 1987).

Don Meredith, *Wrexham FC: Pen Portraits* (Wrexham: 1997).

Jimmy Murphy, *Matt, United and Me* (London: Souvenir Press, 1968).

Peter Parry and Brian Lile, *The Old Black and Green: Aberystwyth Town FC, 1884–1984* (Aberystwyth, 1987).

Roy Paul, *A Red Dragon of Wales* (London: Robert Hale, 1956).

Kevin Ratcliffe, *The Blues and I* (London: Arthur Barker, 1988).

Huw Richards, 'The Gospel According to Saint John the Alchemist' in Nick Hornby (ed.), *My Favourite Year* (London: Gollancz, 1994).

Mario Risoli, *When Pelé Broke Our Hearts* (Cardiff: Ashley Drake, 1998).

Ian Rush, *Rush* (London: Grafton Books, 1986).

Ian Rush, *My Italian Diary* (London: Arthur Barker, 1989).

Ian Rush, *Ian Rush: An Autobiography* (London: Ebury Press, 1996).

Richard Shepherd, *The History of Newport County FC 1912–1973* (Newport: 1973).

Richard Shepherd, *Seventy Years of Newport County Football Club: A Pictorial History, 1912–1982* (Newport, 1982).

Richard Shepherd, *Newport County Football Club: Archive Photographs* (Stroud: Chalford, 1997).

Richard Shepherd, *Cardiff City 1947–1971: Archive Photographs* (Stroud: Chalford, 1997).

Richard Shepherd, *Swansea Town Football Club 1912–1964: Archive Photographs* (Stroud: Tempus, 1998).

Neville Southall (with Rick George), *Everton Blue* (London: B & W Publishing, 1997).

Ceri Stennett, *The Soccer Dragons* (Cardiff: 1987).

John Toshack, *Tosh* (London: Arthur Barker, 1982).

John Toshack, *Gosh It's Tosh* (London: Duckworth, 1976).

John Toshack, *Diario del 'Gales'* (Spain: Editorial LUR, 1987).

Alex Wilkins, *Heroes: Ryan Giggs* (London: Invincible Press, 1997).

GENERAL

John Arlott (ed.), *Soccer: The Great Ones* (London: Pelham Books, 1968).

Michael Blakemore, *Next Season* (London: Weidenfeld and Nicolson, 1969).

Dave Bowler, *Danny Blanchflower* (London: Gollancz, 1997).

Jimmy Burns, *Barça* (London: Bloomsbury, 1998).

John Camkin, *World Cup 1958* (London: Rupert Hart-Davis, 1958).

Eric Cantona, *Cantona: My Story* (London: Headline, 1994).

Peter Chapman, *The Goalkeeper's History of Britain* (London: Fourth Estate, 1999).

Bobby Charlton, *Forward For England* (London: Pelham, 1967).

Hunter Davies, *The Glory Game* (London: Weidenfeld and Nicolson, 1972).

Alex Ferguson, *Managing My Life* (London: Hodder and Stoughton, 1999).

Ken Ferris, *The Double: Spurs 1960–1961* (Edinburgh: Mainstream, 1999).

Ralph L. Finn, *Spurs Supreme* (London: Robert Hale, 1961).

Tom Finney, *Football Round The World* (London: Museum Press, 1953).

A. Gibson and W. Pickford, *Association Football and The Men Who Made It* (London: 1906).

Brian Glanville, *Goalkeepers are Different* (London: Hamilton, 1971).
Brian Glanville, *People in Sport* (London: Secker and Warburg, 1967).
Brian Glanville, *The Footballer's Companion* (London: Eyre & Spottiswoode 1962).
Maurice Golesworthy, *The Encyclopedia of Football* (London: Robert Hale, 1967).
Jimmy Greaves (with Norman Giller), *Taking Sides: The Ten Greatest Football Teams* (London: Sidgwick and Jackson, 1984).
John Harding, *Alex James* (London: Robson Books, 1988).
Nick Hazlewood, *In the Way! Goalkeepers: A Breed Apart* (Edinburgh: Mainstream,1996).
Jimmy Hill, *Great Soccer Stars* (London: Hamlyn, 1978).
Francis Hodgson, *Only the Goalkeeper to Beat* (London: Picador, 1998).
Richard Holt (ed.), *Sport and the Working Class in Modern Britain* (Manchester: MUP, 1990).
Nick Hornby, *Fever Pitch* (London: Gollancz, 1980).
Nick Hornby (ed.), *My Favourite Year* (London; Gollancz, 1994).
Roger Hutchinson, *Into the Light: A Complete History of Sunderland Football Club* (Edinburgh: Mainstream, 1999).
Simon Inglis, *The Football Grounds of England and Wales* (London: Willow Books, 1983).
Simon Inglis, *League Football 1888–1988* (London: Willow Books, 1988).
Peter Jeffs, *The Golden Age of Football* (Derby: Breedon Books, 1991).
Bernard Joy, *Forward Arsenal* (London: Phoenix, 1952).
Stephen F. Kelly (ed.), *A Game of Two Halves* (London: Mandarin, 1993).
Stephen F. Kelly, *The Old Trafford Encyclopedia* (Edinburgh: Mainstream, 1995 edition).
Hugh MacIlvanney, *MacIlvanney on Football* (Edinburgh: Mainstream, 1996 edition).
Tony Mason, *Association Football and English Society 1863–1915* (London: Harvester, 1988).
John Moynihan, *The Soccer Syndrome* (London: McKibbon and Kee, 1966).
Tony Pawson, *The Goal Scorers* (London: Cassell, 1978).
Mark Perryman (ed.), *The Ingerland Factor* (Edinburgh: Mainstream, 1999).
Ivan Ponting, *Arsenal Player By Player* (London: Hamlyn, 1998).
Ivan Ponting, *Manchester United: The Red Army* (London: Hamlyn, 1999 edition).
Dave Russell, *Football and The English* (Preston: Carnegie, 1997).
Len Shackleton, *Crown Prince of Soccer* (London: Nicholas Kaye, 1955).
Ivan Sharpe, *Soccer Top Ten* (London: Stanley Paul, 1962).
Paul Shaw, *The Book of Football Quotations* (Edinburgh: Mainstream, 1999).
Phil Soar and Martin Tyler, *Arsenal 1886–1998* (London: Hamlyn, 1968 edition).
Bob Wall, *Arsenal from the Heart* (London: Souvenir Press, 1969)
James Walvin, *The People's Game* (Edinburgh: Mainstream, 2000 edition).
James Walvin, *Football and the Decline of Britain* (London: Macmillan, 1986).
Jim White, *Always in The Running: The Manchester United Dream Team* (Edinburgh: Mainstream, 1996).
Billy Wright, *The World's My Football* (London: Stanley Paul, 1955).
Percy Young, *Football Year* (London: Phoenix, 1956).
Bob Wilson, *You've Got To Be Crazy* (London: Arthur Barker, 1989).

INDEX